Straight Talk From a Wise Woman
TEARS, TRAUMA AND A HEALING PATH

Written by

Lorna J. Hines, LCSW/R, ACSW

Edited by

Dr. Jennifer A. Reimer
Diane Mendez
Dr. Heather Sanders

Published by

A Sanders Company, LLC®

Cover Design and Interior Art by

Dr. Heather Sanders

Cover Photography by

The lovely woman who took my photo at the Alpha Kappa Alpha Gala in New Jersey in 2024

All rights reserved. 2025 ©

No part of this publication may be reproduced, stored in a retrieval system or transmitted in any form or by any means, electronic, mechanical, photocopying, recording or otherwise without the prior permission of the publisher or in accordance with the provisions of the Copyright, Designs and Patents Act 1988 or under the terms of any licence permitting limited copying issued by the Copyright Licensing Agency.

A CIP record for this book is available from the Library of Congress.Cataloging-in-Publication.

Interior photographs provided by Lorna J. Hines.

ISBN-13: 978-0-9963315-9-3

A Sanders Company, LLC®
Nashville, TN
(615) 988-0030
asanderscompany.com

Printed and bound in the United States of America.

This publication provides authoritative information to consumers. It is sold under the express understanding that any decisions or actions you take as a result of reading this book, must be based on your judgment and will be at your own sole risk. The author nor publisher will be held responsible for the consequences of any actions and/or decisions taken as a result of any information given or recommendations made.

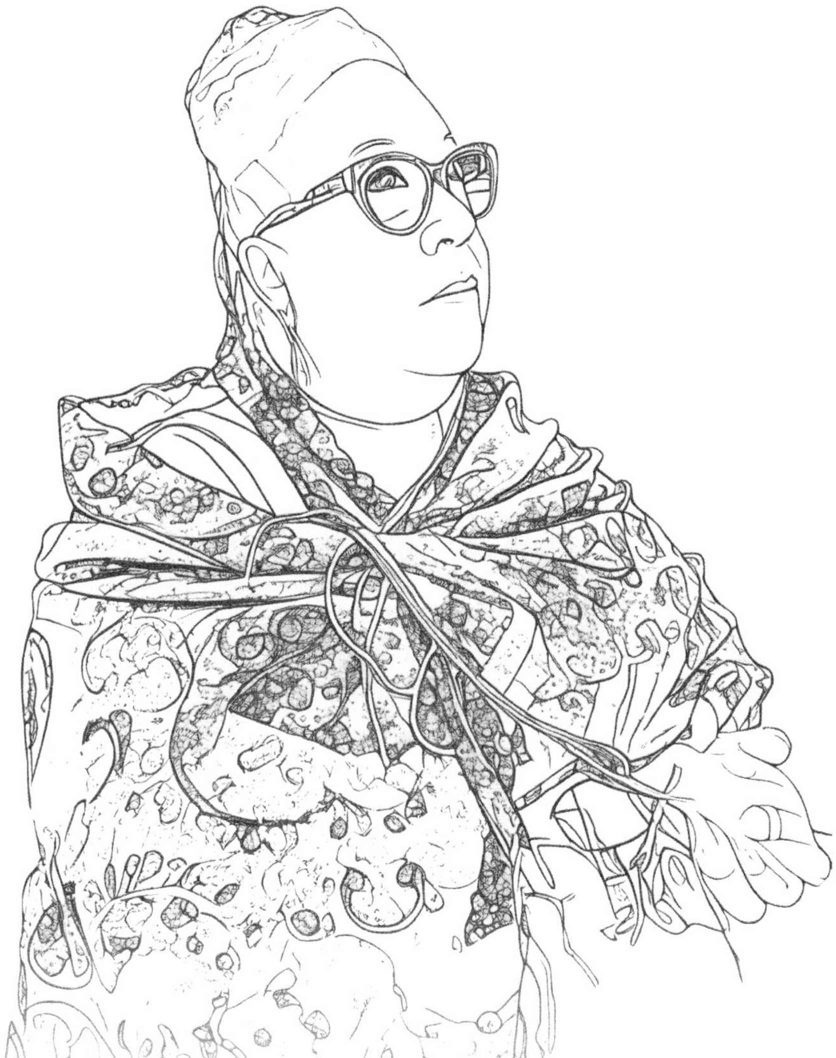

Straight Talk From a Wise Woman

TEARS, TRAUMA AND A HEALING PATH

dedication

This book is dedicated to Spirit, my helpers, guides, family, friends and ancestors whose shoulders I am honored to stand on.

table of contents

11 | FOREWORD

14 | INTRODUCTION: *The Awaited Promise*

17 | PREFACE: *A Life Jacket in a Sea of Despair*

25 | **CHAPTER 1: Black Lives Matter: George Floyd and Me**
- » *Further Uncertainties of (Black) Existence in America*
- » *Sick: A Tale of Two Pandemics*
- » *Bucket Tipping on a National Scale: Jan 6, 2021*

51 | **CHAPTER 2: You Can't Unlock a Door With Keys That Don't Work**
- » *Confronting Conditions of Powerlessness: The Isms that Dim Our Light*
- » *My Life, Your Life: An Intersection of Isms*
- » *What the "n-word" Means To Me*

69 | **CHAPTER 3: The Wise Woman's Family Sojourn—A Path to Understanding Context**
- » *A New Deluge*
- » *A History of Silence and Secrets*
- » *On the Trail of History: From Money, Mississippi to Enfield, North Carolina*
- » *An Immigrant Story: From Strivin' to Thrivin'*
- » *The Story of Gwendolyn Esme: My Mother and My Biggest Fan*

121 | **CHAPTER 4: You Are Perfect: A Conflicting Message in Tumultuous Times**
- » *You Are Perfect*
- » *Tumultuous Times: 50s, 60s, 70s—present*
- » *The Young Wise Woman Finds a Way*
- » *The Wise Woman in the Ivy League*
- » *The Wise Woman Launches Her Career*
- » *Casting off the Stigma of "Less Than:" The Wise Woman Matures*

165 | **CHAPTER 5: The Faces of Trauma**
- » *Filling the Bucket…again (and again, and again…)*
- » *Our Trauma, Our Worldview*
- » *Soul Murder*
- » *Healing Soul Murder*
- » *The Vicissitudes of Soul Murder*
- » *The Wise Woman Succumbs*
- » *Still We Rise*

209 | **CHAPTER 6: Death Is Not Final: The Opportunities and Potential in Loss**

- » *Holy Glory Dancing and Singing Beyond Death*
- » *The Highways and Byways of Grief: George Floyd and So Many Others*
- » *One Journey in Grief*
- » *Death Is Not The End*
- » *Ava's Passing*
- » *The Wise Woman Develops Her Philosophy on Life & Death*
- » *The Wise Woman Embraces the Seven Principles of Spiritualism*
- » *The Continuous Existence of the Human Soul*

249 | **CHAPTER 7: What Is Healing to This Wise Woman?**

- » *All Aboard! Gettin' on the healing bus*
- » *Surrender to Healing*
- » *Sankofa: Or Healing Starts With Knowing*
- » *The Fundamental History aka the Real Story*
- » *Willie McGee and Me*

271 | **CHAPTER 8: Creating Cultures of Healing**

- » *Reframing Our Societal Legacies and Identities*
- » *Disparity, Or Modern-Day Slavery?*

327 | **CHAPTER 9: Healing Our Communities, Healing Ourselves**

- » *Creating Communities of Care*
- » *Warriors or Protectors: Changing Perceptions of Police*
- » *Unraveling Understanding*
- » *Unraveling the Senseless: Reframing Our Personal Pain and Legacies of Trauma*
- » *Divine Healing*
- » *Overcoming Common Obstacles to Healing*

373 | **CHAPTER 10: Where Do We Go from Here?**

- » *Self-Care Means Living Your Life Like It's Golden*
- » *Life Celebrations: Big or Small, They Start with You*
- » *Ordinary People Extraordinary Deeds*
- » *Breaking Away from the Struggles of Life*
- » *Seeking Your Happy Place Within*
- » *Infusing Service and Gratitude*

foreword

Impressive, informative, inspiring and healing!

Maya Angelou said "people will forget what you said, people will forget what you did, but people will never forget how you made them feel". Upon reading "Straight Talk From a Wise Woman"- Trauma, Tears and a Healing Path", one is left with a feeling of hope and trust, that we are indeed not alone, but part of the tapestry of life. Though history and current disparities fill us with fears and anxieties we must learn to cope and move forward.

Those of us who have had the privilege of spending time with Lorna J. Hines, always felt her positive presence. Having a teacher/parent relationship enabled me to get to know her, to know about her outstanding training, parental skills, and expertise in working with others and was always left with a feeling that she admired and respected the awesome task of what we did working with her own children and countless other children.

The experience recounted in Straight Talk was vivid, probing and emotional, it validated feelings we shared. One immediately feels the depth of her compassion and is inspired by her quest to move forward. Learning from our ancestors and others the ups and downs of life, it is the standing up, being mindful of ourselves and others that this journey is often painful but need not be traveled alone.

The story is well written, easy to read with delightful poetic pauses that helps one to stop and examine fears and anxieties. It is the awakening of these unspeakable tragedies that remind us of our plight, yet she brings comfort in sharing coping mechanisms that helps us to keep going.

My personal experience of having grown up in the segregated south, encountering unimaginable obstacles, experiencing fear, having doubts and anxieties as a Black girl were mirrored with Lorna's experience growing up in the north. It clearly demonstrated that hatred, bigotry, the feeling of little self worth have no boundaries, the struggle for human decency can be documented everywhere people of color exist, yet we "still rise", grow and learn-another door opens!

I strongly suggest that you place *Straight Talk from a Wise Woman-Trauma, Tears and a Healing Path* on your night stand, handy to reach. Turn to any page! May it serve as a reminder of our history and guide of how your today's can be better than your yesterday's and that you can do and become a more productive and peaceful person. Say goodbye to stigma, celebrate life! Lorna reminds us, *life celebrations, big or small, start with you.*

Dr. Theodora Smiley Lacey
CIVIL RIGHTS ACTIVIST, EDUCATOR, AND A SCHOOL IN TEANECK, NEW JERSEY WAS NAMED AFTER HER, THE THEODORA SMILEY SCHOOL

The collective grief and anger we felt after George Floyd's death was visceral, with his cries still echoing in our shared consciousness, reminding us that we have yet to heal from this trauma witnessed by the world. Lorna J. Hines offers a lifeline in her profound book, Straight Talk From a Wise Woman. This text is not merely a guide but a transformative journey through the complexities of trauma, resilience, and healing. Hines, a seasoned psychotherapist, skillfully weaves her extensive expertise with the raw, lived experiences of Black Americans, making this work essential for anyone navigating the tumultuous waters of emotional and psychological distress.

Hines' narrative begins with a sobering acknowledgment of the traumas that define so many of us. The poignant framing of individual pain against the backdrop of historical and systemic oppression serves as a powerful reminder of how intertwined our personal struggles are with collective injustices. Yet, rather than succumbing to despair, Hines' voice emerges as a beacon of hope, urging readers to reclaim their narratives and find empowerment within their experiences. This intersectional approach, one that respects the complexities of race, gender, and class, invites a diverse readership to engage with her work, ensuring that Straight Talk resonates far beyond the Black community.

As readers turn the pages of Straight Talk, they will undoubtedly find themselves transformed. Hines provides not just a road map for personal growth but a profound understanding of the interconnectedness of our traumas and triumphs. Her work encourages a radical reimagining of self-worth, reminding us that, despite our struggles, we are deserving of lives filled with satisfaction and success.

Applause for this labor of love from Lorna J. Hines. This book is an invitation to embrace our legacies while shedding the burdens that no longer serve us.

Farah Tanis
GLOBAL ACTIVIST, EDUCATOR, CEO—RESTORE FORWARD AND BLACK WOMEN'S BLUEPRINT

THE AWAITED PROMISE

In the past, I have written in rhyme
I am now challenged at this important time
Let me write quickly whatever comes forth
The inner depths of an expansive mind

As a child and somewhat as I matured
The concept of time has been met
An ambivalent overture
Often resisting waiting
Especially in the venue of mating

Of significance, I am a planner
Likely to anticipate the unlikely
More often than not
Have not done things in a planful way
Always trusting in the power, caring and compassion
Divine Spirit
Who will always have a way

It is with that trust and confidence in mind
I will seize this critical time
To live life as I see it
Doing better
Loving, forgiving and trusting myself
Helping others, doing good deeds, not based on merits
Strengthening belief in
A Loving and Bountiful Spirit

This gestation that I previously referenced
With all of my might
Started long ago
Perhaps several lifetimes
But this recent one I chose
Supported birth enveloped
A multidimensional aura
A rainbow of fragrant roses, crystals and golden light
And the oh-so-gentle hum of OM

And so as the circle of life proceeds
There have been spans of time
Reflected the continuum of life's highs and lows
Many tears flowed
Whether in time of blissful joys or many lows

I am told and believe with all of my heart
This neonate is about to be delivered
Ushered into a life of blue skies, bright sun

And happiness beyond belief
Perhaps with a moment or two
Of serenity and peace

I also have been told
Many whose opinions and beliefs I trust
I have been imbued and infused
With golden light
The Spirit, Helpers, Healers and Guides
All entrusting me with all of their might

I have obtained a great resolve
Dispelling a life—a life with despair
So I have obtained a great resolve
Rather than fill my life with despair, impatience,
Just standing still

Awaiting
I know will come
The divine alignment and rush
Of breaking waters and cries
Life is ushered in

To do what I know is best
To live life, to love, pray, forgive, help others
Knowing the inevitable soon comes
A bountiful and beautiful harvest
A cornucopia of successes
That will fulfill my life with zest

Preface

A Life Jacket in a Sea of Despair

May 25, 2020

Drip drip drip…and the bucket tipped over…The bucket was me, brown and aging, but substantial and useful. Drip drip drip…and the bucket tipped over…The shiny, tough veneer on this symbolic bucket is everything that isn't always enough, the toughness and shininess that can't always hold back the floods. Drip drip drip… and the bucket tipped over. Racism, like water, erodes.

I wrote this book to save my life. In the wake of George Floyd's murder on May 25, 2020, I was drowning in a flood of despair, hopelessness, and so much anger. A notebook was my life jacket. I seized my intuition, my knowledge and wisdom and chose instead to utilize my anger and trauma to transform brokenness into a powerful healing modality, a radically revolutionary remedy to soothe feelings of powerlessness. When I needed a place to unburden myself, writing was not only a safe space but also an empowering one. Indeed, writing has its own power for both writer and reader. As I wrote what was near and dear to me in that heartspace full of many different emotions, I realized I had been seeking an external remedy when, all along, the remedy was deep within my body, mind, and spirit. This book is an act of reclaiming power.

Powerlessness has always been difficult for me. In part, because I was socialized with a powerful understanding of my identity but also because I have always felt the strong sense of power within my soul. I struggle the most in situations where I am treated unfairly. I have had to learn patience and understanding over my years on this earth. The latter being an essential component of achieving wisdom! I truly believe that same spirit force that showed me the way through my trauma after the murder of George Floyd has come to my aid multiple times when I felt powerless.

I have often considered how I've been able to tackle a multitude of life's challenges and wondered what wisdom I might be able to share and pass on. Luckily, throughout my life, multiple forces have come together to place me and keep me on the path towards healing and motivating others. Although I have learned that wisdom does not necessarily coincide with age (I have come into contact with many souls much older than I who have not garnered understanding and learning from their life circumstances), I can say that after six decades on this beautiful earth, I do indeed feel, at this juncture, that I have learned many life lessons. I have taken time to reflect on the many individual and psycho-social patterns that have not served my success and satisfaction. Because my need to live, procreate, and thrive in this environment is embedded in the blood, sweat and tears of my ancestors, I seek to share my lived experiences, to help others who feel the effects of racism, trauma and turmoil.

While I truly feel that I am not at an end point for my quest for wisdom, if my lessons can be of help to someone, why not share them? As the African-American spiritual resounds, "If I can help somebody, then living my life will not be in vain." My vision is that my words may be a soothing balm and a life jacket to many, not only people of African ancestry, but all those who have faced down the flood waters of pain, cruelty, unseen hurts, tragedy, fear, and uncertainty—those yearning for safety and security when they feel like they're drowning. Power, wealth, and social status will not shield us from physical disease, death, losses, traumatic circumstances, and many more. Challenges are inevitable. No matter who you are or where you come from, we all face stuff! I believe that the strategies I've developed to survive and thrive in my own life may help you find a way through the pain. One of my goals is to provide you with a sense of empowerment, hope, and resolve.

As a long-time practicing psychotherapist and clinician, I am thoroughly familiar with the state-of-the-art interventions and treatment focused on addressing a number of emotional and mental health challenges. And there are many wonderful texts that address those themes. Yet, I believe a rehashing of the many years of my clinical experiences will not accomplish the goals I have set forth. Therefore, this book is not meant to be a replacement for medical and/or psychological care. This book does not offer a complete panacea or a cure-all. And it's not a quick fix for life's challenges (even anti-depressants may take at least two weeks to kick in!).

I felt it was important to go beyond the clinical because, ultimately, my wisdom is drawn from many sources, not just my clinical training. My experience has taught me that the desire to help is not enough. The helping must be designed and punctuated with experience, education and training, not only the kind found in books or taught in school. There must be a willingness to bring together all of the important learning tools we acquire, tempered with flexibility, patience, and the acceptance that we might need to stray from the established path. I have tried to utilize all of the tools in my toolbox to write this book for you.

One of those tools is words. Our words have power. I am sure you can easily recall a sentence, verse or lyrics to a song that have a special meaning to you. Words contain the potential for healing, an important truth that I had in mind as I developed this book. One of my major goals is to write with clarity leading to purposeful discernment. So, I wrote an amalgam of essays, short stories, and poems to provide different glimpses into my struggles and triumphs, high and lows, and my never-ceasing effort to do what I thought was right. I begin many chapters with poems I have written, although I do not profess to be an accomplished poet. I write poetry from a spiritual place. I incorporate symbols, multiple examples and personal experiences to illustrate concepts. All these are to ensure clarity. I believe when authors write something that only they can understand, what wise purpose can their writing serve? To make the best of this book, then, I strongly suggest that you read and discern behind the words, finding what may have relevance to your personal circumstances and your journey. There are no right or wrong answers!

When babies are born, they do not have a roadmap to birthing. They are born with the remnants of birth, and often with ill-shaped faces. But to those who love them, they are beautiful, together with their imperfections. And so, too, this book is beloved and imperfect. Rather than following a specific roadmap, leading to possible impossible perfectionism, I decided to just write. I did not initially seek outside advice on this book, fearing that I would have to change the authenticity of my message. I value the opinion of others; however, for this treatise, it was important that I expose my vulnerabilities and take the risks that were important for me to take, especially at this era in my life.

After the initial relief that journaling brought me, it was challenging to seek the discipline and self-confidence, risking criticism and possible hurt, to turn a life-saving instinct into a book that might possibly reach and help others. Fear of criticism, of not being "good enough," and seeking validation from others can and does inhibit us from taking important risks that may lead to greater success and satisfaction in our lives. But I have also learned that criticism will not hurt you unless you let it! Eventually, I discarded the idea of endless research and analysis, as my professional training had instilled in me, focusing rather on what was contained and needed to be expressed in my body, mind, and spirit. My inner knowingness has always propelled me forward in the face of setbacks and hurtful criticism.

Over the years, my wisdom has taught me to temper and balance my desire for success and my fundamental tendency to work hard with a strong sense of wellness and self-care, a work-in-progress that continues to this very day. Since leaving my career as a high-level administrator, I've had to carefully monitor my work versus play. During my extensive career, I was often told I was working too hard, and indeed I was. There were times when I was moving so fast that I did not offer myself the essential time to observe actions, experiences, and myself. There was a point where I worked more than full-time and on constant call as an administrator at a psychiatric hospital; I had a part-time psychotherapy practice and was teaching two courses at a university. These actions did not serve me well. Many loved ones urged me to cut down, but I was so deeply involved that I could not stop. I was finally "stopped" by the rigors of double pneumonia over one summer month. The universe was telling me something. And so I stopped. In retrospect, when I review my circumstances at the time of George Floyd's murder, was I not being self-caring enough? Was I working too hard? And, perhaps, was I out of balance when I learned of George Floyd's murder?

When I feel myself falling back on old patterns of self-doubt, over-working and imbalance, my wisdom and positive self-talk remind me not to recreate the same self-defeating patterns that did not serve my success and satisfaction. As we go through this journey together, dear reader, I will urge you to seek and develop your own self-care plan, focused on enhancing your true life's meaning. Self-care insulates you from the challenges that you will face.

Today, I hear many people speak of the idea of "ancestral wisdom"—a legacy of knowledge and know-how passed down from one generation to the next. My ancestors faced down the very real threats of lynching and the casual violence of a Jim Crow society, and they did not give over to anger, hatred, and revenge. I draw on the strength and sense of these wise warriors, who preserved and, time and again, chose the other way. From them, I have learned how to live, how to carry on, how to choose life over suicide and homicide. Perhaps this is why, in spite of all I have witnessed, I have an inner knowledge and conviction that, in the words of the great African American poet Langston Hughes, "I, too, am America."

My knowing awareness tells me that now is the right time for me to share the wisdom and intuition I have utilized to survive and thrive in the midst of precarity. My knowledge, conviction, and intuition remind me that there are ways and means of surviving—by framing and reframing how we conceptualize the management of tragedy and turmoil. This is both radical and revolutionary. Radical and revolutionary is what is necessary to circumvent tragedy. We know this because we've tried most everything else, and it hasn't worked!

To put it simply, my heart and soul compelled me to continue what remains in my life's desire: to help, promote, and expand the opportunity to provide healing. This book continues my developmental, genetic, historical and life-long purpose to serve and offer care and compassion to others. It includes all of my inner and spiritual resources, as well as lived experience. I hope to provide you with a sense of empowerment, hope, and assurance that coping with trauma is possible. We can have successful and satisfying lives. Triumphant lives.

When the bucket finally tipped, there was so much water. The flood waters rose, and I feared that I would drown in the fear and the trauma, the soul murders, the constant vulnerability. I was reaching out, looking for a life jacket or a safety net. I was drowning in sadness.

Before the rising tides of despair and devastation could pull me under for good, my fingers grabbed hold of a life jacket—my awareness, intuition, and wisdom. The knowledge that there has to be another way. I had so much water and I had to do something with it. I needed to find a place for everything that came spilling out. A safe place. A healing and empowering place.

So, I wrote this book.

Chapter 1

Black Lives Matter: George Floyd and Me.

May 25th 2020: Drip drip drip…and the bucket tipped over…The bucket was me, brown and aging, but substantial and useful. Drip drip drip…and the bucket tipped over…The shiny, tough veneer on this symbolic bucket is everything that isn't always enough, the toughness and shininess that can't always hold back the floods. Drip drip drip…and the bucket tipped over. Racism, like water, erodes.

It's not an exaggeration to say that I was traumatized by the death of George Floyd. What do I mean by trauma? One simple definition of trauma: experiencing something painful or upsetting and continuing to feel pain and distress even after the situation or experience has passed.

The exact moment when I came face-to-face with the death of George Floyd remains fuzzy and unclear. The emotional, spiritual, and psychological devastation I experienced as I watched his death alongside my family makes it hard to remember with exact clarity. I remember the voices of the 911 operators, acting out of compassion, alarmed and sensing something was terribly wrong. Something was terribly wrong. And we all could see it. I had to invoke all of my training and self-care wisdom to quiet my anxiety, sadness, and despair. I remember that I turned to my husband and said that Officer Chauvin and George Floyd must have known each other previously, and that this crazed murder must be the result of an unresolved vendetta. But not even a vendetta can explain what we saw on the screen during those quarantined, late spring days of 2020.

May 25th 2020: Drip drip drip…and the bucket tipped over… The bucket was me, tipping over, watching the faces of the officers murdering George Floyd. When I think about it now, nearly two months later, I remember my confusion. How did a handcuffed black man who was cooperating with the police in a non-violent way end up on the ground, with a white man's knee against his throat? When I close my eyes, I can still see the empty face of Derek Chauvin, especially his eyes, devoid of emotion, as he pressed the life out of Mr. Floyd. There was an almost inhuman vacancy in his eyes. They say that the eyes are the window to the soul. If this is true, then Derek Chauvin's soul expressed deep and unfailing hatred for the black man under his leg. His non-verbal behavior showed the world that he had no sense of George Floyd's humanity, no understanding of their *shared* humanity. Does his lack of emotional expression explain why he did not respond to George Floyd's pleas, crying out to his mother, and his dying words that he could not breathe? There was something deep and disturbing in the blank, empty face of Derek Chauvin. I could easily imagine him as part of a slaughterhouse assembly line, dispassionately and repeatedly killing black people as if his job was to slit their throats, one after another, without emotion or empathy—just getting the job done. Why didn't the other officers respond to Mr. Floyd's pleas? Were they caught up in group dynamics? Or perhaps they, too, did not see or hear the victim's humanity?

What makes George Floyd's life and murder important to me? He came from a seemingly close-knit family, much like my own. Like me, Mr. Floyd was a parent—he had children. Although Mr. Floyd was not living with the mother of his youngest child, he was devoted to his children. Like me, he was a grandparent, and those who are grandparents know the uniqueness of that loving relationship. After his murder, his sister came on television, tears flowing, sadness and despair surrounding her, and I joined the many who cried and grieved alongside her. I later read and saw that he had a girlfriend who was also utterly devastated by his death, and again, I joined in the devastation, as did many others.

Mr. Floyd seemed like the kind of African American man my family might've known—a nice guy from the neighborhood, perhaps down on his luck. As I write this, I can think of many men who are currently unemployed, seeking any type of job to support themselves and their families.

As I watched, alongside the world, how could I not feel the pain of centuries of dehumanization? I was watching Mr. Floyd, but I was also seeing other African Americans, my family, people that I have known in this life, and people I know only from the pages of books, photographs, or as spirits, others who have been devalued, objectified and treated as inhuman. I was flooded with memories of murders.

George Floyd's calculated murder served to remind me, and perhaps others, of the lengthy catalogue of murdered, unarmed black people. Although I have witnessed and been impacted by the murder of many unarmed and innocent black people, there are several in particular that have left me shaken, frightened, and at times enraged and burdened with a sense of powerlessness. These pages are an incomplete chronicle of some of those lives. There are so many people whose names I do not know, may never know.

May 25th 2020: Drip drip drip…and the bucket tipped over… The bucket was me, tipping over, watching the faces of the officers murdering George Floyd. Drip drip drip…Racism, like water, erodes.

1939, Café Society in Greenwich Village, New York City: African American jazz singer **Billie Holiday** performs Abel Meeropol's song, "Strange Fruit" for the first time. To me, and to so many others, the song is a tribute to all of the unnamed black men and women who have been traumatized, tortured, beaten, and killed at the hands of white people. This entry is for them. You are remembered.

May 8, 1951, a state penitentiary in Mississippi: Willie McGee is executed by the electric chair after being accused and convicted of the assault and rape of a white woman in a case that went through three controversial trials and won international attention. Despite evidence that the police forced a confession from Mr. McGee and violated his constitutional rights, and despite the support of public figures such as William Faulkner, Bella Abzug, and Josephine Baker, McGee is finally found guilty at his third trial on March 6, 1948. The jury deliberates for less than one hour.

August 28, 1955, Money, Mississippi: A 14-year-old African American boy, **Emmett Till**, is brutally tortured and lynched while visiting relatives. Emmett was originally from Chicago. While visiting Money, he's falsely accused of inappropriate behavior with a white woman, Carolyn Bryant, whose husband owns a local grocery store. When the news spreads of the allegation, white vigilantes arrive at Emmett's house and take him away. His body is found almost unrecognizable due to the beatings and torture, yet his mother insists on an open casket at her son's funeral. She wants the world to know what has been done to her son. Those responsible are later acquitted of all charges. Many believe Emmett's murder signaled the beginning of the Civil Rights movement. Will the same be said someday of George Floyd?

June 12, 1963, Jackson, Mississippi: Civil Rights activist **Medgar Wiley Evers** returns home from a NAACP event and is shot and killed by a sniper bullet. Earlier that evening, President John F. Kennedy had addressed the nation, calling white resistance to civil rights a "moral crisis." The African American community responded to Evers's murder with a "tide of anger." Although the FBI identified his murderer as white supremacist Byron De La Beckworth, two all-white juries failed to convict him. Finally, 30 years later, a racially mixed jury found De La Beckworth guilty of the murder of Medgar Evers. In 1963, the NAACP posthumously awarded Medgar Evers the Spingarn Medal for services to the African American community.

March 21, 1981, Mobile, Alabama, late in the evening: **Michael Donald**, 19, is visiting his sister. They are watching TV when he says, "I am going to the store to get a pack of cigarettes." He never returns. The next time his family sees him, he is hanging from a tree. He's been kidnapped, tortured and lynched. They call his death "the last American lynching." Initial investigations yield nothing. The police arrest three men who turn out not to be the perpetrators. The family holds an open casket funeral, a grim reminder of Emmett Till's funeral, refusing to cover up the consequences of racial violence from the nation. Michael's family, especially his relentless mother, continue to advocate, looking for justice. Eventually, through the help of advocacy agencies and strong police work, the KKK are found responsible. Michael's mother files a wrongful death suit against the KKK that effectively bankrupts the organization. One of the murderers is sentenced to death in 1997.

March 3, 1991, Los Angeles, California: Following the horrific beating of **Rodney King**, I develop panic attacks at the mere sight of policemen. One afternoon, while living in the suburbs, a police detective knocks on my door. As I began to panic, breathing quick shallow breaths and on the brink of fainting, I am certain the young detective is also terribly frightened. He explains in a sympathetic voice that he's only investigating a report of a robbery and checking in with people in the neighborhood.

April 10, 1990, Teaneck, New York: In a town far away from Minneapolis, Minnesota, 16-year-old **Phillip Pannell** is shot in the back by a white police officer, Gary Spath. I'm utterly devastated when I hear the story; the new racial divide that grew following the murder in a town that boasted of diversity—a living example of multiculturalism—has a profound personal impact on my family. While picking up our small children from after-school programs, I find myself in the middle of an angry, white crowd that has gathered to support the officer who's been charged with manslaughter. All I can do is pray as I instruct our girls to hide below their seats in the event of shots fired or a mob attack. Somehow, we make it home, seeking the solace and safety of our humble abode. To this day, I recall my fear and panic—not for myself but for our daughters, who quite easily could've been caught up in this melee.

February 4, 1999, New York City: I could have easily bumped into the West African immigrant **Amadou Diallo** prior to his murder because he lived very close to the area where I grew up; as a child, I would have walked through his street. My family and I would've walked up and down Westchester Avenue in the Bronx, purchasing fruit or pizza, or going to the drug store. How was it that this unarmed young man was murdered by a shower of bullets as he ran for safety into his apartment building? None of the police officers stood trial for his death. Later on, around 2000, I had the occasion to meet and speak with Mr. Diallo's father. I admired this pious and intelligent man who spoke to a group of mental health professionals regarding the violence suffered by his son and family. There was no hint of anger or frustration as he spoke. And now, as I recall the meeting, my admiration continues.

February 26, 2012, Sanford, Florida: I cry rivers of tears when I learn of dear **Trayvon Martin**'s murder. And again when President Barack speaks those wise words, "this handsome young man could have been my son." I cry for him, his parents, and the black mothers and fathers throughout our nation. I cry for his innocence and the fact that he will never enjoy going to his prom, never graduate from high school, never go to college, never have the opportunity to be a fine husband and father.

November 22, 2014, Cleveland, Ohio: Trayvon's tragic scenario repeats in a life much too short-lived: **Tamir Rice**, the cherub-faced youngster whose only crime is being a kid playing with a toy gun. The Cleveland police claim that Tamir was warned three times to drop his toy gun. These claims are never substantiated. Multiple investigations into the Division of Police reveal a pattern of the use of excessive force. Records unearthed tell the chilling history of Police Officer Loehmann, the officer who shot Tamir, who had resigned from a previous department as a result of "suffering a dangerous loss of composure during firearms training." Could these documents have indicated a problem more serious and substantial than "a loss of composure"?

July 17, 2014, Staten Island, New York: The death of **Eric Garner** is also an awful reminder of the murderous effect of chokeholds. It is difficult, if not impossible, to fathom the escalation needed to go from the sale of loose cigarettes to murder at the hands of police officers. How did such a thing happen?

August 9, 2014, Ferguson, Missouri: Young **Michael Brown** has graduated from secondary school and has plans to become a heating and cooling technician when he's murdered by a white police office named Darren Wilson. He's suspected of robbing cigarillos from a convenience store. During his arrest, 18-year-old Michael Brown, 6'5" and 290 pounds, struggles against the

Officer Darren Wilson, 6'4" and 210 pounds. And yet, during subsequent questioning, a fully grown Wilson states: "when I grabbed him the only way I can describe it—I felt like a 5-year-old holding onto Hulk Hogan. That's how big he felt and how small I felt just from grasping his arm."

There is a sad and tragic poignancy to Darren Wilson's words, to the way that they invoke and describe a significant part of the historical experience of African Americans. For centuries, African Americans have struggled with the harmful stereotype-turned-mythology of the "brute negro" who must be restrained and put down like an animal to prevent angry, violent, bent-on-raping-white-women black men from running amuck. Even the landmark American film, *The Birth of a Nation*, which, in 1915, revolutionized the American film industry and is still one of the most famous and most-viewed films in American history, drew on the stereotype of the "brute negro" as a central part of the plot's tragic and melodramatic success. Maybe my readers will remember the iconic scene where the young white heroine commits suicide by jumping off a cliff rather than succumb to being raped by the brutish escaped slave who chases her through the woods. Enslavement, Jim Crow, mass incarceration, police brutality, continuous structural inequalities and obstacles to equality in all aspects of our lives are the legacy of such violent, dehumanizing myths.

What makes George Floyd's life and murder (as well as so many others I've discussed) important and relevant to me? His life, Michael Brown's life, the lives of all these ordinary Black Americans, are in alignment with my own life. Their lives could be—are—mine, are the lives of family, my friends, all of my loved ones who experience the everyday racism of being black in America.

I was horrified to learn that in Ferguson, Missouri, where Michael Brown lived, the police routinely profiled young black men as a means to earn income for the impoverished town, guaranteeing that many black people would be challenged and arrested by the police, purely for profit. These actions reminded me of the new type of enslavement for African Americans—the carefully calculated plan to keep blacks in their place without opportunities for success. How different was this from sharecropping, both formal and informal laws of Jim Crow, the KKK, redlining, voter suppression, health and wealth disparities and the many other forces of continued enslavement? They are all the mechanisms by which white society attempts to manage and control African Americans. These were all the things my ancestors found ways to *survive*.

July 13, 2015, Waller County Jail, Texas: I continue to suffer with a sense of bewilderment at the death of **Sandra Bland**, stopped for an innocuous traffic violation and wrongfully imprisoned. While in jail, Ms. Bland allegedly committed suicide. I grieved alongside her family and friends. As other black people share a sense of mistrust in our criminal justice system and its capacity for lies, I, too, wonder if conspiracy exists.

July 6, 2016, Falcon Heights, Minnesota: **Philando Castile** is a school cafeteria manager, fatally shot by police during a routine traffic stop. As Mr. Castile reaches for his identification (as requested by the officer), he's shot dead. The story is familiar. The police thought he was reaching for a gun and said that they feared for their lives. And I wonder, with doubt, horror, and dismay, whether the so-called routine traffic stop was not also part of a formalized profiling intervention, tacitly approved by the Police Department of Falcon Heights, Minnesota? I think of

Diamond Reynolds, Mr. Castile's girlfriend, and their innocent youngster, forced to witness this horror, forever traumatized by the tragic and unnecessary murder of their loved one. I align myself with this thought—the thought of never being able to forget the memory of a murdered loved one. I know that such experiences were an open invitation to a sense of powerlessness, chronic sadness, and despair.

June 17, 2015, Charleston, South Carolina: I hold in my heart the **nine African American parishioners** in the Emanuel African Methodist Episcopal Church in Charleston, South Carolina. They weren't killed by police officers but by a hateful assailant whom they had welcomed into their congregation, in line with the Christian doctrine of loving one another as God loves all of us. They offered him the right hand of fellowship, when, in fact, his plan was a calculated and murderous scenario. How can I forget their spiritually focused Home-Going service where our President Obama eulogized these fallen heroes? And not one individual will forget his rendition of "Amazing Grace." I continue to cry for these fallen martyrs who never saw the evil in their midst as their minds and spirit focused on the teachings of God.

September 6, 2018, Dallas, Texas: I continue to find difficulty in talking about the murders which have taken place in the sacredness of the home. Do you, reader, recall the execution of **Botham Jean**? He is shot by Police Officer Amber Guyger while simply eating ice cream in his living room. Guyger claims she thought he was in her apartment.

October 12, 2019, Fort Worth, Texas: Equally incredulous is the murder of **Atatiana Jefferson** in her home, her castle, enjoying video games with her nephew. The police officer indicated he was responding to a call regarding an open door. I wonder, with frustration and despair, if this was a scenario of "shoot first and ask questions later," assuming a black person was armed? Equally disturbing is the loss of the victim's father who died of cardiac arrest shortly after his daughter's murder. Might he have also suffered from what's known as "broken heart syndrome?"

August 30, 2019, Aurora, Colorado: The friendly, innocent face of **Elijah McClain** haunts me because it was only recently that the public was made aware of his murder. Despite his slight build, he, too, was placed in a chokehold which led to his untimely death at the age of 23. The sadistic callousness of the police officers, two men and one woman, who took pictures reenacting Elijah's murder reminds us of the existence of the objectification, hatred, and heartlessness among some police officers.

February 23, 2020, Glynn County, Georgia: I recall with horror the murderous intent of the white man and his son, hunting for a black man to kill, and coming upon an unarmed young man whose only crime was an early morning jog. I speak with reverence and sadness recalling the murder of **Ahmaud Marquez Arbery**. The sheer premeditation of his murder defies imagination, but reminds us of the hatefulness, malice, and desire among some white people to kill African Americans. These perpetrators were not police officers, but they share the same disregard for African American life. What motivates this hatred?

There is something bone-chilling in the pre-meditated acts of terror by those motivated by a racial hatred so meaningful that they would take the time and effort to drive, in some cases many hours and across state lines, to commit their crimes. Derek

Chauvin may not have planned the murder of George Floyd, but he, too, seemed able to remove and blind himself from the humanity of the human being beneath his knee. What compels a person to such violence? How is it that these killers do not have the ability to call upon wisdom and intuition or a higher power? How do they come to believe that there is no other way? Is it their anger and frustration, the weight of carrying these emotions, that police who kill African American people carry with them, what they shoulder when they put on their uniform and strap on their weapons?

March 13, 2020, Louisville, Kentucky: **Breonna Taylor**, a 26-year-old black woman and EMT is horrifically gunned down by a flurry of bullets in her own home. The reasons for this monstrous crime defy a logical explanation. How do you explain this loss of a young woman in the prime of her life, gunned down by police, the same officers meant to be her allies in service to the community? What can be said to her family, friends and loved ones? We are bereft—there are no words for this crime.

March 23, 2020, Rochester, New York: As I write this chapter, I have just learned of the death of **Daniel Prude**, who, according to a report by the *New York Times*, was placed in a mesh hood by police officers and held face down on the road until he died of asphyxiation.

March 29, 2021: Chicago, Illinois: Police shoot 13-year old **Adam Toledo** after a chase. Body camera footage shows young Adam complying with the officers' commands to drop the weapon he's carrying. After tossing a handgun under a fence, Adam is raising his hands when he's shot eight times. Eight-tenths of a second have passed between the moment when police see Adam holding a gun and the shots that ended his short life. Adam

Toledo is part of the Latine community, who not only share our African ancestry but also the violent effects of racial profiling and victimization at the hands of American law enforcement.

April 11, 2021, Brooklyn Center, Minnesota: **Daunte Wright** is shot by police during a traffic stop related to expired registration tags. When the police discovered a warrant for Daunte's arrest, they attempted to haul him from his car. During the ensuing scuffle, an officer pulls a gun and shouts, "taser." Seconds later, Daunte, shot, loses control of his vehicle and collides with another car. He is pronounced dead on the scene. Later, Police Chief Tim Gannon says, "It is my belief that the officer had the intention to deploy their Taser but instead shot Mr. Wright with a single bullet"

April 20, 2021, Columbus, Ohio: 16-year old **Ma'Khia Bryant** is involved in an altercation with two other girls. The police are called and Ma'Khia is shot and killed outside her foster home

August 23, 2020, Kenosha, Wisconsin: **Jacob Blake** is paralyzed after being shot seven times in the back while opening the door to his car where his three young children were waiting.

January 7, 2023, Memphis, Tennessee: **Tyre Nichols** is dragged form his car before being pepper sprayed and tasered by police officers who had stopped him for reckless driving. Mr. Nichols ran to his mother's house, where he was punched, kicked, and further brutalized by law enforcement. Medics on the scene did not administer care for 16 minutes after arriving. Tyre died in the hospital from his injuries three days later.

As I write my book, I know there will be more and more deaths that I cannot record. I feel as if I am constantly updating this chronicle as each new year, month, week…every time we learn of another tragedy. If I recounted here every single unjust loss of life at the hands of the police, I would never finish this book. But they are with me. Their stories are here, guiding my hand. Billie Holiday sang of "Strange Fruit" hanging from the boughs of poplar trees in the American South; in my mind's eye, I see the bodies of black people hanging like so much laundry on a never-ending clothesline that stretches out past the horizon. Eventually, I will turn these pages over to editors and publishers and there will come a time when I can no longer record these deaths here. But each will be etched in my mind, body, and spirit. And each will add to the trauma and turmoil that I experience. The narrative of violence and murder of black people by police is ongoing.

The recent documentary depicting the forced confessions of the Central Park Five left me fearful, tearful, and hopeless regarding our criminal justice system. You can read more of their tragic story in Michelle Alexander's book, *The New Jim Crow*. This is a must-read for all. Alexander outlines why the United States has the largest prison population in the world, comprised mostly of African Americans—people who look like me. She goes on to show how once African Americans are released from prison, they face a lifetime of bias and impossible odds when it comes to seeking a better life, regardless of their status.

What do the police see when they see the faces of black people, including my own? What is this visceral reaction that white officers have towards people of color? What layers of judgements and assumptions do they view us through? Do they come into the police force in this way or is their humanity eroded in some way by the structures and practices of American law enforcement? Unregulated police brutality speaks to the design, formation, and institutionalization of American racism. It speaks to the need for the fundamental changes our society needs to modify the role of police office from warriors to protectors and promoters of the safety and security of all people who live in this country.

Even Representative Tim Scott, a black Republican, admitted that he has been profiled and stopped by police on numerous occasions despite his unwavering support for President Trump and other GOP colleagues. Neither his class, education, nor political allegiance mattered to the police stopping Rep. Scott—he was treated as an average black man by police who only saw a potential criminal.

The recent passing of **Mr. John Lewis**, the tireless Civil Rights activist, reminds me of those who have sacrificed their lives in the fight to end legal segregation. I think of **James Chaney, Andrew Goodman**, and **Michael Schwerner**, a brave trio of young men, one black and two white, who were brutally murdered by the KKK in June 1964. My consciousness cycles through the decades and I think of the death of **Heather Heyer** in 2017. Ms. Heyer, a white woman, was killed while protesting against white nationalism in Charlottesville, NC, when James Alex Fields, Jr. drove his car into the crowd, injuring thirty others. These murders represent the seething hatred many whites also feel towards those who ally themselves with African Americans and anti-racism.

In actuality, the murder and victimization of all the lost souls I have described resonate and relate to my own life and circumstances. Perhaps George Floyd (and the many I have talked about and the many that are unknown to me) and I have a deep and ongoing connection based on our common racial heritage. I easily could have been one of those murdered. Like Mr. Floyd and so many others, I have been racially profiled, stopped by police in New York City, New Jersey, and New York State, for no other reason than "driving while black." While trying to arrive on time to pick up our children, I have been often stopped on the New Jersey Turnpike, an infamous profiling venue for African Americans. During the last time I was stopped, I candidly asked the young, white trooper why he had stopped me. He admitted that he had made a mistake, yet the encounter rendered me powerless, angry, and much too late to pick up my children.

In hindsight, the scenario could have had more dire consequences—I am thankful that I got away with my life. I am thankful that I had received "the talk" on how to respond to a police officer when stopped—a routine educational process for many African Americans. I have been followed in both high-end and neighborhood stores as another possible criminal. In Neiman Marcus, while looking for a handbag, I was dismissed so rudely that I vowed to never return to that store. Is what separates Mr. Floyd's fate and mine sheer luck or the divine intervention of my Higher Power? I will go through this broken, beautiful world knowing every day that it could have been—it could be—me who is stopped. And killed.

*May 25th 2020: Drip drip drip…and the bucket tipped over…*For me, every act of racism and violence has been another drop in the bucket, eroding my belief that somehow things will get better tomorrow. Each instance of dehumanization, inequality, racial profiling, police brutality, institutional racism, disrespect, fear of destruction, an existence of inner uncertainty, fear and constant anxiety brought me closer to my tipping point. Racism, like water, erodes.

Even if we may dismiss the traumatic events that live within us, their presence is there. I'm not just talking about clinical PTSD, but also the way certain images, sounds, smells, and other small details can bring back painful memories or haunt our conscious and unconscious minds. It was the haunting image of black men hung from trees in the South during legalized lynchings that inspired "Strange Fruit." Can you recall the terror in the eyes of African-Americans as they crossed the Pettus Bridge in Selma, Alabama? Or displayed in the actors' eyes in the movie *Rosewood*? I will never forget the impact of the movie *Schindler's List*, which depicted Jewish people in the horrors of the Holocaust. I could only watch a small portion of *Twelve Years a Slave* which portrayed the brutality of the slave/caste system of my forefathers and mothers. I can now add Derek Chauvin's face and expressionless eyes in the midst of murdering a black man to the list of my personal traumatic hauntings.

I have not mentioned the numerous trans people who met their demise simply due to the color of their skin and their gender identity. Or the many mentally ill and substance-abusing black people whose lost lives could've been saved with stronger infrastructure, access to affordable health care, and the right to a basic standard of living. Their loss is equally disturbing and equally traumatizing. And what, again, do I mean by "trauma?" *Trauma: experiencing something painful or upsetting and continuing to feel pain and distress even after the situation or experience has passed.*

As I watched, alongside the world, how could I not feel the pain of centuries of dehumanizing trauma and powerlessness? It was through the multiple lenses of past and present structural problems that I watched this tragedy and its aftermath unfold.

I was watching Mr. Floyd, but I was also seeing other African Americans, my family, people that I have known in this life, and people I know only from the pages of books, photographs, or as spirits, others who have been devalued, objectified and treated as inhuman. I was seeing Emmett Till, Dr. Martin Luther King, Jr., Malcolm X. I was seeing a history of a people. I was seeing myself.

Sick: A Tale of Two Pandemics

Is it far-fetched to suggest that the vacant, hate-filled eyes summoning the death of George Floyd were also a reflection of murderous COVID's devastation? Is it possible that my own experiences with COVID, and the experiences of those around me, including and especially Black Americans and other minorities, intensified the trauma of George Floyd's murder? Is it too radical to offer that, during the tumultuous times of 2020-2023, America was experiencing two pandemics? One, a long-standing national sickness called racism, whose symptoms were fresh in our bodies and souls after the murder of Mr. Floyd. The other was the destructive spread of the novel coronavirus, COVID-19. Indeed, as I reflect on my intense reaction to the death of Mr. George Floyd, these two illnesses are deeply intertwined.

From late winter and into the spring of 2020, many of the counties where I lived succumbed to high indices of COVID. In fact, the county where I reside had the highest numbers in the state, possibly due to our proximity to New York City. Within my neighborhood, COVID victims posted signs at their doors, reminding us all of the potential of contagion. A sense of dread prevailed. In my own life, many loved ones were impacted, as well as the loved ones of my patients. Many became ill, while others died. For Black Americans, it was a time of fear, sadness and despair as we watched how our communities were disproportionately affected by the virus.

As the numbers of those impacted by COVID rose alarmingly, our national media was ablaze with coverage of George Floyd's murder and the subsequent protests. Many of us found ourselves in a highly uncertain and frightening time. The reaction from those in leadership and the government was equally disorienting and fearful. Contradictory information, political double talk, scientists facing off with world leaders over the validity of facts and scientific knowledge…the world felt chaotic, topsy-turvy. Many African Americans began to feel an increased sense of alarm. Would this plague be yet another example of the generational trauma that many black people have experienced over the last 400 years?

And so George Floyd's murder on top of another pandemic, on top of the many disparities experienced by African Americans, on top of years of generational trauma, on top of my own very personal and specific experiences with violence, trauma, racism, and sexism in all aspects of my life (more on this in Chapter 2) marched like an army of darkness to challenge my personal body, mind and spirit.

In early August of 2020, I woke to an otherwise routine Monday. I felt as if I had a cold but wasn't alarmed. As my symptoms worsened, I wondered if I'd caught a nasty virus. At that time, I had no thoughts that I could be suffering from COVID. Our family was careful! We always wore and frequently changed our facial coverings; we only went out when absolutely necessary. Upon returning, we would wipe down our shoes with disinfectant and remove our outer clothing. We made our own hand disinfectant and had no visitors coming to our home. We were safe (or so we thought). However, as I began to sink deeper and deeper into illness, I knew this was no cold or summer flu. And so by Saturday, I found myself alone in my house with a raging fever, an unrelenting cough, and trouble breathing. My family members had all gone out. Panic set in. I thought about how I did not want to die alone in my house; I couldn't bear the thought of my loved ones coming home to find me dead. Isn't our thought process ridiculous at these crucial times?

As the hours passed, I became weaker and weaker. I wasn't sure if I could walk on my own. I certainly knew that I could not drive myself to the hospital. Eventually, I called an ambulance, was placed on a stretcher and rushed to my local hospital where testing revealed that I had, indeed, caught the dreaded COVID-19 virus. After receiving oxygen and IV fluids, I felt strong enough to return home. Little did I know the worst was yet to come.

Despite antibiotics and regular doses of Tylenol, my fever would not break, and my cough worsened. I could not eat, sleep, or rest. My family members tested positive, although their symptoms were not as severe as mine. Two days after my first visit to the hospital, I returned due to my cough and shortness of breath. For 12 hours or more, they monitored my plummeting oxygen levels. They sent me for a CAT scan that indicated I had pneumonia. Doctors and health care personnel demanded I permit admission to stay overnight. The Attending Physician of the COVID ward was summoned. The nurse assigned to my care tried her best to exert her knowledge and authority, even resorting to bullying. However, I summarily refused to be admitted. Why, my dear reader, would I do such a thing?

My answer is simple and spiritual. As the physicians and nurses discussed my case, I saw myself in a vision being wheeled into the hospital ward and never getting out. I knew it was concrete guidance from Our Loving Spirit. For me, that was Spirit's message to seek an alternative. Despite the ire and confusion from hospital personnel over my decision, I left. I summoned all of my strength to walk out the hospital doors without fainting, because the staff refused to offer me a wheelchair or assistance. I told myself: *you can make it, and you better not fall or faint!* Self-talk can be powerful!

The next two weeks were horrific. The fever, weakness, shortness of breath and coughing continued. Sores and inflammation in my mouth and throat meant eating was out of the question. My dear husband would force sips of water and clear broth down my throat. There were times when I knew death was surely near. I could not even pray, although I consider myself a prayerful individual. When I had moments of clarity, I learned numerous prayer groups and healing sessions had begun on my behalf.

A conversation with a good friend (who is also a stellar midwife) finally changed the course of my illness. I explained my symptoms and she mailed me herbal remedies and immune boosters with careful instructions. She explained the importance of the pneumonia in my chest; this made sense and was helpful. I followed her advice and instructions carefully. By mid-September, I was able to tolerate smoothies and light soup. A telehealth visit with my primary care doctor indicated that though I was out of the woods I should not return to work.

Nearly three years later, I continue to experience what is called "Long-Haulers Symptoms," yet I am able to work, to love and to pray.

Bucket Tipping on a National Scale: Jan 6, 2021

I had barely recovered from the worst of my COVID trauma when another national emergency rocked our nation. By January 6, 2021, our national sickness was raging. Divided by the results of a brutal presidential campaign and with no COVID vaccine in sight, we were a society at war with ourselves. As we battled the symptoms of a global pandemic, we were also suffering from the symptoms of our other disease—distrust, hatred, denial, outrage, and fear manifested as we tried to have national conversations on race, gender, sexuality, poverty, and so much more. Like my body, that worn bucket, bruised and battered after my long struggle with COVID and more, our nation had reached a tipping point.

As I attempt to recall where I was and what time of day it was when I first heard of the event taking place in Washington, D.C., on January 6, 2021, my mind remains fuzzy. However, the faces, devoid of guilt, respect or self-awareness, of those who stormed the capital without hesitation, are forever marked on the inner recesses of my brain, body and spirit. I can recall the scene perfectly—the faces, the energies, the costumes, and the passion to destroy.

I was particularly struck (alarmed, really) when I recognized the same vacant, dissociative look of Derek Chauvin in the eyes of the insurrectionists. Their zealousness, although chaotic and frenzied, felt almost orchestrated. And because it took quite some time before we saw a robust response from local police, the National Guard, or the military, I wondered if what I was seeing could be the beginning of a civil war. I was frightened because I recognized people from my extended neighborhood amongst the violent groups. I feared becoming helpless, hopeless, and unprotected in the event of spreading unrest. I wondered with a sense of incredulity—am I really in the United States?

In my many years upon the earth, I've seen my fair share of criminal behavior go unpunished by police and, in some instances, even instigated by the police. From junior high school onwards, I witnessed the beatings and torture of people who looked like me in the American South during the Civil Rights Movement. I had watched the televised accounts of water hoses set upon innocent men and women whose only crime was wanting a soda or cup of coffee at a local lunch counter. I knew that such simple wants could end with being bludgeoned and beaten without mercy. This was what I was seeing on January 6th.

I was reminded of the days when the infamous Ku Klux Klan ruled our South, boasting amongst its membership those who had sworn to keep citizens (all citizens!) safe. In this version, the victims of beatings and terror were those sworn to "protect and serve" their constituents. How could they possibly hold back a wave of insurrectionists, so high on zealotry and conviction that they had traveled (thousands of miles, in some cases) to incite criminality, terror, and chaos? How could we protect ourselves from a dangerous group, acting under the support and encouragement of a U.S. president? What could we do as we watched law enforcement struggle to contain the violence while my fellow citizens hurled chants to "hang" our Vice-President against the walls of the Capitol Building? Of course, I was scared!

As I watched the potential fall of our democratic nation, I asked myself: what does this mean for me and my loved ones? What does it mean if the person in charge of our nation could call for an end to who and what we purport to be? That a tremendous lie, that surely all logical and sensible people could not believe, could cause the end of our sacred nation was unfathomable. How could so many citizens have lost their sense of reason, blindly following the incoherent messages of an egomaniacal mad man who showed little regard for the wellbeing of the country he was supposed to be leading? Given what I know and have experienced over my long life, is it crazy that as I watched the January 6 insurrection, I feared that the eradication of Black Americans, and other minority groups, might soon follow?

The events of January 6 exposed the tenuousness of our democracy, and thus, the tenuousness of my very existence as a black woman in the United States. This precarity is an ongoing uncertainty, mistrust, and fear that I (and others, maybe even yourself, dear reader) live with every day.

We are also living through a moment in our history when everyone's lives are at risk due to unprecedented levels of gun violence. Another symptom of our national underlying dis/ease are the seemingly endless mass shootings. With each new horrific and traumatic shooting, we mourn the lives of victims and their loved ones, offer "thoughts and prayers," yet are unable, as a citizenry, to take effective legislative action to reduce the occurrence of these senseless murders. Hardly anyone in this country does not know someone whose life has been affected by gun violence. A very good friend shared that her mother lived close to the supermarket in Buffalo where many Black Americans were needlessly killed on May 14, 2022. We are still trying to understand the tragedy in Uvalde, Texas, and the loss of both children and adults. Reasonable people can't understand how and why assault weapons are available as tools to kill other humans, creating mayhem, chaos and tremendous loss.

We are a sick country. While we may have come through the worst of the COVID-19 pandemic, we are still suffering from the effects of a pandemic of hatred and fear against those perceived as different. Now, more than ever, we the people are in need of a healing balm.

Again, dear Reader, you may ask, what has compelled me to share these stories here and now? Because they add more dimensions to the multi-faceted trauma I have experienced. Because I want to show you how interconnected and intersectional these traumas are. Because it is my hope that these stories can assist you in understanding why my bucket tipped when it did. And because I want to capture, drop by drop, how so many physical, emotional, and spiritual injuries deluged my personhood until all I had left were the words with which I am now writing this book.

Chapter 2

You Can't Unlock a Door With Keys That Don't Work

My own life's story has coincided with the critical events of the 1960s and 1970s and onwards to our current epoch. We cheered as schools were desegregated; we cheered for a "war on poverty" that might end our hunger; we cheered when we were informed that universities and colleges would seek to recruit minority students, when laws were enacted to prevent segregation in housing and employment. Many of us bought into the rhetoric and false information that justified the incarceration of millions of African American people, especially men, and the racial profiling that allowed this system to flourish, unchecked. And perhaps, people of color, such as I, falsely conspired with whites, thinking that laws, policies and procedures would, indeed, make our lives better.

Decades have passed since those days of early optimism, and we are only now beginning to have national conversations about the failure of the Civil Rights Movement and the reality of racial disparities in our country. How do we fully understand where we find ourselves currently? Nearly sixty years since the passage of the Equal Rights Amendment, and the sojourn of Black Americans towards full emancipation, personhood, and equality still continues. How much has changed since Dr. Martin Luther King Jr. outlined the three "major evils" facing African American communities—"the evil of racism, the evil of poverty and the evil of war"—in a speech he delivered on May 10, 1967? Our society's so-called fixes for injustice and inequality (of all types!) have never addressed the intersectional and overlapping social, political, and economic forces that work to disempower African Americans, people of color, the poor, immigrants, women, and LGBTQIA. You simply can't unlock a door if you don't have the right keys!

Confronting Conditions of Powerlessness: The Isms that Dim Our Light

Racism, sexism, classism, ableism, ageism, antisemitism, homophobia, and discrimination of all types are isms that create conditions of objectification and powerlessness. They are the things that make us feel "less than" because of one or more aspects of our identity. Experiencing isms impacts our health, wealth, and opportunities. Isms take their toll on us, emotionally, mentally, physically, and spiritually.

In order to understand isms, we must remember that they are based on the judgments we have about others, and they involve the exertion and control of, and by, power. *Isms* are implemented, maintained, and controlled by those in power, often driven by a fear of losing that power. The threat of powerlessness can drive even well-meaning people to acts of greed, selfishness, and self-preservation, at the expense of others. There are people who believe that many of the assets or privileges they possess shield them from powerlessness. And they will do nearly anything to protect that privilege.

A "zero-sum paradigm" is the idea that progress for some must come at the expense of others. Clinging to that false logic, some people will act against their own self-interest, simply to block the progress of others. Nowhere are the examples more compelling than in the history of race-based lawmaking in the United States. In her best-selling book, *The Sum of Us: What Racism Costs Everyone and How We Can Prosper Together*, author and policy-maker Heather McGhee recounts how in the 1950s and 1960s, white city officials opted to drain their public swimming pools rather than integrate them with their black neighbors. She also documents how white people will lower the sale price on their home when they see that black people are moving in, just to get out of the neighborhood as quickly as possible.

I saw such "white flight" happen first-hand in the neighborhood in which I grew up. My neighborhood began to change ethnically sometime during the 1960s, when there was a mass movement of white ethnics from Manhattan and the surrounding boroughs to Long Island's suburban Levittown or New Jersey. Indeed, within New Jersey's affluent Bergen County, it is a well-documented fact that as Black Americans began to move into various neighborhoods in Teaneck and Englewood, white homeowners fled, often taking less money for their property. And as they moved out, additional people of color moved in.

Such demographic changes were not simply the result of individual racism. "White flight" and "ghettoization" were supported and created through American institutions and law. Official practices such as redlining helped to cement and formalize the creation of ethnic enclaves, racial segregation, and planned communities, enabling whites to hold on to the most desirable real estate and housing locations. You can read more about this in *The Possessive Investment in Whiteness: How White People Profit from Identity Politics* by the historian George Lipsitz. While some Black Americans successfully used legal redress to "sneak" into these communities, they were often subject to various racialized and violent acts. My uncle, for example, managed to obtain housing in a privileged, white neighborhood, only to have a cross burnt in front of his house. Many African Americans were (and are) torn between wanting the best for their families but also knowing that they might be subjected to racial violence.

Power is precarious. History and personal experience indicate that the ownership and possession of power and privilege is dependent upon and supported by external circumstances—the people, places and things that support your power. The history of various white ethnic groups illustrates my point. Upon arrival to the United States, the Irish, the Polish, and peoples from southern and eastern Europe (including Jews), were not considered legally "white." They suffered from discrimination and ghettoization. They experienced incredible amounts of powerlessness. Yet, over time, as the definitions and meaning of whiteness, specifically, and race in general changed, these white ethnic minorities were able to assimilate into a more privileged status due to their lighter skin. You can read more about this story in *Whiteness of a Different Color: European Immigrants and the Alchemy of Race* by Matthew Frye Jacobson.

The truth is, isms and the accompanying fears of powerlessness, affect all of us, regardless of whether or not we consciously count ourselves amongst a minority group. However, our experiences of isms are not always equal. The concept of intersectionality can help us understand how identity impacts experiences of trauma and powerlessness.

My Life, Your Life: An Intersection of Isms

I often conduct an exercise in classes asking people to identify what they see as the most salient part of their identity. One student told me her role as a mother was the most important factor about her identity. Many students focused on just being white and had little understanding of their ethnicity and what that meant for them and their families. I offer this exercise to help students recognize the difference between how we may perceive ourselves and how others may perceive us. This exercise helps students begin to think about intersectionality.

We will be forever grateful to Prof. Kimberlé Crenshaw who developed the concept of intersectionality. In its most broad definition, intersectionality refers to the complex nature of personal identity: who we are is a web of traits and characteristics, the things we inherited and things we have chosen, the way we see and define ourselves and the way others see and define us. Intersectionality helps us understand and conceptualize, in a more holistic way, the number of roles, classifications, and groupings that represent a person's identity and lived experience.

But Prof. Crenshaw had the specific experiences of black women in mind when she developed the legal definition of intersectionality. She used this concept to illustrate the overlapping discriminations of race, gender, and class that limited working-class black women's opportunities and their abilities to seek legal recourse. She noted how there were laws to address racism in the workplace and laws to address sexism, but there were no existing laws that addressed the simultaneous condition of being black and a woman and experiencing discrimination that was both race- and gender-based. Black women were falling between the cracks and gaps in the American justice system.

What we can learn from Crenshaw's concept of intersectionality is that some people's intersecting identities put them *at greater risk of* experiencing specific forms of powerlessness related to overlapping isms: violence, poverty, second-class citizenship, and a life-long quest for equality. In other words, it's impossible to separate personal, individual experiences of powerlessness with the social institutions that perpetuate disparity.

Particularly for African Americans, our opportunities (and lives) have been curtailed by a combination of isms, including racism, but also many other intersecting forms of discrimination. Consider the identifying intersections that impacted George Floyd's life and death. His vulnerability was a combination of circumstances, including his gender, his socio-economic class, his build and stature, and the neighborhood he lived and shopped in. Indeed, had Mr. Floyd been employed, he might have been at work on Monday, May 25th 2020, instead of out buying cigarettes. Consider the common stereotype of a criminal: a black man in a poorer neighborhood. Here we can see the intersecting prejudices across race, gender, and class.

Individuals such as myself and George Floyd, who experience more than one of these modes of oppression, may not know which one came first, or which are present in any given situation. Faced with attempts to control or shut down our power, we may feel overwhelmed by oppression, pain, hurt, and fear. All these things end up in that bucket, filling it up, tipping it over. *Drip… drip…drip…*

As I review my own life, I have struggled with the feelings of powerlessness brought on by my own intersectional identity and the subsequent experience of overlapping isms. When I was a child, my doting godmother often lovingly called me "half breed," referring to the fact that, like her, I am of African American and African Caribbean ancestry. My mixed heritage is an example of intersectionality; each of these cultures and ethnicities have different socio-political-economic expressions (you'll read more about these differences in the following chapters where I share the histories of my maternal and paternal ancestors). Later, I would come to understand the negative connotation of "half breed" for myself and others, but as a child, I understood her words as a proud expression of my multifaceted heritage and identity.

It's worth repeating: our identities may be numerous and multiple, but our various parts are not always treated as equal. In the case of African Americans, it often feels as if our race, designated by our skin color, defines our existence. Our darker skin sets us apart, regardless of our other identities. And this one single aspect of difference can reverberate throughout every aspect of our public and private lives. One single black person can simultaneously experience multiple disparities—in access to health care, education, employment, voting rights, and the justice system, among others. This is why, even my own class status, education, and profession have not insulated me from racial profiling. Now, as an elder, I understand that my identity is truly multidimensional, and not only because of my ethnic and racial background. I understand that who I am is a mixture of how I see and define myself and how I am seen and defined by others. But it has taken me a long time to reach this position of clarity. In fact, I would offer categorically that inwardly and outwardly my race and ethnicity have played the largest part in my identity—and I am not alone in this experience.

What the "n-word" Means To Me

Flashback to sometime in the 1980s. I was driving on Route 22 towards Plainfield in New Jersey with a white female colleague. It was around that time when the evening's darkness is about to set in. I was nearing an intersection where I needed to be in the left lane, when a person behind me started blowing her horn for me to move. Although I was relentlessly trying to move over so the car behind me could go to the right, but I was not fast enough. As the driver passed us, she stopped, rolled down her window, and said, "I hate you, you black n*****, bitch."

I felt like someone had stabbed me. All I could do was scream. After the hurt subsided, I felt a powerful landslide of anger. I replayed the incident in my mind's eye, imagining going after my assailant and ramming my car into hers, just trying to get these awful feelings to stop. Not only was I called the "n-word" and a bitch, but I was also told that I was hated by a complete stranger! Was this an example of racial, sexual, or ethnic oppression? At the time, my inner voice told me that I was feeling all three at the same time. And that is why I screamed.

For African Americans, the "n-word" is never just the "n-word." When white people call black people by that name, they weaponize language. The word becomes a weapon. And, like a weapon, it's meant to harm. To be called the "n-word" is to be wounded; indeed, when that woman shouted those words at me, I felt as if I had been shot. The word is the blade of a knife, the bullet of a gun, the hand that punches or slaps, the foot that kicks, or the knee that kneels on our neck. For African Americans, the "n-word" is never just the "n-word."

Andrew Hacker, a noted historian and political scientist at Queens College in NYC, writes about the significance of the "n-word" in his book, *Two Nations: Black and White, Separate, Hostile, Unequal*. He writes that there's more to the word than a textbook definition. Every time a black person hears that word, it brings up an entire history of racial discrimination and violence. It calls to mind every murder, rape, lynching, every feeling of powerlessness, going all the way back to the slave ships. From slavery through Reconstruction, Jim Crow, the Civil Rights Movement, the murders of Rev. Dr. Martin Luther King, Jr. and Malcom

X, through the years of "welfare queens" and "crack whores" and mass incarceration, that word is an expression of all of the most dehumanizing aspects of black history. The word negates and erases the beauty and strength of our African ancestors who built and maintained powerful, successful communities, especially in West Africa, whose legacies live on in the DNA of many African Americans. Gender biases, class wars, a generalized fear of what's different—all can be present in one moment of powerlessness. The "n-word" is more than a racial epithet, it is the ultimate way to make us feel as if anything can be done to us because we have no power. It is a word meant to kill and disarm; it is a word that captures, in 6 letters, the entire objectification process. When someone uses that word on you, you become the object. You are stripped of your humanity. You are nothing more than that word. Your mind, body, and soul are murdered. Your personhood is erased, replaced with that word. You become the word. And nothing more.

This is what I saw in the eyes of Derek Chauvin. In that deep emptiness, that endless blankness, I knew that George Floyd was, to him, nothing more than an object. Nothing more than one more n*****.

Drip...drip...drip...another drop in the bucket. Drip...drip...drip... racism, like water, erodes.

Crazy, Out of My Mind

During my mental health career in state government, one of my well-meaning white staffers once said to me, "I don't know how black people do it. I would be crazy, out of my mind, living in this society." And as he said this, I thought of those times when, yes, I *did* feel crazy, alone, alienated, and angry.

How does one survive such debilitating emotions was the question he didn't ask. Surely, my colleague wasn't suggesting that suicide or homicide was the answer? This is surely not an option for us. Having my feelings, experiences, and background validated helps me. Such was the case earlier this very week when I happened to be watching one of the more feeling-focused television shows called, "A Million Little Things." One of the main characters, Rome, is a black man whose racial-ethnic identity has not been part of his character arc. Indeed, the show has not freely or regularly explored issues of race and ethnicity, although sexual harassment, suicide, infidelity and stigma were all part of the show's themes. Rome is portrayed as "just one of the guys," along with two white buddies. However, during this recently aired episode, Rome is confronted by a white man in a sports stadium while he's taking a video. The interaction becomes increasingly confrontational as the white man escalates the argument, but Rome remains "cool." His white friend intervenes and ends up punching the white confronter, knocking him to the ground despite Rome's urgent requests to calm down. After being arrested, Rome and his friend are sitting in a police car when Rome brings up the fact that although they're close friends, his white friend does not fully understand Rome's "world." Rome goes on to say something like, "do you know why I wore this button shirt today? Because I knew I was likely to be the only black guy here, and I wanted to make sure I looked my best. You know, I couldn't wear a hoodie like you because it would be assumed I am a hood." His words were validating for me. They echoed in my ears and touched my heart, because fairly recently I had been followed in a department store by a plainclothes security person (although I did not look like a "hood"). This incident was one of thousands that have happened to me throughout my life. A week before, the same thing happened to my husband while he was shopping for clothes for our granddaughter.

Probably due to the way in which I was socialized, I've always felt it necessary for me to be prepared and "on" when I am in public. I have often heard from my elders that, as a black person, I always have to be better—far better than the average person. I expect to be judged on my appearance, including my clothing, hair care, hygienic standards, etc., and so it is essential that I am always *more than* presentable. These experiences of having to behave and "be" in a certain manner are part of what it means to be black in America. And when you consider how impossible it is for *anyone* to meet these standards, it is surprising that more black people do not suffer from traumatic stress, as my former colleague implied when he said he'd be "crazy out of [his] mind" if he were black. Although fictional, Rome's poignant words reminded me that I am not crazy.

Overcoming the Challenges of Class

Because my early life was dominated by my experiences of being female and black, I did not feel the full impact of class difference until I went to college. In part, I believe this was because much of my childhood and adolescence were spent in my neighborhood or similar neighborhoods in New York City. Most of my friends and schoolmates were from a similar, working class to lower-middle class socioeconomic strata. All of us went to public school; many families owned their homes or were struggling to do so.

College was a rude awakening. Many of my classmates did not have to work, did not need a scholarship to attend college, and had large allowances, cars, and lots of clothes. Many had never visited the parts of New York City that I lived in, and thought danger lurked everywhere. In fact, my freshman-year roommate fit that description. She was from a very typical New Jersey suburb, and when she told her mother she had a black roommate, her mother said it "would be a good thing for her." To this day, I don't know why!

I found peace when I found my social group, students like me who had no interest in my socioeconomic status, past or present. This grouping was diverse and included a number of white folks. In fact, we embodied intersectionality! Such was the case with our student government, which was governed in large part by what many would call "hippies." The black student group and the student government worked together. We were also friends, spending time together, helping each other study, and seeking advice about teachers and assignments. Many of them supported black studies and the hiring of professors of color. They were understanding and listened patiently to my feelings and anger regarding racial issues and the continued face of racism on the campus. Our multidimensional group demonstrated how intersectionality and solidarity across differences can create opportunities for sharing resources and power. We enjoyed some successes, albeit limited ones, by embracing and working with our differences.

As I began to find my center and grounding with my peers, my confidence grew. And I believe this is a key factor in coping with issues of class differences and feeling stigmatized. Once you learn that discrimination begins with the belief that one class is better than another, and then you work to unlearn that belief, you can more easily find common ground. With a sense of equality, your confidence and sense of self and self-efficacy begin to grow. And so, together with my social grouping and the safety net provided by my surrogate campus mother, Mrs. G., a loving white woman from Wales (more on this in Chapter 4!), social class differences were not a significant part of my early life experiences.

From Surviving to Thriving: The Key is Intersectionality

There is not one aspect of an African American's experience that is not impacted by race. Not only unequal access to resources and social discriminations, but also the toll that intersecting experiences of powerlessness and isms take on our sense of self-worth and identity. If we speak up about our challenges, we may be accused of "playing the race card." We might suffer the double jeopardy of simultaneously experiencing racism and having the validity of that experience questioned or denied. We might begin to question our own experience of reality, or believe that maybe others are right, and we are "crazy," "overreacting" or even delusional. This type of gas-lighting can create or compound trauma. At times, existence itself may feel like an insurmountable challenge to African Americans.

How does one survive? I am reminded of the saying, "walking by faith, not by sight." I have often found myself navigating these issues feeling as if I am walking in a dimly lit corridor, without enough light to really see what's going on, but having faith that somehow the answers to these challenges lay beyond the darkness. Like many, I continue to tread alone in this darkness, always looking towards the light. I hold onto my life preserver in the sea of despair.

Before we can unlock the door with the right keys, we need to know why our existing keys aren't working. While many see the Civil Rights Movement as the culmination of the struggle for racial justice in the United States, the truth is that we still have a way to go. Unfortunately, the Civil Rights Movement did not adequately address issues of intersectionality amongst African American people. To this day, legislation, policy, and other vehicles for social/economic/political change have yet to fully incorporate the intersections of race, class, gender, sexuality, etc., when framing issues around race. To finish the social justice project of the Civil Rights Movement, we must understand how important intersectionality is for the lived experiences of formal and informal racist practices; we must challenge ourselves to go further to creatively and strategically address racism.

When we admit to ourselves that we have yet to conquer these evils, how do we stop ourselves from feelings of powerlessness, hopelessness, rage, and despair? How is it possible for African Americans to remain peaceful in light of such callous violence? How is it that we have not taken to the streets, taken up arms, and returned the violence, an eye for an eye and a tooth for a tooth? And you may ask, how is it that I have not resorted to violence? How can I carry the weight of so much trauma and not retaliate? I would be lying to you, my reader, if I told you that I have never thought of violence. I, too, have been enraged at times. I, too, have felt my blood sing with revenge, with the temptation to hate all white people. I, too, understand hatred.

In the aftermath of my emotional turmoil following the death of George Floyd and the overwhelming evidence that the Civil Rights Movement has failed our country, I asked myself in silence and fear, where do I go from here? What separates me from the likes of Derek Chauvin or the Oath Keepers? What separates me from the white nationalist terrorist, lurking on chat boards in the darkest places of the internet and carefully crafting devious plans? Must I succumb to the rage, a sense of powerful alienation in the country in which I was born? Where do I find solace and perhaps instances of triumph? Will it come from writing the pages of this book? As I began to re-frame my disillusionment, fear, and rage, I found a renewed sense of urgency to think through our traumatic histories, national and personal, individual and familiar, and offer strategies for managing pain. I began to refocus on healing.

Again, my thoughts turned to my own family. The death of George Floyd flooded me anew with admiration for my ancestors who were able not only to survive but also *thrive* when faced with circumstances of powerlessness and dehumanization. I think of my great-grandparents born into slavery in the South. I think of my grandparents born into a society ruled by the laws of Jim Crow. Did not my own ancestors suffer—and survive!—a similar dehumanization? Were they not also brutalized under a system that coded such brutality as legal and necessary? I felt the recognition and understanding of their history wash over me. In their stories, I find strength and determination—for how can I not offer myself the same opportunity to persevere and prosper?

The truth is, simply reacting to powerlessness and oppression isn't enough. Instead, we need to take an active part in addressing and eliminating forms of oppression through training, teaching, advocacy, politics, art, writing, religion…whatever way we feel called upon to help. Later in this book, I share some holistic strategies for healing and eradicating the trauma caused by conditions of powerlessness. At the heart of all my healing modalities is the conviction that differing worldviews do not make others deficient or pathological; instead, by understanding others' worldviews, we raise our consciousness and increase our inner self-knowledge. Feelings of hopelessness and despair keep us from fulfilling our divine purpose and threaten to dim our light. This is why we have an urgent need—an opportunity—to embrace holistic change and healing. But in order to know where we are going, we have to know where we've been.

Chapter 3

The Wise Woman's Family Sojourn: A Path to Understanding Context

Many who are perhaps wiser than I insist that, in a spiritual sense, we choose our families before we are born. Cultural anthropologists, ethnographers and mental health professionals agree that we learn much of who we are from our families. If I had to do it all over again, I would indeed choose to grow up and be reared amongst my clan. The lives and stories of my family have woven themselves into the fabric of my being; they are the seeds sown into the rich soil that nourished me into who and what I have become. I embody all the choices, good and bad, of my ancestors. So, who are these people, these ancestors of this wise woman? I am a combination of all of them. And this is their story—my story.

A New Deluge

In the aftermath of Mr. Floyd's murder, I began having lucid dreams. Various family members visited me, gathering around offering their support and love from the spiritual realm. And I needed it. My intense emotional reaction to the death of George Floyd had left me in a dark place. I examined and reexamined my emotional, psychological, and cognitive status. Had I been working too hard? Not sleeping enough? Neglecting my own self-care? Was I suffering from undiagnosed Post Traumatic Stress Disorder or perhaps Acute Stress Disorder? Was this yet again, Complex Trauma? My musings failed to provide me with an explanation.

The presence of my family members in my thoughts and emotions got me thinking about my family's constellations and sojourns. I am part of an ordinary family bound together by extraordinary intersections. My family's contexts are rife with poverty, domestic violence, alcoholism, drug abuse, unemployment, infidelity, a lack of, and poor, communication, unresolved anger, undiagnosed Post-Traumatic Stress Disorder and much more. But I am also part of an extraordinary family bound together by our ordinary intersections—of hard work, of strong moral and ethical values, of education, of a commitment to doing what it takes to thrive, of hope for and investment in children. However, as African Americans, my family experienced these challenges within the context of larger *isms*—the social, political, and economic inequities and disparities of structural and institutional racism.

My relatives grew up enslaved and in a post-enslavement society, negotiating the world of Jim Crow, which was designed to re-enslave African Americans, celebrating the Civil Rights Movement, and navigating our present national racial reckoning. Surely they, too, confronted circumstances of trauma and turmoil. In particular, I felt the presence of my Great-Grandfather Ceasar, who, after being wrongfully accused of shooting the sheriff's deputy in circumstances that remain unclear, disappeared into the velvet folds of a Mississippi night with the law hot on his heels (this was around the turn of the 20th century). Why was he accused of this crime? Was it because of his marriage to my white Irish great-grandmother in a time when interracial marriage was illegal? Was he seen as a ravager of white women or a violent "negro" who needed to be confined? Was it because he was seen as threat or a challenge to the strict caste system of Money, Mississippi in the early 20th century? Was he being chased because he was black in the Jim Crow south? Was my Afro-Caribbean grandfather who worked as an engineer on the Panama Canal denied employment in New York as an engineer because the white bosses assumed he lacked intelligence and skill simply because he was black? What about my maternal grandmother's constant sexual harassment?

As I re-visited the circumstances of my ancestry, I began to consider anew how my family's socialization process has been impacted by challenges in handling trauma. What strategies or insights might I learn from re-visiting my family's stories (and secrets) that could help rescue me from the seas of despair, the flooding of feelings of powerlessness? Might their experience with coping with trauma help me to understand my own reactions to the murder of George Floyd? Indeed, when I reconsidered my own family's experiences in the aftermath of the death of George Floyd, I opened the floodgates to a new deluge of questions.

Separated by more than one hundred years, but how different, really, were the realities faced by my great-grandfather and George Floyd? In a different story, my great-grandfather would have been captured, brutalized, and lynched, a practice that has changed in form but not in intent. Are not both men victims of an unjust justice system? Was watching the murder of George Floyd in 2020 so traumatic because it hurts to think that perhaps centuries of the systematic brutalization and murder of African Americans has been for nothing?

What would these ancestors have to say in response to the murder of George Floyd? Perhaps Great-Grandfather Ceasar and my other ancestors had a higher tolerance than I for the dire and inhumane? For the everyday traumas of being black in America? How would they respond to my reactions? Might their background and experience have impacted their reactions? Was there some thread of ancestral wisdom and psycho-spiritual fortitude, passed on through my family, that helped *me* survive and thrive? What secrets am I only beginning to understand now? Would a review of my family's identity help me to understand my own socialization process? What might I learn from my family's context that might help me understand how I learned to manage and thrive through trauma?

Like George Floyd, I was reared in a family that believed in a vision of a fully integrated community and society which provides equality and opportunity to all. However, unlike other cultures that expect children to follow in the footsteps of their parents, perhaps inheriting a generations-old business or profession, my family expected each new generation to improve upon the last, rising higher up in their perceived social strata. My family valued professional success. This meant higher education. The credo

I grew up with was "do the right thing" in spite of what others do or think. But what if these expectations were unrealistic and even unattainable? Is it more advantageous to expect the worst? Has my experience with the promises of freedom and opportunity that come with integration made me more susceptible to being thrown off course by injustice?

With George Floyd and Great-Grandfather Ceasar in mind, two sides of the same coin, I embarked on a journey into my family's past, intent on understanding my reaction to current circumstances, hoping that whatever I might discover would also help others.

A History of Silence and Secrets

Much of what I have learned about my family's history was shared orally or not at all. While some can turn to genealogical records going back centuries or can easily discover their pasts in history books, African-Americans have had poor access to our historical narrative, and only recently have we had any role in shaping it. Our records were concealed, badly recorded or not at all, withheld, and lost. At the same time, African-Americans inherited a rich legacy of oral tradition from our African ancestors. Both the legacy of a strong oral tradition and the paucity of written historical records have contributed to the important role that storytelling, songs, and even prayers, have in passing down the traditions and histories of African American culture. I've come to realize, however, that our oral traditional is as much about the unspoken as it the spoken.

In my relatively short lifetime, I can think of so many important facts about our history that have only recently emerged.

Consider *Rosewood*, the movie depiction of the 1923 Rosewood massacre in Florida, as well as recent films such as *Amistad, 12 Years a Slave, Harriet*, and the various documentaries which have addressed the destruction of "Black Wall Street" in Tulsa, Oklahoma. Did you know that slaveholders developed journals that focused on ways to make their "holdings" more profitable? These journals detailed the proper way to punish slaves, breeding suggestions, all of the ways in which their "objects" (my enslaved ancestors) could yield maximum profit. Let us not forget the so-called mental health diagnosis "drapetomania," which was given to slaves who wished to flee their horrific enslavement. Or the fact that experimental surgical operations were performed on enslaved women without anesthesia. Such horrific facts don't appear in our history books; they don't sit comfortably with our beloved images of Dr. Martin Luther King, Jr. and Rosa Parks during Black History Month.

To understand why so much of our history remains unknown, we have to go back to slavery. Slavery and its aftermath fractured families. Overtly and covertly, our families were encouraged to keep secrets to survive. Willful denial and cognitive dissonance were all mechanisms to cope with the challenges and difficulties of being black in a white-dominated society. We felt ashamed of ourselves and our histories. It didn't help that what we now call the Black Experience wasn't taught in any of the schools that I attended. Without a larger narrative in which we could situate ourselves, understand ourselves, and envision our lives as part of a larger legacy, we felt "less than," a psychological-social-economic-political state that those in power were happy to maintain. We kept silent about sexual violence, our unequal access to education and resources, the times we sided with a victimizer in order to survive, poverty; we kept quiet about hating our skin color or the texture of our hair. Secrecy was a veil we wore to cloak our shame. And this was no different in my family of origin.

My paternal grandmother could often be heard admonishing that "children were seen and not heard." These infamous words might be familiar to you, as well. In retrospect, I wonder if her admonitions conditioned me to not seek answers to the questions that resonated within me. And while my grandfather was an avid storyteller and jokester, especially after huge family dinners, he rarely talked about his birthplace in Enfield, North Carolina, his parents or his siblings. I knew nothing of his early life despite being the eldest grandchild and often referred to by him as "beautiful princess." Although I was an outwardly inquisitive, warm, and friendly kid, I did not ask questions about the origins and life stories of my grandparents' parents.

Shortly before he succumbed to a lengthy illness, my father spoke for the first time about my Great-Grandfather Ceasar. He uttered the disturbing words, "he shot the sheriff." At that time, my father was in his 70s, suffering with the debilitating effects of chronic heart failure, mild to moderate dementia, and a number of other chronic illnesses that impacted his daily life activities. So, my initial reaction was disbelief. Was the loss of oxygen to his brain making him babble? Yet, later, when I heard those same words whispered hesitantly on the phone by my second cousin—as if the police or sheriff would arrive at any second and cart dear Great-Grandfather Ceasar off to the gallows—I knew there was much more to the story.

It was time. I heard the voices of ancestors telling me to pull back that veil of secrecy and release the shame that still silenced my family's history. It was time to tell the stories.

On the Trail of History: From Money, Mississippi to Enfield, North Carolina

In 2009, my award-winning journalist daughter and I traveled through the Mississippi Delta and up to northeast rural North Carolina doing extensive research in libraries and courthouses, reviewing census records, newspaper clippings, rolls of microfilm, and interviewing local people, trying to find any written documentation that might shed some light on the mystery of Great-Grandfather Ceasar's fate. Eventually, we pieced together not only his dramatic tale but much more about our family's long and fascinating history.

Great-grandfather Ceasar's parents, Fred and Annie Hines, were born into slavery circa 1820 in North Carolina. Before Annie died and Fred re-married multiple times to women younger than himself, the two were "blessed" with a dozen children, one of which they named Ceasar. Ceasar was described as "coal black with black straight hair and gleaming white teeth." Ceasar was born in 1862 or 1863 in northeast North Carolina. Known as a "good shot" by relatives, Ceasar worked as a farm laborer in the post-Reconstruction period and later entered the ministry. His wife, my great-grandmother Jane Harris, was born on the Isle of Man. She was white and a milkmaid by profession. Jane milked cows and also knew how to separate the milk from the cream, prepare the milk for drinking, make butter and buttermilk, and even make cheese. Jane relocated first to Dublin, Ireland, before coming to the United States to seek a better life. Ceasar met and married Jane Harris around 1880, and they settled in northeastern North Carolina, each taking a manual labor job on local plantations.

Jane and Ceasar's story is quite extraordinary for the times in which they lived. Their passionate love affair defied the boundaries of race and law. During years when interracial marriage was illegal and punished, formally and informally, with great violence, they risked everything to be together. It's quite possible that the family avoided potential controversy by claiming that Jane was "mulatto." If this is true, Jane was willing to strip herself of the rights and protections that she would've had as a white woman in order to marry Ceasar.

From a photo passed down from grandfather, as well as how I see her in my mind's-eye, Jane was a beautiful woman. In the photo, she is unsmiling. This was typical of the time period, but my intuition also tells me that she was cautious about expressing her emotions and preferred actions and behavior over words that, at times, might have appeared empty and meaningless. She was dark-haired and tall in stature, especially for a woman of her time. She valued the importance of family, loyalty, hard work, and thrift, but especially the loving and passionate relationship that she had with Ceasar. As an immigrant from Ireland, it would make perfect sense that she sought an existence that required immense hard work and diligence but also predictability, safety, security, and love. And so, against all odds, they entered into the bonds of matrimony and travelled to Money, Mississippi, where they acquired a shot-gun house (a narrow, rectangular style of housing popular in the American South in the post-Civil War years) and settled into a life of hard work and domesticity.

Jane and Ceasar were likely part of the odious share-cropping system. In the post-Reconstruction-Jim Crow era, sharecropping was a system of farming and land management that replaced the slave system in the South. African American families rented a plot of land from the owner, as well as all of the implements needed to plant and grow their crops. All of their supplies had to be purchased from the owner's "company store," where owners had complete control over the prices. Owners could raise prices at will, hike up interest rates, and create situations in which it was impossible for sharecropping families to ever pay off their bills. If, for some reason—and there were many reasons—a family could cultivate a good crop, they incurred even greater debt, digging themselves deeper into a hole they could never climb out of. Many families suffered this fate, without resources to feed or provide for themselves. Sharecroppers had no legal recourse, as it was understood that the local authorities supported land owners. Debtors could be jailed, beaten, and even killed, for running away or otherwise trying to escape the bonds of debt-slavery. It was an impossible situation. This devastating period in the United States' history was superbly portrayed by Cicely Tyson and Paul Winfield in the 1972 movie, *Sounder*. It was into this world that Jane and Ceasar's children were born, including two daughters named Bertha and Martha.

Money, Mississippi

You may not know that Money, Mississippi is a significant location for African American history. It is the town made infamous by the torture and murder of young Emmett Till (whose story I chronicled in Chapter One). The once-thriving town never recovered after Till's torture and murder. The town has become an ironic play on its own name. During our visit to the area, my daughter and I found not money, but its lack. The store where Till allegedly made remarks to a white woman was boarded up. There were no stores or other indications of a thriving community. Surrounding the town are soybean farms, a church cemetery in need of great attention, and so-called historical slave houses where guests could re-create the living conditions during slavery. We were dismayed to see the dire poverty and remnants of segregation that continue to exist.

As part of our journey, we went to the local cemetery to see if my great-grandfather was buried there, or if there might be some information about him there. The cemetery stood, overgrown and unattended, next to a small, white stone community church that looked as if it might be the center of activity for the locals but also in a state of a disrepair. It was nearly impossible to read the names and information on the headstones in the cemetery, despite being the burial site of the renowned blues musician Robert Johnson. Local lore says Johnson sold his soul to the devil for his blues talent. The depressing reality of deterioration and neglect conflicted with the signs attesting to the historical importance of Mr. Johnson and his musical legacy.

Indeed, I felt conflicted and confused in the south. I was disturbed by the terrible poverty amongst people of color, the vast economic disparities between blacks and whites, the horrific lack of employment and opportunities for blacks, and the stark reality that people of color did not have, and still do not have, a fair shot. It was alien to me, dangerous. A place where people get lynched. In so many places, we could feel a certain tension in the air.

It was obvious to us that members of the black community who still live there continue to feel the sting of Emmett Till's murder. Although there were a few houses, my daughter and I met a lovely elderly couple who offered us a seat on their porch. They shared that when they were much younger, they could not sit quietly on their porch, minding their own business. Any white man could come up to them and ask them why they were not working. If black people did not offer a reasonable explanation, uncertain consequences would occur. This practice was part of Jim Crow's insidious "Black Codes," a series of informal laws and practices meant to terrorize free black people. Can you imagine an experience of not being able to sit quietly minding your own business without being accosted, without fearing dire consequences? I was shaken from speaking to so many people who had been personally affected by the child's torture and murder. It hurts to think that perhaps Emmett Till died in vain.

As a result of the town's infamous and troubled history, initially, most people thought we were there to do research on Emmett Till, and they expressed a willingness to help in any way they could. So, while visiting with locals, my daughter and I often shared what we knew of Great-Grandfather Ceasar's story: According to Martha, their eldest child, Ceasar was observed running through the long, shot-gun house, which was shaped, as the name implies, like a shot-gun, with the sheriff in pursuit. That day, Great-Grandfather Ceasar escaped the law. When I told one woman the part of the story where my great-grandfather allegedly shot the sheriff, she said, "Good." It was a chilling response. Clearly, this was an area steeped in a history of injustice.

Later, I wondered why her answer stayed with me. Didn't I also understand the impulse towards vengeance? Didn't I also know the trauma that invites rage and cold-blooded brutality? If this was the world that produced my ancestors, certainly they, too, must've felt the same anger, the same sense of retribution and vengeance. What tools and strategies did my family use to avoid giving into racial hatred and violence? How am I part of that familial legacy?

One woman in particular would provide the missing key to unlocking the secrets of Great-Grandfather Ceasar's story.

Searching for Great-Grandfather Ceasar

My back was aching from poring over newspapers and microfilm. The clock ticked and I was anxiously aware that the library was closing. This was our last day—our last hour—for conducting research, and the pressure was on. But I was exhausted. An earnest and attractive librarian wearing glasses, whose hair was coiffed in waves and curls, was eager to try and help. She was dressed fashionably, but with an understatement that conveyed she took herself and her job seriously. I was asking her for some last-minute help when I noticed a caramel-colored African American woman standing nearby, whose name I later learned was Vera, filling out her t-shirt and jeans with gorgeous curves. Unlike the librarian, this woman wore her hair pulled back and was dressed more casually, yet there was a spiritual or angelic presence that surrounded her. She asked me about my research and listened compassionately as I related Great-Grandfather Ceasar's story. When I finished, she said, "I know your story."

When she uttered those words, all of the exhaustion and tiredness fled from my body. I was filled with a sense of optimism and hope—my family's experience was finally validated! Vera's great-aunt had told her the story of Great-Grandfather's Ceasar's dramatic flight from Money and Vera knew that her family had lent a helping hand to mine during those difficult days. She told us about the odd hours of the night when there might be a knock at the door and her father would dress quickly and slip out in the night. She emphasized earnestly and passionately how African-Americans helped one another during these times. "My family helped your family," she said candidly.

She told us the story of how the community helped Ceasar leave Money after the shooting, recalling how often her family had re-told the story over the years. Jane and the children remained in Money and received support, protection, and emotional care from the Black community. She was proud that her family refused the self-hating "Uncle Tom" stereotype, never once turning in their brothers and sisters. The strong spirit of mutual aid and community prevailed, and her family helped my great-grandfather escape the lynching that certainly would have been his fate if he'd been apprehended by the white authorities. As she went on to talk about how African Americans in her community learned to keep secrets for a long time, I became tearful, in part out of exhaustion and also from a strong sense of validation. Rather recently, I have come to the firm conclusion that there truly are no accidents. Often, accidental meetings are the ways in which God makes their presence known.

Although there were no written records to "prove" what Vera shared with us, I had faith in the oral traditions that have long defined our African American communities. When Vera told us that, in the story passed down in her family, Great-Grandfather Ceasar escaped town on a boat or train, that clicked with the fragments of information we already had. And it made sense that Ceasar would've ended up in Florida if he had been forced to leave Money via one of those routes. Forever grateful for Vera's divine intervention, my daughter and I left Money, Mississippi with a quiet joy tucked away in our hearts. We continued our search.

Prison Pipelines Past—Still Present

After Ceasar's flight from Money, the trail goes cold until he resurfaced in Enfield, North Carolina, where my grandfather was born. We don't know exactly when, how, or why Jane and the kids left Money and ended up in North Carolina. But that is where Ceasar was ultimately reunited with his family. Our extensive research indicated Ceasar spent time in Savannah, Georgia and Florida. He may have also been conscripted into a chain gang or sent to a prison farm, such as the Parchman Farm in southern Mississippi, to perform hard labor, possibly on trumped-up charges. It was understood among the black population that they may be subject to profiling and sent to Parchman Farm without cause. They shuddered at the possibility, as everyone knew that being sent to Parchman was a death sentence. The mere mention of the name could frighten people. Parchman was a prison pipeline for black men. Once incarcerated, these black men became a source of free labor for the community, a lucrative business for the local and, ultimately, national economy. When I think of my great-grandfather's father's history, I can't help but think of today's practice of racial profiling, the prison pipeline, and mass incarceration of African Americans. My mind considers the targeted ticketing of black men in Ferguson, MO—a blatant way for the town to make money and the cause of Michael Brown's unnecessary death. A history can't repeat itself if it never actually ended.

Dear Reader, do you remember my brown bucket, tough and aging from this book's previous pages? Do you remember the *drip, drip, drip* filling my bucket as I watched the murder of George Floyd on television? When I think of Parchman Past and Parchman Present, I feel the *drip, drip, drip* of more drops in the bucket. More pain and powerlessness fill me when I reflect on our history of limiting the lives and opportunities of African Americans. From enslavement and Reconstruction onwards, there is a clear pattern of injustice in the service of reinstituting enslavement. Because isn't the current day stigma associated with being branded as a "felon," simply a new way to permanently enslave a people, even perhaps for transgressions as small as writing a bad check or stealing cigars from a convenience store? I am seized with a sense of sadness and despair when confronted with the ugly face of American racism, how intricately woven it is into every aspect of the fabric of American life. I think not only of institutional, structural racism, but also the casual and informal racism of everyday life, the implicit and subtle ways that inequality and violence thread themselves into your perception. For my readers who may not have experienced these circumstances, they make you feel as if there is nothing that you can do to change any of it.

Today, Parchman is still up and running as a state penitentiary. It has been cited by government for its deplorable conditions, poor food, a general lack of care for its inmates, and a high inmate death rate. In short, a continuation of past policies.

A Family Reunion

For Ceasar, however, God had other plans. Instead of dying from starvation, exhaustion, and overwork in a prison farm or chain gang, he made his way to North Carolina and rejoined his family. Was it Ceasar's past experiences that gave him the fortitude to survive those years of hard work, separated by his family, constantly looking over his shoulder, afraid the sheriff would find him? Did he call out to God during his time of torture and turmoil? Did he feel that God kept him safe and secure, allowing him to return the loving arms of his family?

How incredible it must have been for Ceasar to walk up the road and see his family in the far distance, calling out the names of his beloveds, beckoning them to come as he trotted alone with fatigue, malnutrition, thirst, and loneliness. How incredible it must have been for him as Jane and the children surrounded him, hugged him, and held him close. Did he wonder if he was dreaming? Did he wonder if it was all just a figment of his imagination? I picture my ancestors savoring the moment of this blissful reunion. I picture them as they lead my great-grandfather to the family's compound, supporting his weary body with their own, uttering loving words, reminding him that now he was safe in the secure arms of his dear family and that there was no need to worry. As Ceasar listened to these tender words from his people, his family, he quietly uttered gratitude and thanks to the wonders of God, who had led him home.

Perhaps his gratitude to God sparked a spiritual awakening in Great-Grandfather Cesar because, upon his reunion with his family, he was called to the ministry. In the height of the Jim Crow era, black ministers were deeply involved in the socio-political circumstances of their parishioners. Indeed, from Reconstruction onwards, black ministers in the South would play vital roles in burgeoning the Civil Rights Movement and my great-grandfather was no exception. We know for a fact that his ministry and activist work focused on the vast inequalities between black and whites. Ceasar established close alignments with ministers in the area. On Sundays, Ceasar would invite all the local ministers to his home, where they were offered sumptuous, down-to-earth, home-style cooking. During these supper meetings, the gathered men of God would discuss the inhumane, illegal, and immoral practices of Jim Crow in Enfield. They would denounce the use of violence to keep African Americans "in their place," while also praying for the white elites whose fear was responsible for the threat of lynching. As they discussed the precarity of black lives, they also strategized how the Church could address these horrific circumstances as socio-political and spiritual advocates. However, Great-Grandfather Ceasar's dedication to Christianity and social justice prevented him from obtaining gainful employment, and so Jane continued her pattern of caring for the family and meeting all needs. Ministry and farming structured the daily lives of Jane, Ceasar, and their children.

Jane knew how to work the land. She maintained a bountiful garden filled with every kind of fruit, vegetable, and herb that she could grow. She also fished and cooked, kept house, washed and ironed the clothes, and entertained Ceasar's fellow ministers. Jane was known for her cooking and would prepare elaborate, tasty meals drawn from the fruits of their labor, the bounty of their garden and small farm. The choicest pieces of meat, game, and fish were offered to the guests, the men were fed first, before the women and children. I know this because my grandfather, Joseph Ceasar Hines, remembers getting stuck with the less desirable bits and pieces from their limited supplies.

Perhaps the strain of caring for a large family without economic aid from her husband became too much for Jane. Perhaps Ceasar felt he could no longer minister and contribute to local activist causes while being the head of a family. We can only speculate as to the reasons why Jane and Ceasar ultimately split. When the eldest of their children moved to Norfolk, Virginia, they offered Jane the opportunity to join them and have an easier life. In Virginia, she worked as a cook and also in a bakery. By the 1920 census, she was listed as dead. She's buried in the family plot in Virginia.

Movin' On Up: From Enfield to NYC

In search of further information about the fate of Great-Grandfather Ceasar, my daughter and I traveled to Enfield. We found the town neglected and in economic decline. The house where my grandfather had grown up was no more. The town was split down the middle by a railroad track. Despite beautifully printed signs advertising economic recovery programs, we found no sign of recovery. We found a place of confusion and depression. Empty storefronts. A business that advertised itself as some kind of lending company had a long line of black people coming in and out. Through the window, we could see a white man seated at a desk.

The obvious signs of poverty impacted me. I was struck by how much penury my family had lived through, how much sacrifice and hard work it had taken to rise into the lower middle-class in which I was raised. I was struck, too, by how unchanged such conditions are for so many black people in America. How much violence could we avoid if black people had greater economic opportunities? How much of police brutality and the destruction of black lives in an unjust justice system is linked to poverty?

Ultimately, my daughter and I were unable to locate records of Great-Grandfather Ceasar's death in Enfield. Locals suggested that we visit the black-owned funeral home in the nearby city of Rocky Mount—perhaps they had arranged his burial. Although they did not have any record of his death, they referred us to the local "colored-only" cemetery where all black people in the area had been buried. The cemetery was in a state of disrepair. It was difficult to read the engravings on the headstones. Still, we scoured graves, headstone by headstone and, despite the overgrowth and debris, located what we believe is Ceasar's gravesite. According to his headstone, Great-Grandfather Ceasar made his transition in 1917.

It was in the grim landscape of Enfield, against a backdrop of destitution, determination, hope and the drive to thrive, where my gray-green-hazel-eyed and fair-skinned grandfather, Joseph Ceasar, began his life's story. He was one of many conceptions and births following Great-Grandfather Ceasar's return to the family. As a young man, Joseph Ceasar suffered from a respiratory ailment and needed to leave Enfield. He signed on with the railroad, hoping a different climate would improve his health. Later, he worked a variety of jobs, including service work in various eateries, and he would often admonish me to never eat in those places. The only other story he shared was the weekly Sunday visits at his parents' home, where preachers would gather for dinner upon the invitation of Ceasar. I remember his bitter complaints, remembering how his father's guests received the best parts of the chicken, leaving him only a back or a wing. I was never clear about my grandfather's schooling. I suspect he had very little opportunity to attend school, but he did attend night school as an adult. We often made fun of his attempts to speak Spanish after learning some words at night school.

Eventually, Joseph Ceasar made his way to Richmond, Virginia, where he met and married my beautiful, chocolate-skinned and soft-spoken grandmother, Mary Booker Hall. Mary was highly educated, worked as an accountant in Richmond, and was skilled in the domestic arts. Her father, Roderick Hall, was also chocolate-skinned with black, straight hair. According to family lore, he used patent medicine for various ailments. Little is known about my great-grandparents; however, in my grandparents' wedding picture, Mary's parents are present to serve as witnesses. This precious photo tells more than one story. In the picture, my grandfather is wearing a suit and derby hat. My grandmother is wearing her best dress. But it's not a big white dress and there are no bridesmaids and groomsmen in matching outfits flanking the couple. Their service was a civil one; there was no church. Indeed, weddings were often simpler in those days, and when I look at their picture, I am often struck by how much the culture of weddings has changed in just a few generations.

The couple moved to New York City and settled in the mecca of Harlem. Their strong bonds of marriage and mutual goals of thrift, hard work, and goal-setting allowed them to invest and buy property in the Bronx and Manhattan. Like many African-

Americans, the ownership of property indicated financial solvency and success. Grandpa, or Daddy-Daddy as I affectionately called him, was known for being thrifty and knew "how to save a dollar out of fifty cents." Without a doubt, the seeds of hard labor and thriftiness were sown into him by his mother, Jane. He loved to fish (as did my father, who passed it on to me), and if he caught fish, the family ate fish every day. It was the same with the numerous vegetables he harvested from the gardens where he lived. He knew how to make the best use of all the resources available to him, a survival strategy that I have also inherited (in my own way).

Joseph Ceasar and Mary had four children. Intelligent and high-achieving, all of Joseph Ceasar and Mary's children completed or had some higher education—one became a physician. My was father the eldest and, in most respects, the most brilliant, especially in technical subjects. In an ironic twist of fate, he ended up being the least formally educated of his siblings. My father's lack of professional achievements was another family secret. Much of this era and history were shielded from me, perhaps due to embarrassment, or perhaps the family had agreed to "let bygones be bygones." Or perhaps it was related to the burgeoning conflict between Daddy-Daddy and my father. No doubt city life in Harlem offered my father opportunities for frolic and fun, which would've been unthinkable for his father, who grew up on a farm where survival was dependent upon hard work. My mother served as the historian on this issue, sharing that my grandfather was particularly strict with my father, who was, after all, his first-born and namesake. One summer when my father was somewhere between his tweens and teenage years, he was punished by having to stay indoors for the entire summer! I imagine that left an indelible mark on their relationship and my father's psychosocial and emotional health. His greatest supporters in the family over the course of his entire life were his mother and sister, who always referred to him, lovingly, as "Junior."

Unlike his brothers and sisters, for whom home life, studying, and school were enough, my father needed more from life. He joined, or perhaps was drafted, into the military. I know little of this part of his history, and our efforts to locate records or official information from the government left us empty-handed, full of questions. While I knew he spent time in the Navy, he only ever spoke of his time in Alaska, where he worked on communications equipment and devices, perhaps honing and developing his technological acumen. He never spoke of combat or the horrors associated with war. It was only many years after his death, through mediumship, that he indicated to me that he had experienced the traumas of war. I learned of a number of high-level medals received during his time in World War II, but why and how he earned them, for what particular acts of brave service, remain unknown. After his tour of duty ended, it appears my father went to City College and also worked. It was at a work venue where he and my mother met and planned their life together.

The values of thrift, education, and the yearning for a better life are themes that unite people of African descent throughout the African diaspora. We share common desires: to work hard, to provide for our families, to raise children who will have better, easier lives than us, and to honor our communities. Great-Grandfather Ceasar and Great-Grandmother Jane desired these things. Grandfather Joseph Ceasar and Grandmother Mary desired these things. George Floyd desired these things. And my mother's family also shared these yearnings, despite the fact that they were born and raised thousands of miles from Money, MI and Enfield, NC.

An Immigrant Story: From Strivin' to Thrivin'

My maternal side of the family boasts roots in the beautiful island of Barbados, with ties to St. Lucia, Jamaica, Trinidad, and Panama. Like the rest of the Caribbean, Barbados had been colonized by Europeans. Barbados had been a British territory and even the local "Bajans" nicknamed their island, "Little England." All nations of the United Kingdom had their presence on the island—English, Welsh, Scottish, and Irish. You can still feel the traces of British culture and values on the island. For example, the island is divided into eleven parishes, based upon the role and relationship with the Anglican Church. Examples such as this speak to a complex legacy of both colonial violence and, over time, cultural affinities.

The island's colonial past and postcolonial present shaped the choices available, and the choices made by my family. Like other colonized places, the Caribbean islands were valued for their resources. Europeans coveted the rich soil, ideal for planting cash crops such as sugar and tobacco. They also saw, in the native populations and, later in the slaves they abducted and imported from Africa via the slave trade, a lucrative source of cheap labor. By the late 19th century, which is about as far back as I can formally trace my ancestors, the island's resources had been well depleted by the British. They had taken all of the best land. Independence came, but with it a struggling economy and limited opportunities. When my grandfather sought employment as an engineer, he ended up in Panama. Enticed by the promise of American citizenship, he joined thousands of other workers who were promised citizenship in exchange for their labor in the construction of the Panama Canal. My family is full of stories of male relatives who worked on the Canal and obtained citizenship –a way of manifesting a dream of a better life. Given a choice, I wonder if my relatives wouldn't have preferred to stay on the island, surrounded by family and friends? The same choice (or lack of choice) faced my grandmother, Edith. She, too, left the island for the shores of New York, driven by the promise of a better life.

I now understand the choices that shaped the arc of my maternal ancestry were based on the necessity to live. They did what they had to do to survive in an environment grown out of and adapted to trauma and exploitation. But what does colonial trauma have to do with? It may surprise some of my readers that I can see the patterns created by a colonial mindset in the murders of African Americans by police in the United States. But it doesn't take much re-framing to see the routine stops and ticketing of Black Americans by the police as a way to increase the coffers of the government. It's not much of a leap from chattel slavery to Michael Brown or George Floyd. Seen from the point of view of history, from the eyes of the colonized, such race-based exploitative practices are not so different from colonial policies that squeezed out riches exploiting the labor and resources of the Caribbean. From the eyes of a people who have lived under colonialism, the brutal policing of black people that can end in their death is just an echo of the iron shackles, the plantation overseer's whip, the Jim Crow noose, and the riot police baton.

As I gather these threads of narrative together in order to write this book, I am beginning to truly understand how, because the history of my family of origin is also the history of a series of choices made in response to exploitation and racial trauma, the life and death of George Floyd was always going to be personal. In the wake of his murder, I find myself wondering what my grandparents would have done if they had known that the country in which they would raise their children and grandchildren, amidst the promises of integration and equality, would so often fall short, so often resemble the scarred and struggling land they left behind…would they have made the same choice? If my grandfather had known that, in the United States, he would be unable to work as an engineer and would be forced to drive a taxi in New York City, would he have left the Caribbean? Or, knowing that their grandchildren would all graduate from high school and even go on to complete higher education, would that have been enough to convince them their choice was the right one?

These questions may seem futile—after all, we cannot change the past. We can, however, re-frame it. My maternal family's story is, in many ways, a classic immigrant tale. I can chart the stages of departure, arrival, striving, surviving and, by my generation, integration and thriving. We are an American success story. But, I would argue, behind our American success story is an American survival story. And it is this story that has no clear ending, no final resolution. The emotionless eyes of Officer Derek

Chauvin reminded me that our American survival story is a precarious one. To survive in America is an everyday struggle. The moment in which we become too comfortable, too convinced that our class status (or other aspect of our identity) will insulate us from violence is to forget how thin the veil between worlds can be. My ancestors knew this, and they did not forget. With their wisdom guiding these words I, too, will not forget.

Grandma Edith

My grandmother, Edith Amanda Hoyte Pilgrim, was born to Samuel Hoyte and Amelia Ann Stewart in 1898 in a town called Chalky Mount, Barbados, a name it earned due to the presence of chalk in its hills. Chalky Mount resides in a parish called St. Andrew, nicknamed "Scotland District," and the prevalence of Scottish surnames (such as Hoyte and Stewart) are legacies of slavery and the plantation system. Slaves, of course, were given the surnames of the family who owned them. I don't know how the family supported themselves, although farm animals often appear in the stories. For example, my grandmother, the youngest of the family, was born premature and nursed from a cow. Exhausted from numerous births and surrounded by many children, her mother just wasn't able to nurse her herself. My grandmother attended school. Indeed, school features often in stories of her early life. School provided a structure to her daily life: rising early, going to school, coming home for a lengthy lunch, and then returning to school. Alongside education, religion was an essential part of her family's existence. The religious values of the Anglican/Episcopalian faith infused everyday life, as well as other folk spiritual practices.

Sometime around the tender age of fifteen, in the year 1913, Grandma Edith decided to board a great ship bound for New York City. Through a cousin, Edith had secured employment as the "upstairs girl" in the home of a wealthy white family in Dobbs Ferry, New York. It was common for immigrant communities to rely on and provide mutual aid and connections through social networks in order to help one another. And so, Grandma Edith did not have to pass through Ellis Island and remained proud of the fact she did not require the humiliating "delousing" cleansing treatments given to immigrants upon arrival.

Edith and Preston in Hell's Kitchen

Not long after her arrival in New York, Edith met the dashing, tall, dark, handsome and intelligent Preston Egbert Eggergton Pilgrim. I'm not sure exactly how Edith and Preston met, but the diasporic Barbadian community was a close tight-knit group, depending on one another for mutual aid, bonds of love, sharing cuisine from home, friendship and community. I do know that the love story between Preston and Edith was fueled by intense passion, religious fervor, and a complete synergy of goals and aspirations.

Preston, affectionately called "Pilly," emigrated to the Big Apple from Barbados and Panama via the building of the Canal Zone in Panama. He and his fellow countrymen worked 24/7 to complete the canal. Their accommodations were meager, and so to save as much of their earnings as possible, they slept in shifts. Some of my kinfolk remained in Panama after completion of the Canal, like my great-uncle whose descendants remain there to this day. I know of the existence of these relatives because of the financial aid Edith sent her family in Panama and Preston sent his family in Barbados throughout their lives.

Once Preston came to New York City, he wasn't able to continue work as an engineer. The walls of racism, classism, and immigrant bias proved too sturdy to break. However, undaunted and refusing to fall into sadness and despair, he worked any and all jobs he could find, especially as the years of the Great Depression stretched on. Things were very different in those days. Not only were unjust exclusion from jobs much more explicit, people were more likely to utilize their multiple talents and skills at different jobs. Preston worked as a building "Super," drove a cab, and ultimately purchased a medallion, which allowed him to own his own cab and work entirely for himself without being tied to any particular taxi company. It was a sign of success and independence. He worked hard and saved his money so that he could, like so many immigrants, bring his family members over. Preston sent for his brothers, McKinley and Gordon, and his sister, Rosa, for whom he wanted to provide a better life.

Together, Edith and Preston brought ten children into the world during their marriage. Only five—Oslyn, Carlton, Daisy, Eunice, and my mother, Gwendolyn—survived into adulthood due to the tragedies of disease, accidents, and poverty. Their first child stayed with Edith's parents in Barbados, later returning to New York City to join her parents. One of Edith's children succumbed to viral meningitis and the another was the victim of a horrific childhood accident. Although the details are unclear, my second eldest aunt, Daisy, who was a child herself, may have accidentally turned over the contents of hot water onto her baby brother who subsequently succumbed to his burns and died.

Like so many of my family's histories, this story remains cloaked in secrecy. What I know of this tragedy, I know from its effects—Aunt Daisy struggled her entire life with feelings of guilt and responsibility for the death of her sibling.

The growing family, like the rest of the nation, did their best to make ends meet during the Great Depression. In those days, Hell's Kitchen was a neighborhood many immigrants called home. African Americans families who migrated to the North from the South lived side-by-side with families of Caribbean immigrants and shared many cultural traditions. It was not uncommon for multiple families to reside in a small apartment, sharing whatever they had with one another and neighbors in need. Money was always a problem for families residing in New York City's lower east side. Yet people came together, cooking, eating, laughing and crying, managing their lives with limited financial income and sharing their triumphs, joys, sadness and despair. My aunt retold the story over and over of coming home from school frightened, fearing she'd find her family evicted and their belongings on the street. In this grim often-bleak but joyful context, Edith and Preston worked hard to keep a roof over the family's head and food on the table. After working long hours, Preston would tread home monotonously to find a hot meal of traditional Barbadian fare and a loving wife who was bathed, wearing a clean dress, awaiting news of the day. In spite of all the challenges they faced, their love for each other and the bond between them was strong.

Although their passionate marriage flourished, there were times of conflict and discord due to financial hardships. My family remembers seeing many hungry children around the

Pilgrim house at dinner-time, knowing they'd receive good food from generous Edith. In spite of their own financial troubles, my grandmother dedicated herself to helping those in need. Clearly, I have inherited this genetic proclivity! Although Preston would accuse her of "picking up strays" and increasing the number of mouths he had to feed, Edith's need to help was also deeply rooted in her understanding of the commandment to "Love Thy Neighbor." I imagine she often faced moral, ethical, and religious conflicts when faced with desperate pleas from friends and family.

On the Origins of the Wise Woman's Faith: A Tale of Two Traditions

My family did their best to preserve the values of their family and their faith, despite significant obstacles. My family turned their challenges into opportunities, transforming a source of powerlessness into empowerment.

In Harlem, Edith & Preston needed a community with whom to share their religious life, including baptisms, confirmations, and Sunday school for their children. According to the family lore, my grandfather, who obviously exhibited many leadership qualities, arranged a meeting with representatives of the Episcopal Diocese of New York City. That meeting (there were perhaps more than one) resulted in the designating of St. Andrew's Church in Harlem (at 127th Street and Fifth Avenue) as a New York City historical landmark in 1967. (The multiple award winning African American actress, Cicely Tyson, was known to attend this church, often veiled to conceal her identity from prying eyes!)

At the time, the church was being supported by the Diocese; my family and many others set about repairing and enhancing the beautiful building, making it a cornerstone in our family's history. All of Edith and Preston's grandchildren and many of the great-grandchildren were baptized and confirmed there. It was the regular meeting place of our families, especially during the holidays. It was there that I saw my great-uncles decked out in splendor, sporting formal morning coats with tails, ascots and white gloves, as they ushered worshipers to their seats. It was there where extended family peppered me with questions about school and my future plans, greatly influencing my determination to succeed. Their love and nurturing had a profound and everlasting effect on my spirit and soul's expression.

Like many other communities in the African diaspora, we practiced a unique blend of religious-spiritual beliefs. For many, religion and spirituality are not necessarily the same thing. In fact, some people see the two as conflicting. That was not the case for my family and their community; for us, these two were never in conflict. Each had their place in our daily life. The religious values of the Anglican/Episcopalian faith infused everyday life, especially the Lenten to Resurrection season of the Christian calendar. But equally important were folk culture and folk spirituality. It was a common occurrence for my Grandma Edith and my aunts to openly talk about spirits, burn lots of different colored candles, *and* pray when addressing and offsetting life's challenges. Grandma Edith, who was definitely an intuitive healer and medium, explained in detail that a candle was a way of making a prayerful wish to God. She described how the dressing and handling of the candle were part of the sacredness of this practice. This indeed was an opportunity to share your concern with God as well as Angels, Archangels, Blessed Mother and many other saints, helpers and inspirers.

Grandma Edith loved to tell us the story of the Good Friday murder. The story goes that, on Good Friday, a husband in her parish killed his wife. There was a great deal of blood at the site of the murder, which caused a commotion in the parish. After the murder, blood mysteriously reappeared every Good Friday. Combined with the story of the crucifixion that Grandma Edith read us, we easily slipped into the reverent silence demanded of us every Good Friday from noon until 5:00pm. We also fasted during those hours, dining always on fish in the evening.

Having grown up in this manner, there was no demarcation between our religious views as Episcopalians and our spiritual views. Ultimately, it was all part of a larger, holistic devotion to God. This multi-faceted devotion, which was such a vital part of my ancestors' daily lives and my upbringing, would serve as a springboard for my on-going search to combine religion and spirituality in order to come closer to God, a journey which I will share in more detail in the following chapters.

Sadly, in the 1920s, racism prevented the full inclusion of Black Americans in both traditional and less traditional religious-spiritual spaces. It may surprise my readers to learn that, during this time, in big Northern cities like New York, churches remained segregated—blacks and whites were not allowed to worship together. For example, my family members were prohibited from attending the "whites only" Episcopalian churches in New York City.

As a faith practice, spiritualism had been an integrated haven for worship throughout the 19th century within the Northeast. Sometime in the 1920s, the National Spiritualist Association of Churches adopted a resolution to discontinue integration in their churches and to have African Americans initiate, plan and develop their own churches. Thus, racial segregation proved once again to be an obstacle for the full participation of Black Americans in traditional and more radical faith traditions, regardless of geography.

What is Spiritualism and What Makes it Important to Me? The Wise Woman Shares

But why am I talking about spiritualism and not any other faith tradition? In addition to being practiced by the Royal Court in England and being a significant part of United States' social history, the Spiritualist church has played a significant role in my own life. My own research into this tradition informs my perception of its significance.

Spiritualism is a philosophy, a religion, and rests much in science and rational thinking with essential foundations in love and caring for one's fellow human being. It arose out of free-thinking individuals who found themselves at odds with conventional 19th century beliefs such as the necessity of slavery and the opposition to the women's suffrage movement. As a result, the more traditional dogma that is associated with other mainstream religions such as Catholicism is not present in Spiritualism. Spiritualists believe in the importance of acknowledging, understanding, and accepting personal responsibility for our thoughts, actions, and feelings while on the earthly realm. In Spiritualism, there is no heaven or hell—we all are responsible for the good and evil things we think and perform. Instead of the promise of heaven or the threat of hell, those who adhere to this religion utilize Seven Principles to guide their lives. Fundamentally, Spiritualists believe in the presence of God in all aspects of life and death, as well as the wonderful opportunity to develop a personal relationship with this wonderful force. Spiritualism offers the opportunity to worship a gender-inclusive God.

There are many Spiritualists who refer to God as Father while others utilize Mother/Father. In either case, equality between males and females is a given. Spiritualists believe life continues beyond death and, therefore, the process of mediumship can connect with and contact those in the spirit world. Mediumship is also seen as a wonderful opportunity for healing for both spirit persons and those on earth. I was led into Spiritualism by the belief that every human being is imbued with the presence and light of God. As I studied, meditated and initiated conversations with a loving Spirit, I also found evidence of that Spirit within me. I later utilized this knowledge and experiences in designing healing modalities and care work, which I will share with you in greater detail in the second part of this book.

Meanwhile, back in New York City...

Once again, my family turned their challenges into opportunities, transforming a source of powerlessness into empowerment. According to the family lore, my grandfather, who obviously exhibited many leadership qualities, arranged a meeting with representatives of the Episcopal Diocese of New York City. That meeting (there were perhaps more than one) resulted in the designating of St. Andrew's Church in Harlem (at 127th Street and Fifth Avenue) as a New York City historical landmark in 1967. (The multiple award winning African American actress, Cicely Tyson, was known to attend this church, often veiled to conceal her identity from prying eyes!) At the time, the church was being supported by the Diocese; my family and many others set about repairing and enhancing the beautiful building, making it a cornerstone in our family's history. All of Edith and Preston's grandchildren and many of the great-grandchildren were baptized and confirmed there. It was the regular meeting place of our families, especially during the holidays. It was there that I saw my great-uncles decked out in splendor, sporting formal morning coats with tails, ascots and white gloves as they ushered worshipers to their seats. It was there where extended family peppered me with questions about school and my future plans, greatly influencing my determination to succeed. Their love and nurturing had a profound and everlasting effect on my spirit and soul's expression.

   As the family conflicts grew and anger flared, the handsome Preston increasingly stayed away from home. When he did return, he was often met with fiery anger and perhaps a few dishes thrown at his head. During those times, he referred to his wife as "mad Miss Edith." Subsequently, he developed a relationship with another woman and left the family. In his final act of desertion, he left my grandmother a widow at the tender age of 36 when he passed away due to kidney dysfunction. He had been a cabbie, and it's likely that he developed his kidney problem from having to hold his urine for hours on end. (Kidney problems manifest amongst a number of my family members, including myself). Preston's paramour was thrust into despair, could not live without him and died shortly thereafter. While I did not have the chance to meet Preston, I would have liked to. Still legally married, Grandma Edith arranged his funeral and burial in the St. Michael's Episcopalian cemetery in Queens, New York. Like many widows of the time, she wore only black. Despite the complications in their marriage, it's interesting to me how Edith still felt obligated to assume the cultural mores around widowhood.

After the death of my grandfather, my uncle felt obligated to assume the role of family patriarch. I am certain this was a hard decision for him and the family because it meant leaving school. He worked at a variety of odd jobs, culminating in a successful career as a butcher. I am reminded again of George Floyd, who was also actively seeking steady employment. Indeed, the long tradition of valuing hard work and steady employment is something that is often missed in the public perception of black people.

The American Dream vs. Powerlessness

My family felt the full force of race-based discrimination when they undertook the ultimate symbol of the American Dream—home ownership. After Preston's death, Edith and her children bought a home in the northeast Bronx. Ours was the first Afro-Caribbean family to own a home in the neighborhood. Like Harlem, the northeast Bronx was originally the site of white ethnic home owners. Once our family established themselves in the neighborhood, more people like us moved in and the white folks began to move out. Caribbean immigrants and people of African descent saw an opportunity to realize the American Dream through home ownership and education. However, the American Dream would prove to be elusive and more challenging for my family and the other African American families in my neighborhood. While home ownership and education offered measures of empowerment, both official and unofficial redlining policies and practices worked against us. Unfair and race-based practices, supported at the local, state and federal levels, victimized people of color. In those days, it was common practice for the contract mortgage system to sell African Americans on the promises of the American Dream while actually crafting contracts that left them without complete ownership of their homes. Immoral middlemen found ways to scam many out of their hard-earned money.

Although our family placed a sizable down payment on our house and obtained a mortgage, local citizens protested to our presence by taking our family to court, citing our poor character as a legal basis for nulling the mortgage. If you've been following my family's journey so far, you'll know a fair amount about what kind of people they were—hardworking folks with strong religious beliefs and a commitment to family; they were involved in the local community and generous to their neighbors and friends. Nonetheless, my relatives had to "prove" that they were "suitable" to occupy a house that they had legally purchased, hiring an attorney, obtaining character letters from a variety of people, including their priest. In this case, the law worked in favor of my family, and they were allowed to keep their home.

Alas, our collective history is littered with examples of families who were not so lucky.

After passing the legal "test," more covert attacks sought to demean my family and terrorize us into leaving the neighborhood. The women in my family would be accosted on their way to work, asked to clean the houses and sidewalks of white homeowners for a few cents a day. For my relatives who held respectable jobs, these requests were humiliating. My female relatives would also be "mistaken" for prostitutes and were regularly propositioned on the street. For the black women who did clean the homes of white families, it was not uncommon for them not to be paid at the end of a day's work, supplied with a lame excuse or given old clothes or cast offs in lieu of cash. Such treatment increased the sense of powerlessness within African American communities.

The "Black Hand"

Thrust suddenly into the role of the sole breadwinner and head of the household, Grandma Edith and the children faced the arduous task of doing more than surviving. Grandma Edith rolled up her sleeves, working at various jobs during the night shift so she could be at home during the day to care for her children. She shared stories of constantly having to fight off would-be nighttime attackers who assumed, because she was a woman of African descent and on the streets after dark, she must be a prostitute. She spoke with candor about being grabbed and taunted with, "girlie, you are coming up to my room." Her response was often providing her attacker with a hardy punch in the mouth.

Despite her personal struggles, Edith's belief in the value of education for her children and herself proliferated. My mother and aunts all attended school regularly, supported by unannounced visits from my grandmother. One day, another student claimed that when she looked at Edith's daughter, my aunt, she saw a "black hand." In those days, the "black hand" had enormous cultural significance for Italian people. This sighting or signal was associated with terrorist gangs, and to see it was not only a bad omen, but it was also a threat of being harmed or killed. In essence, my aunt was being accused potentially of harming or killing a fellow student. My grandmother was an unwavering advocate for her children—completely unafraid of the barriers of class and race. She did not hesitate to explain to school officials that my aunt knew nothing of "black hands," and demanded all the rights and protections that public education could offer her daughter. When she wasn't defending her children's rights to education, Grandma Edith was taking steps to ensure her rights as well. Growing up, I saw the pamphlets and books she studied diligently in preparation for her citizenship exam.

Thanks to my grandmother's unwavering beliefs and my uncle's sacrifices, the girls continued their education. All of the girls earned degrees and landed illustrious careers in nursing, fashion design, politics and government service. Like their parents before them, they stressed the importance of education to their children. Their mantra was, "your teacher is your best friend."

The Story of Gwendolyn Esme: My Mother and My Biggest Fan

There was always something special about Gwendolyn Esme. One of my dearest friends often said she heard music surrounding my mother when she entered a room. She was born at home in Hell's Kitchen. Was it the time of her conception and birth (on June 17th in 1923) which granted her special energy, vitality, charm, charisma, intelligence and wit, and her unique her capacity to engage and inspire others? Was it her love and devotion to Jesus Christ? Whatever it was, Gwendolyn was the most adventurous of her siblings—always seeking and exploring.

Gwendolyn was an avid student, quickly grasping concepts and developing academic skills. At 16, she graduated with honors from Morris High School. Morris boasts other important alumni, such as Col. Colin Powell. She also enjoyed basketball and other youth development activities at St. Augustine's Church in the Bronx. She adored music and dance, especially jazz. As she grew older, my mother expressed many feelings through dance, studying ballet and modern dance.

Gwendolyn was the first to leave the nest, her adventurous spirit taking her away from the New York metropolitan area. After studying at Columbia, she decided to join the war effort. She was recruited to build and design airplanes due to her excellent technical aptitude on a number of entrance examinations. This opportunity required that she move to Rome, New York. So, move she did. And not only did she excel at her new job, but she also worked tirelessly for the local black community.

When Gwendolyn returned to New York City, her leadership and imagination inspired her to develop a social club that supported African American soldiers. At the time, there were few places for black soldiers to socialize, as formal and informal segregation and racism dominated the social landscape. Like her mother Edith, Gwendolyn loved to help others and continued to perform acts of service throughout her life.

After the war, many African Americans sought employment as civil servants. My mother also took a clerical job for the federal government. It was here that she met the handsome, intelligent, and hazel-eyed Joseph C. Hines. People say that opposites attract, and this was certainly the case with my parents. Joseph was the introvert and Gwendolyn the extrovert. However, in spite of their different personalities, they shared mutual goals, including the desire for a family. Sadly, I know little about their courtship. My mother often talked about my father as the person who went to the coffee shops to get food for the other employees. She remembered how often the staff wouldn't pay Joseph back for the things they had ordered. My mother watched this scene repeat while Joseph, too shy or kind-hearted, didn't speak up. A champion for fairness, my mother spoke to Joseph about being taken advantage of by their colleagues. I like to think that he was charmed by her care and concern for him.

A Marriage and Mutual Goals

Gwendolyn and Joseph were wed in October 1947 in New York City. Their wedding celebration was featured in the society columns among the black elite in New York City, with formal black and white pictures. Growing up, I heard time and time again about their glamorous wedding. Special lace was ordered from Spain for my mother's veil. At least seven or eight bridesmaids wore beautiful gowns and ornate headpieces, while my father and the male members of the wedding party wore elegant tails. Many friends and family clamored for an invitation—it was *the* event of the season.

During the early years of their marriage, the couple worked together designing their home within the larger family compound in the Bronx. They set mutual goals, including planning a pregnancy. They waited six years before conceiving me. When I was born, they named me Lorna Joiselle, after my father's sister, Loraine, and my father, Joseph. As a father, Joseph was dutiful and attentive—he changed diapers, made formula, and sterilized bottles. He fixed things when they broke down and exercised his technical skill in the house. I vividly remember when he purchased a kit to build a television. Our home was the site of visitors who showed up weekly to view this marvelous invitation. Together, my parents helped to plan, initiate, and design an essential mutual aid society called the Progressive Benevolent Society.

As a way to exercise power when surrounded by powerlessness, Gwendolyn joined, and was an outstanding member of, the Jackson Democratic Club in the Bronx. The Club, as it was affectionately called, was the place to address all concerns; housing, employment, medical care. In those days, various government programs offered equal access to different affordable housing projects and employment opportunities that supposedly relied on open and transparent process. In reality, these programs were anything but. Public housing was rife with unofficial official racisms and segregation. Everyone knew that there was one "projects" for poor whites and another "projects" for black people. As a consequence, people of color needed the right information in order to fully access these services (for example, finding out the exact date of a certain employment test or where to submit an application). The Club helped folks get the information they needed to access these resources, as well as access to local politicians who would sit down with community members and listen to their concerns. The Club, and other organizations like it, helped to circumvent the structural racism built into the public assistance systems. My entire extended family was involved with The Club, a powerful example of how the value of helping others infused my family and community.

It is unclear when their marriage began to deteriorate, another missing chapter in my family's history, another silent, unspoken story. I only have fragments of memory to try to paste together the events during this time. Sometime during my toddler stage, my father's drinking escalated. He began to spend more time outside of the home, drinking with friends. Communication and intimacy suffered. I have a hazy memory of picking up the telephone and hearing a threatening male voice on the other end. Later, I learned that my father had been having an affair with a married woman, and this woman's husband had called to threaten our family. Likely as a result of the drinking and difficult family life, my father lost his job as a civil servant for the Treasury Department. This was a major blow for the growing family.

The arguments escalated, at times moving from vocal to physical outbursts. Eventually, I believe my mother consulted the family doctor for advice and intervention. In an effort to help my parents stabilize their marriage, my paternal grandfather intervened and suggested my parents move and care for buildings he owned in Harlem. It was there when, during one very horrific verbal and physical altercation, I awoke, confused and afraid, to my parents' loud voices. Ultimately, this opportunity did not work out and I never knew the reason why. Shortly thereafter, without discussion and explanation, we returned to the family compound in the Bronx.

Little Lorna Goes to the Hospital

Somewhere between the ages of six and seven, even in the midst of my parents' deteriorating relationship, I began to have trouble seeing the blackboard in school. And, like most parents, their attention turned to my needs. I was tall for my age, and for some unknown reason, when the teacher had us line up, I was always placed in the back with the boys. While many kids my age looked forward to sitting in the back of the class so that they could pass notes and pray they would never be called upon by the teacher, for me, it was torturous. My complaints about not being able to see the blackboard increased and, eventually, I was taken to the optometrist for an examination. I was diagnosed with near-sightedness and needed glasses. This diagnosis has been with me my entire life, with an increasing deterioration and a more profound need for glasses.

While I am not completely sure why a physical exam was also necessary, I was taken for one at Jacobi Hospital in the Bronx. Jacobi was a brand new public hospital, clean with a number of modern conveniences. When I visited, this beautiful space was resplendent with mapped markings indicating where you could find the pharmacy, clinics, etc. It was a joy for me to be there— I even loved the clean smell of rubbing alcohol. I felt assured people could get well here. At that time, the only other public hospital in the Bronx was Lincoln Hospital, and it had a terrible reputation. It is difficult to believe that care in public hospitals was free, including medicines. I believe that has impacted my belief in "free" medical care for all.

My physical included a urinalysis, and when the report was shared during a follow-up visit, my mother and I were told I required hospitalization for additional tests and assessments. I remained in Jacobi Hospital for many months with an unclear diagnosis. Days were spent undergoing physically intrusive tests (doctors attempted to inset a tube internally in order to try and catch my urine before it went to my bladder), as well as endless x-rays with no conclusive diagnosis. I dreaded the tests and missed my family. I was terribly lonely. In those days, health professionals had a poor understanding of child development and children's needs. Children were treated like any other hospital patients. As a result, my parents were not allowed to visit me at the hospital, except during strict visiting hours. They certainly couldn't spend the night. I remember counting the hours and minutes until visiting hours would open and I could be with my family. It was also a frightening time for me. I was afraid, not understanding what was happening to me and why I had to keep enduring round after round of tests when, in general, I wasn't in any pain or physical distress. My only escapes were attending half-day school and enjoying the food they served at the hospital.

After months of fruitless hospitalization which brought no conclusive results, my aunt, a nurse, intervened and had me transferred to the private hospital where she worked, located in what now is called the "South Bronx." She was a fierce advocate and had spoken directly with an imminent urologist. It was a very old hospital, not at all modern like Jacobi, and the food was awful and no schooling to boot. However, shortly after my admission, my kidneys were tested with dye and a diagnosis was reached—there was a congenital deformity in the duct from my bladder to my kidney, which required surgery.

This was scary news for my family, as we all knew that kidney problems ran in the family. The ghost of Grandpa Preston's death as the result of kidney failure haunted the family. So, as they so often did in times of turmoil, uncertainty and feelings of powerlessness, the family came together. They prayed. And prayed. And prayed some more. They relied on each other and put their faith in God and their community. Despite their fear, they refused to lose hope and were determined that I receive the best possible care. There is nothing like the illness of a child to bring parents together. And, indeed, my parents bonded together during my hospitalization and surgery. In the days before my surgery, there was little to do to occupy time other than waiting for visits from parents and relatives. I recall my father surprising me by bringing me the family's television (he carried it to the hospital on his back) so I could have something to enjoy during this extended stay.

On the day before the surgery, my maternal grandmother prayed over me and told me she had contacted Billy Graham for prayers for my healing and recovery. I received cards and pictures from the students in my class. After the surgery, all I remember is pain, moaning, crying, and being told by my mother that they had given me as much pain medication as possible. I also recall horrid dreams the night after the surgery, and a nurse being with me as I yelled that something was trying to turn me into a Z. However, the operation was a complete success, and the repair remains functional to this very day.

The Secrets Came With Us

From then on, we experienced a series of moves: Queens, then back to the Bronx (not in the family compound). Yet the silences and unspoken secrets in the family followed us into every new abode. My parents' relationship continued the downward spiral, as did my father's drinking. It is unclear if my parents were unemployed during this time. These were things that we didn't talk about. In spite of the confusing and unclear economic circumstances, I can't recall a day when I went to bed hungry—a testament to their stability as parents, the strength of my extended family, and the cultural values and mores of solidarity among African American families. I recall my paternal uncle bringing us shopping bags full of meat; I remember my mother throwing a Saturday night rent party. For those who don't know, a rent party is a very festive affair. There are admission fees, dinner on offer, music, dancing, and a poker game. The party's hosts receive a portion of the poker game's winnings.

During those times when money was tight, my father did people's taxes in return for gifts instead of money. One day when I was around ten years old, he brought home a pictorial essay that he had been gifted in kind for his work. The pages dramatized the treatment of the women who were imprisoned in the infamous "Tombs" in New York City. The pictures showed the filth, dirt, and tears on the faces of many women, huddled together in large cells with only one toilet to share between them. I read and re-read the essay in disbelief that people, especially women, could be treated so horrifically. Even though I was only a school-aged youngster, I heard something within me promising that, someday, I would do something to help these women. Looking back, I believe the seeds of my care and concern and my desire to help others were sown throughout my childhood, but this particular experience gave a fuller expression to what my inner knowingness already understood. I told myself, "I can do something to help these women."

My parents' relationship continued to be strained and conflicted during my school-age years. I remained in the Bronx compound during the week, attended school, and joined my mother in her apartment on the weekends. She had found employment in civil service, working in the U.S. Passport Agency. She began her career there as a clerical worker and moved up the ranks until she was made Office Manager for the entire agency. My father was a shadowy figure. From time to time, I'd find traces of his presence, bottles of gin in strange places like the dirty clothes bin.

During a brief journey towards reconciliation, my sister (now deceased) was conceived and born in 1959. However, shortly thereafter, they separated. My parents finally divorced when I was fifteen. My father paid child support every two weeks until I graduated from college; although he was jailed briefly for not paying. After that short stint in jail, he never missed a payment.

When I cast my mind and heart back to world my father lived in from the perspective of my many decades, I believe that the wear and tear of unacknowledged trauma affected my father in profound ways. I can imagine that years of enduring racism, obvious and subtle, challenged his sense of self. He may have suffered from "invisibility syndrome." Invisibility syndrome is a clinical term used in psychology to name the experience of feeling as if your personal identity and ability are limited and undermined by racism and powerlessness. Did he feel unseen, even worthless in the society in which he lived? Was he burdened with the weight of all that went unspoken?

I believe my father was a complicated man, driven by love for his children but haunted by ghosts and secrets that drove him to self-medicating and coping strategies, such as alcohol. Of course, my father's drinking was never discussed openly in the family, another dark secret. Many would call him a "functional alcoholic" because he continued to be gainfully employed.

When my father hit rock bottom, concerned neighbors would contact me. Each time, we would seek rehab and other forms of intervention. Eventually, my father connected with Alcoholics Anonymous, creating a support network that led to his sobriety. From then on, we were able to connect and create a loving father-daughter relationship. But the damage done to his body could not be reversed. My father succumbed to chronic heart failure, diabetes, neuropathy, hypertension, and arthritis in 2000.

After my father's death, I found a letter that he had written to my mother around the time of the rent party. I vividly recall the words he wrote to her: "I love you so intensely that I hate you." As I read the letter and tried to make sense of it, I felt confused.

To me, these words are indicative of my parents' conflictive relationship and the tumult and chaos that it engendered. It is also indicative of my father's mental health and his emotional issues. From undiagnosed PTSD to his self-medicating and alcoholism, my father's life contained many, many dark secrets.

On both sides of my family, people kept secrets. As I began to collect the stories of family, I felt as if I was slowly but surely discovering the keys that fit the locked doors of my family's past. One day, while I was searching for stories about my father, I happened to catch an interview on NPR with Bridgette McGee-Robinson. Like myself, Ms. McGee-Robinson is an African American woman who was investigating her family's past. In search of answers around the death of her grandfather, Willie McGee, Ms. McGee-Robinson unearthed a painful family secret—in 1945, Mr. McGee had been accused of raping a married white woman, arrested, put through a sham trial, and eventually executed in the electric chair in the state of Mississippi.

Despite gaining national attention, Ms. Robinson-McGee's family had remained tight-lipped whenever she had asked about her grandfather's fate during her childhood. It was only later that her aunt divulged that the family always believed that Mr. McGee had been involved with the woman and the accusations of rape were a consequence of their relationship being discovered during a time when anti-miscegenation laws were still in place. I felt a strong connection to this woman, her story, and the story of Willie McGee (whom I had never heard of before). On both sides of my family, people struggled with unresolved emotional pain and the suffocating silence of shame –"that's just not something we talk about." I remember feeling so moved that I immediately penned the poem, "Willie McGee and Me," which I share with you in the following pages. Another door had been opened.

And as these doors opened and I peered inside the rooms of history that had been locked for years, I saw of the potential ways trauma and dehumanization could be transmitted from past to present, from my ancestors to me. Yet, this family socialized and inculcated me into my community and society, and I have always depended on the higher mission, vision, and values of our family. In the decade that passed between the day I first heard of Willie McGee and the death of George Floyd, I have been working hard to unlock the essential elements and energies of survival that have carried not only my family, but so many families, through times of powerlessness and trauma. For me, this has meant re-visiting the story of my own coming-of-age during the tumultuous decades of the 1960s and 1970s as a story of survival. With the wisdom of years, I cast my mind back to my own origins, sifting through the experiences of racial and gender-based trauma, but also the strengths and successes that carried me through. I understand my ability to survive and thrive not only as a kind of personal success, but as an ancestral inheritance. And, as I continue to write my way through my feelings of despair in the months since George Floyd's death, more doors continue to open. Each click of a lock opening reveals another side to the story—a story that is not purely mine to claim, nor does it belong solely to my own ancestors. This story is a story about surviving the traumatic experience that is America.

Chapter 4

You Are Perfect: A Conflicting Message in Tumultuous Times

You Are Perfect

I heard these illustrious words uttered
I suppose it does not matter
Whether it was radio, television
Or, whether the words were articulately
Spoken or muttered

The significance of the words
Had less to do with the author
And much more to do

With camels, mammals
And other herds

I wondered with awe and determination
About the situation and venue
And perhaps even nation

Was it here or there?
North or West
East or South
Or some still unknown place
In our vast hemisphere

However the importance
Has more to do
With the meaning and significance
More for me than you

As a young child growing up
In the fertile Mecca of the now
South Bronx, County of Kings
And yes the vast village of Harlem
I was assured that I possessed the
Undeniable stamp
Of the right stuff!

This poem's significance
May not be important to
Joe, Mary or Sue
But I respectfully beg you

To Listen as my heart strings
Mutter This Important
I Love You

As a young mite my world
Was surrounded with
Black, Brown, High Yalla
Complexed Folks
Who cared more than
You could imagine about
This attractive colored girl

They focused as best as they could
In creating the fertile ground
Good seeds, and fresh water,
Loving care and gentle ministrations
That would create a healthy crop
Of youngsters whose internal foundations
Started with solid mahogany wood

You must know by now
That I am talking about
My own special familial mixture who
Made the Middle Passage internment
And ended up in the Caribbean and Down South

I didn't fully know it as a tot
But now I am grown and
Thanks to Our Savior, Creator and Sustainer
I have learned a lot

In spite of the oft times harsh words
Floggings and such
In the main
I was surrounded up and down
In and Out
In a loving environment
That has meant so much

Now that I gained in age, experience and
A pound or two
I have also noticed the importance of this stuff
To me and to you

Many of the blood and fictive kin
Who have gone ahead
To prepare that special inn with Our Creator
Have continued to communicate
Their messages of love
Through Sensations, Dreams, Smells, Accidents
Which are often difficult to decipher within

But the importance of the poem
Lies in the essential fact
That I am assured that their
Love has continued in spite
Of the fact that their presence
Is no longer intact

I must remember this important fact
When it's time for me
My Loved Ones to make

Their way to the other side
There is one certain thing
That Love Always Survives

And so for those present
And those who have passed on
Please listen to this message
Which is not meant to prolong
The inevitable fact
Love Goes On

    I focused this chapter on my own experiences of the revolutionary changes which occurred in American society during the mid-20th century. Movements such as the Civil Rights Movement, the push for gender quality, and mounting activism within gay and queer communities, for example, addressed the horrific isms of the time. It was a time of equal horror and celebration. And yet in many ways, the murder of George Floyd has suggested to me, and others, that those isms we thought we'd vanquished in the 50s, 60s, and 70s haven't gone away. *What are the similarities between those decades and the present moment of the early 2020s? What are the differences? What has prevented us from following through on the significant changes we made during those decades? How do we understand what happened during that time period, through my life's lens?*

Tumultuous Times: 50s, 60s, 70s—present

I was growing up in the midst of revolutionary changes during the 1950s, 1960s and 1970s. My family watched in earnest the beginning of the Montgomery Bus Boycott in December 1955, just a few months after Emmett Till's lynching in Money, Missouri. I was four years old. As a girl and preteen, I believed segregation and "colored only" signs were a thing peculiar to the south. In New York, the north, we were spared such violence (so my young mind thought at the time). However, the events of 1955 signaled the beginning of the Civil Rights Movement and my introduction to the realities of racism and the struggle to end it through newspapers, radio, television.

I have a particular memory of watching the news coverage of the murder of four little girls attending the 16th Street Baptist Church in Birmingham, Alabama, in September 1963. During that time, I was attending Junior High School. Although I was a good student and did not get into fights, I remember having an argument with a white girl that culminated in some pushing and shoving. I accused her of being prejudiced and racist. A white, male teacher intervened, saying, "Everyone is so upset with the killing of the four girls in the south." It was then I made the connection between what I saw on television of the murder of these little girls and the bombing of their church. The realization of my hurt was clear—up until then, I had felt a separation between me and the events in the South. I was brought up to believe segregation and "colored only" signs were a thing peculiar to the South. In some ways, being in the North—in New York—made me feel as if I was "better than" those Black Americans in the South. However, the realization that one of those little girls could have been me, my siblings, relatives or close friends, was real. While we all mourned their passing, I could also feel the rising tide of anger, frustration that churned and bubbled, seeking an outlet for the energy that screamed, "I can't take it anymore!"

Indeed, my adolescence coincided with a great national reckoning with race, class, and gender. There were messages of violence, but there was also a message of hope and change. I experienced and saw the devastating effects of sexism, racism, classism, homophobia, domestic violence, poverty, sexual abuse and unexamined privilege. Yet, like many others, I chose to celebrate our victories in gaining social equality while remaining keenly aware that more work was needed to heal our society.

Now, so many years later, as I sit here and write my past through the lens of the recent death of George Floyd, I wonder if it's actually worse, in some ways, to have grown up believing in the promises of the Civil Rights Movement. We believed that we were watching the dreadful apparatuses of institutional racism crumble before our eyes. We believed that the Civil Rights Movement would resolve racism, and we believed it would stop the systematic and reckless violence towards black people. And yet, decade after decade, we've watched as our loved ones continue to be beaten and killed. In those days, we despaired that there was no one on TV who looked like us. Now we can turn on the television and watch members of our communities brutally murdered by the police. Which is worse? What do the life and death of George Floyd mean to me? A loss of hope. A reminder of those terrifying images and a sense, not that history is repeating itself, but that we have never left history.

Visibly Invisible

Chaos and conflict were all around me, on the nightly news, on the streets, between my parents, *and* within the Bronx compound. As grand matriarch, Grandma Edith ruled the roost. She was a force of tremendous support known to interfere in all aspects of family life, including child-rearing, financial matters, couples' relationships, and more. At times, her strength and power emasculated her sons-in-law. My informed reader should keep in mind that even with four separate apartments for the different family members, we were deeply enmeshed. Doors were left open, children and adults alike roamed between the various rooms and apartments. There was not much privacy.

My grandmother was especially strict with me. I was not allowed to have or attend sleepovers, or engage in the kind of typical, all-consuming preteen friendships. I never understood why these experiences, which seemed so normal to my peers, were denied to me. Later in life, I understood that her strictness came from her fears over my safety. She feared that I would be raped, or sexually abused, or become pregnant, and that the trauma of these experiences would prevent me from completing my education. Through her fears, she silently communicated to me that men were unpredictable and dangerous. My subsequent confusion and ineptness around my own sexuality likely has some roots in the unspoken messages of my grandmother and my own inability to fully interpret her coded, secret messages. As a result, I fulfilled my need for connection with after-school activities, reading, and listening to music.

Outside of our home, life was just as confusing. I grew up in a household with expanded understandings of traditional male and female roles. My grandmother, mother and aunts were as equally skilled with hammers, nails, and paintbrushes as they were in the kitchen. They could DIY around the house with the same ease with which they adorned themselves with beautiful dresses and elegant perfumes. And my father and uncles were avid cooks. Despite the variety of roles men and women in my household performed, I was confronted with troubling expectations around what attitudes, behaviors, activities, and jobs were "for girls" and those which were not. My burgeoning adolescence brought a sense of unhappiness, powerlessness, and dread. Like many others, especially girls and young women of color, I internalized the contradictory messages of the times. I wanted to be a part of the change, but at the same time, those persistent isms, racism, sexism, classism, ableism, etc.) birthed feelings of self-hate, disgust, powerlessness and hopelessness, compounded by the psychological, physical, intellectual, and emotional changes of adolescence. I was haunted by the social constructions of female beauty that looked nothing like me, yet I was cherished by my family and friends. Their love and support were constant, even as I doubted my own abilities and attributes. In both my inner world of self and family and the outer world that surrounded us all, I faced contradicting messages about who and what I should be, and who and what I was. This contradiction was the inspiration for my poem, "You Are Perfect," which opens this chapter. Through the rhythms of poetry, I am trying to recapture the confidence of knowing one is valued, the pride of African American communities, and the knowledge that one's blackness is deeply and profoundly beautiful. Unfortunately, for myself, like so many other black girls, those positive foundational messages of self-worth were eroded over time by the endless barrage of social scripts that told me that my skin color, hair texture, body shape, and glasses were all symbols of my imperfection, which I should relentlessly fight to suppress.

Many of the negative things I told myself during my coming-of-age years came from what I was and wasn't seeing in the explosion of popular culture during those years. Although I was too young to listen to the radio, I heard my family talk about Major Bowes, who hosted amateur entertainers on his radio show from 1935 until his death in 1946 (although the show with his name ran until 1952). I suspect there were few, if any, people of color. It is hard to believe that radio had once been the only form of entertainment. However, by the time I was old enough to understand, radio had died out and television rose.

I searched for my place on the television shows I watched with my family. I grew up watching Amos and Andy, which began on the radio around 1928 (well before my birth) and was played by two white men. In 1951, the show aired on television, but it was removed because of their portrayal of black stereotypes. To be honest, I laughed at the funny parts, including segments where Sapphire yelled at Kingfish, a depiction of the so-called "angry black woman." It would be remiss if I did not mention the character of Stepin Fetchit, who personified the historical racial caricaturing of African Americans (although the actor who played him, Lincoln Theodore Monroe Andrew Perry, ended up being one of the few black millionaires!). These reminiscences served as a reminder of racial caricatures and have a particular significance for black people. Part of the historical (and on-going) objectification process to transform people of African descent from members of a civilization of culture, language, riches, education, higher learning into sub-humans only fit for enslavement, relied on the cultural narratives and representations of black people. And so the "Mammy," the "Coon," the "Pickaninny," the individual happy to serve whites, amongst other caricatures, were all invented, and expanded (i.e. black people are not intelligent, don't suffer pain as do whites, etc.) to the present day. The movie *The Birth of a Nation* released in 1915, focused on the "brute negro" and disseminated the belief that black men need to be contained, jailed or killed to prevent the rape of white women and a miscegenated society. Looking back, it seems that in order to make a living at their craft, black actors and entertainers portrayed roles that perpetuated these myths, like the mammy or lazy coon. In fact, many of the flagrant disparities in education, housing, employment, medicine, criminal justice, voting, and the law, which continue today, are all based on racial caricatures and the implementation of these caricatures in the basic institutions within our society. Perhaps our nation's tradition of objectification and racial caricaturizing remained preconsciously or unconsciously in the psyche of Officer Derek Chauvin. As his cold, blank gaze rested on George Floyd, what did he see? From a psychological standpoint, was he viewing a caricature? Did he see the brute Negro who needed containment and incarceration?

It was difficult for my own children, and the students I have had over the years, to believe there were no people who looked like me on our large black and white television. Cartoons and kid shows like *Wonderama* never featured a person of color. My cousins and I watched the Bozo The Clown Show after school, searching for a youngster who looked like us. The same was true for the Disney shows at the time. While Annette Funicello was featured, I never saw young women of color. Grandma Edith's favorite variety show, "Lawrence Welk," had few, if any, people of color. I do recall a gentleman who was a tap dancer. This was likewise the case with *The Dick Clark Show*. The show's young dancers were all white, although black music featured prominently in the R&B and rock tunes. I could only dream of appearing on that show, dancing the monkey. There was always hope while watching that somehow, next week, a person of color would be included. Maybe there would be an opportunity for me! When there was an identifiable person of color, it was such a novelty that we would telephone family and friends, telling them to turn on the TV immediately. Television made some slight shifts in 1956 when Nat King Cole had his own television show. Ed Sullivan, who hosted a weekly Sunday night television show, aired entertainers such as Harry Belafonte and Sammy Davis Jr.

Like many youngsters of color during that time, the idealized family on television, including "Father Knows Best" and "Leave it to Beaver," mirrored an idealized perfection neither I, nor my family, would ever achieve. My hair would never maintain the glorious pageboy style of June Cleaver or the flip adorned by Donna Reed. Oh, how I tried to look like these women. With curlers, papers, and different styling gels, I soldiered on in a relentless, unachievable battle to capture their style. These women never looked tired or worn out, as many of the women in my life appeared. They didn't work. Most of the women in my family worked—long and hard. The women in my family faced layoffs and worried about finances, things I never saw depicted on the television screen. TV moms managed their households always looking fashionable, in a clean home with milk and cookies prepared for the children when they came home, and a hot meal for dinner when Father came home from work. I often thought about the differences between those TV families and my own, and I often blamed myself for somehow not being good enough.

With the wisdom and distance of time and age, I now know that those immaculate styles were unattainable for everyone who wasn't a movie star. The white women of my generation also felt the pressure to look and be like these women, and few to none actually lived that life of seamless, sweat-less, stress-less perfection. But nobody shared the secret…that this TV life was impossible! In those decades of television, we believed that what we saw on TV reflected our reality. We didn't question what we were shown.

Later, in my early teens, I did see people who looked like me on TV. But not in a way that gave me any joy. I cringed in terror as I watched people who indeed looked like me being beaten, tortured, hosed down with water from hydrants like animals, and jailed without just cause. But it wasn't until 1971, when Don Cornelius chanted "Soul Train," that I could finally watch a show where many of the participants looked just like me and were not caricatures, stereotypes or victims of violence.

The horrifying lack of people who looked like me, coupled with socialization and marketing sending powerful messages about beauty, womanhood, and desirability, led to negative beliefs about my hair, skin color, clothes and my need to wear glasses. I often would hear, "Men don't make passes at girls who wear glasses." My skin color, hair texture, body type, and other attributes have historically been seen as an antithesis to the cherished standards of (white) beauty within our nation and other parts of the world. My worldview as a school-aged youngster did not include the understanding of, or pride in, the fact that my physical characteristics were highly valued in the birthplace of humanity, Mother Africa.

As I review and re-orient myself to the past, I do recall the confusing messages I received regarding myself, especially in relation to my peers, my teachers, and others. In the late 1950s through the 1960s, the youngsters I yearned to emulate were featured in teen magazines, and all of them were white. Their clothes, hairstyles, even the social activities they were allowed and encouraged to participate in, were all unreachable gold rings on the carousel of my life. And yet how much I wanted them! Around 1970, the first Black Miss America contestant was so awe-inspiring that we talked about her for days. Yet, by the time "Black is Beautiful" sloganized the 1970s, I was already a college student, and while I certainly appreciated the sudden celebration of being—and "looking" black—I had already spent two decades internalizing the social stigma of being "different" and "less than."

My hair was a particularly sore spot. A phrase that rings true in my memory: "Your hair is your crowning glory." But what if you have no "crowning glory" or perhaps your hair does not conform to the accepted standards for "crowning glory?" For many African American girls, our hair is a major battle, an unceasing conflict. Looking back, I can see that my hair was a beautiful mass of thick tight curls. It looked best in its natural state, perhaps box braided or in cornrows. However, those "less than" styles were associated with unattractiveness and non-adherence to a standard of beauty I would never achieve. I fought a doomed battle, trying to force my hair to conform to styles and standards that were impossible for my hair's natural texture.

And so, memories: the washing, drying, straightening and styling of hair that took all day. Scenes infused with trauma, especially during the summer months when the heat and humidity were formidable opponents to the straight locs we valiantly fought to achieve. At some point, both my mother and my aunt lost the battle with my hair and found the cash to send me to a beautician. But the battle continued. The beautician who tried to earn a living out of an impossible task of multiple appointments, juggling schedules, overbooking, combined with a clientele who were often late, took ages to complete the task of straightening and styling my hair. Beauticians wanted to cut my long, beautiful tightly curled hair, but my mother refused. After years of enduring chemicals and heat, pain and suffering, I found my voice in natural styles. From "afro" to braids, twists, and other styles, which were in synergy with my identity, I fell into my current style of locs which perfectly matches my lifestyle, identity, and my own standards of beauty. I stopped trying in vain to obtain a prize that was, in fact, not a prize, but a detriment to my own unique and effortless beauty.

Safe Spaces

I found ways to cope with the juxtaposition between what the world was telling me about my physical appearance and worth, and how my family and community supported and cared for me. To ease the pain and confusion of such conflicts, I turned to movies, music, and books.

Movies were my passion. My Saturday and Sunday afternoons from age ten onwards were spent watching old movies on a black and white television in our living room, which was the only TV we had in the house! I loved the story lines, the drama and acting. I watched movies starring Shirley Temple, whose dancing I thought I could imitate. My youngest aunt, who was an avid movie goer and radio listener, introduced me to many of the "old" Hollywood actors: Bette Davis, Joan Crawford, Lana Turner, Vivien Leigh, Katherine Hepburn, Ingrid Bergman, Mickey Rooney, James Cagney, Humphrey Bogart, Cary Grant, Clark Gable, Spencer Tracy, to name a few. She taught me the names of the less famous actors like Andy Devine and others. The first time I saw *Gone With the Wind* in black and white, I was inspired because I saw black actors. As you may know, Hattie McDaniel, who played Mammy, won an Academy Award for Best Supporting Actress. My family members often reflected with hope on her achievement. I also loved Ethel Waters in *Pinky* and *The Sound and the Fury*. Even now, the memory of Juanita Moore on her deathbed in *Imitation of Life* brings tears to my eyes. As she faces death, she is also confronted by her biracial daughter's hatred for being half-black but raised to believe that she was white (although the actor who played her daughter was not actually biracial).

Music, in particular, helped me cope with pain and sadness. Like many public schools at the time, the New York City public education system had resources and support for some students.

Although it's hard to imagine this now, in my elementary school years, mornings were devoted to academics and the afternoon were spent with music, led by two gifted teachers. I was among the few students who were exposed to music. My family gave me an old, damaged violin that had belonged to my cousin. Somehow, my teacher repaired it, and I played the violin from elementary school through junior and high school, both in school and a community orchestra. I attended private lessons as well, which cost $1.50 per lesson. In these lessons, I not only practiced and improved my technique, but also experimented with writing music. Participating in bands and concerts was particularly important for me. Playing alongside others is profoundly different than playing alone. As I put bow to strings alongside other musicians, I felt empowered. I could feel the enormity of what we were doing, expanding all possibilities. I participated in multiple concerts, including a major one towards the end of the school year, which was an important occasion for me and my family. I was even amongst those who attended Leonard Bernstein's "Young People's Concerts" in Carnegie Hall. I remember playing the musical score from the movie, *Exodus*, whose expansive music gave space to the pain and longing in my heart and mind.

For me, music and the playing of the music was an opportunity in a symbolic, but also very real, way to give voice to my feelings. In my family, it was not permissible to show anger, to talk back, or to appear rude. We did not speak about our intense emotions. So, where do you find a place for these teenage feelings, full to bursting with intense emotions and physiological expansions? What do you do with these feelings? Music unclogged my bottled-up emotions and allowed me to vent and express what I felt inside. I could feel my complicated emotions emanating from the notes and melodies of music. At times, music acted as a medical panacea, lifting me from a sea of despair into a sky of hope, filled with faith. And through music, I could contribute to something that was bigger than myself. When I was playing music, I felt myself a part of that bigness, the energies coursing through me and around me helped me understand the power that existed inside. These experiences helped me find my voice— the voice that I needed to give presence to the feelings that were inside of me that I couldn't/wouldn't necessarily put into words. The language of music connected me to the pain that I was feeling at the time but could not find words for. All the sadness and despair, and some of the anger and frustration, that I felt I could not express at home, took shape and form in music. I stopped playing the violin in my senior year of high school. At the end of the school year, the music teacher, with whom I had taken private lessons, handed out achievement awards. Despite the years spent under his tutelage and my strong performances, I was the only senior music student who was not given an award. There was no one I could appeal to intervene in this obvious snub. It hurt me so greatly that I never picked up the violin again.

If I wasn't playing music, I was listening to it. I had no money to buy records, so I listened to the music that was available in the household. During my pre-teen years, from around 6th grade onwards, I was obsessed with my mother's Jazz records. On the weekends, I could be found listening to Carmen McRae, Nancy Wilson, and Nina Simone. Simone is widely known for her political songs, but I loved the way she performed the music from Porgy & Bess, especially "I Loves You, Porgy." In my mother's apartment, I would sing along with these jazz singers, trying to imitate the cadence and emotion, because it resonated with me.

Listening to music and singing along offered me another opportunity to release the different emotions I was feeling at the time. As I listened and sang along to "I Sold My Heart to the Junkman," I could relate to offering aspects of my heart to someone who didn't appreciate their worth. The soulful, searing songs by black jazz singers chronicled the highs and lows of being black in the United States, providing me with a window in the intimate, emotional worlds of other black people. As I entered adolescence, the events of the Civil Rights Movement also increased my interest and understanding of black people in America and throughout the world. The protest music of the era resonated with me. I was listening to Sam Cooke's, "A Change Is Gonna Come," "Strange Fruit" by Billie Holiday, "People Get Ready" by the Impressions, and "Mississippi Goddam" by Nina Simone. Through these songs, I began to apprehend the connection between culture and socio-economic and political realities.

It was during this time that I began my love of history and literature. In Junior High, I learned much about world history, including an understanding of people in Africa. I threw myself into reading, especially authors of the Harlem Renaissance: Richard Wright, Langston Hughes, Claude McKay, Ralph Ellison, and Zora Neale Hurston. Later, the words of writers such as James Baldwin, Toni Morrison, Alice Walker, and others, captured my imagination and inspired my quest for self-knowledge. Poets also caught my interest, including those who chronicled the Black Nationalist Movement: Amiri Baraka, Sonia Sanchez, Askia Muhammad Toure, to name a few.

It was through my alignment with these gifted writers that I began to fully understand and resonate with my identity as an

African American. In books by African American writers, I saw the opportunities that existed for me. Reading the written words of these authors—and even listening to their live presentations—inspired me. I began to see myself in the worlds they described. When I encountered Pecola Breedlove, the young protagonist of Toni Morrison's *The Bluest Eye* who longs for blue eyes, I could relate. Just as Pecola believed that if she had blue eyes, all her problems would be solved, I, too, had studied the actresses on TV, thinking that if I could look like them, I'd have no problems—I would be whole, healed, and happy. With incredulity and awe, I recall Baldwin's depiction of a young woman's loss of virginity. I wondered how he could so thoroughly understand what it felt like for a young woman to lose her virginity. I could feel and experience his words, sensing there was something special in them, and that ultimately helped and healed me. I realized that if talented black people could produce such wonderful written words that perhaps I, too, could join them. However, I did not have a black educator until graduate school. Therefore, most of my study and understanding of black people has been self-taught. Often, I faced the awkward situation of having to justify ideas, arguments, even facts, to teachers who were not educated in the history and cultures of black people. It was tempting to remain quiet and avoid conflict with my professors. But I didn't. My inner knowingness propelled me forward and gave me the courage to question and gently push back, a quality that continues to serve me to this day.

While poetry, fiction, and non-fiction were positive outlets where I could read about the lives and experiences of people who looked like me, I had few resources to answer the many questions my burgeoning womanhood raised. Chief among the taboo topics was sex and sexuality. And yet they swirled around me, a confusing and sometime traumatic whirlwind of hormones, emotions, and situations. I was horrified to learn that one of my friends had been impregnated by her own father. While her family remained together, my classmate was placed in a home for unwed mothers. Her brother, who was also a friend of mine, sobbed violently as he recounted the story, filled with shame, cloaked in the need for secrecy. I wasn't sure how to support him and what to feel. Marked forever by this incident, incest later became a focus of my work.

I was not well-equipped to understand my own sexual feelings and the sexual attention I would receive from others. In retrospect, there were many times I haphazardly stumbled into this arena like a bull into a china closet. I was taught the protocols associated with menstruation, and that babies could be conceived from sex. However, I missed out on the complex and intricate aspects of sexuality, rendering me ill-prepared to handle the attention of the males I came in contact with. It's said that feelings about oneself begin on the inside and then appear outwardly. If this is true, and I believe it is, I had little understanding of my beauty, sexual allure, and effect on men. This developmental delay, or perhaps lack of competence, continued well into my adult years, causing many situations in which I missed or did not understand what I now view as obvious cues.

"If I love you, I have to love what comes from you"

High school and college were a time of pain and sorrow but also a time of triumphs and joys. During my junior year of high school, my mother met and married my stepfather, Alex. I had always hoped for a reconciliation between my parents, even though they had been apart for many years. I think there is always a tendency for children in the midst of separation and divorce to hold onto hope, and I was certainly among them. However, around 1965, my mother "accidentally" bumped into a charismatic and dashing gentleman whom she had known during her childhood and adolescence. An ex-Marine and widower with two grown children, Alex offered my mother the opportunity to have a stable partner and companion in her life, sharing social and civic activities, taking vacations, and creating a home life, even while Alex suffered from untreated PTSD, which he tried to soothe with alcohol. Eventually, their relationship transitioned into marriage, and my sister and I became part of a blended family. Alex told her, "If I love you, I have to love what comes from you." And to that end, he did his best to play the "surrogate" father, as my own father was physically and emotionally distant at this time. And perhaps best of all, from my mother's newfound relationship, I gained an additional elder brother and sister who helped me enormously in my transition from adolescence to adulthood. Although Alex and my mother separated in the early 1970s, he and I remained close until his death in 1985. Even in the years after his death, my step-siblings and I continue to support, encourage, and care for each other, our children, and our grandchildren.

I did, in fact, feel my stepfather's love when it came to supporting my health and well-being, particularly during a bout of anorexia in my teen years. It was 1965 or 1966, and my mother, grandmother, sister and I had gone out to fancy restaurant for a special Mother's Day lunch. A day or two later, I fell ill with violent vomiting, diarrhea, nausea, and an inability to eat. After a week or so, I was taken to Jacobi Hospital in the Bronx, which was the new state-of-the-art public hospital, and treated with a course of antibiotics. The diagnosis was salmonella. (We later learned the restaurant hired migrant employees and hand washing was not encouraged.) I remained ill from May until September. During that time, I was unable to eat. I felt like I would never be able to eat again; it was as if my stomach had shut down. My family was very worried. The doctors could not offer an explanation other than the parasites within me had turned into Shigella. I must have been drinking liquids because I did not present with dehydration. I recall sitting on the steps of our house in pajamas during the summer months as my cousins played outside, feeling a sense of sadness and despair. Offers for my favorite foods were met with 'no thank you.' My grandmother threatened me by telling me that I would die if I continued to refuse food. My wise uncle told me he knew why I was not eating—I was angry, he said. He was right, but I couldn't feel it and I continued not to eat. My father was summoned at my mother's urging, despite the fact that they were estranged from one another.

Although my mother was a woman of considerable strength who knew how to take care of her family and gets things done, she felt powerless to help me. At the time, my father was working in the admitting office for a hospital in the Bronx. It is probable that as a hospital employee he developed relationships with many of the physicians. To that end, I suspect he sought advice from one of his physician colleagues who advised him to bring his ailing daughter to his office. Whatever the backstory might have been, my father picked me up, stating, "we are going to a doctor to help with your eating problem."

Upon arrival at the doctor's office in the Williamsburgh section of the Bronx, the tall, white, and efficient-looking physician, dressed in formal attire on a Saturday morning, spoke directly to my father (and not me). He performed a perfunctory examination, listening to my heart and lungs, and taking my blood pressure. He said to my father, "she appears high-strung." He recommended weekly B12 injections to manage the problem, and we continued with the treatment plan for a number of months.

It was Alex who helped me to eat again. His reaction to my non-eating was simple. He invited me to take a walk with him and said, "Let's get a hot dog from the 'dirty hot dog man'." The 'dirty hot dog man' refers to a familiar New York City sight—the ubiquitous sidewalk carts selling hot dogs with condiments such as mustard, ketchup, sauerkraut, or onions—or the works! I nodded and began eating on that day and continued eating thereafter. My stepfather normalized eating for me and helped me much more than he knew. The healing elements of a relationship can never be underestimated.

My stepfather was also my advocate when it came to my education. In my senior year, I struggled with trigonometry. My teacher was fairly new to the United States and had a heavy accent. As the story goes, Alex and my mother went to a parent-teacher conference and the teacher told them that I had to work harder and be a better student. According to my mother, my stepfather listened intently to the teacher and then said something to the effect of, "Perhaps if she could understand you better, she would be a better student!"

The Young Wise Woman Finds a Way

While I anticipated and prepared for entrance into college, the Civil Rights Movement continued to unfold, as well as the role and responsibility of community involvement in education. During this time, I sought out help from many in deciding vocational and career choices. While I always felt healing was an intrinsic part of my genetics, I was discouraged from pursuing medicine. Looking back, I'm not sure if this discouragement was based on my gender, race and ethnicity, or socioeconomic factors. Similarly, at one point, I was told I was "not college material" and I should seek higher education in a community college. This was confusing since I was a B+ student with lots of service-oriented and community activities. I respected my teachers and guidance counselors. Yet, their discouragement did not sit well with me. Did I dare to believe there was unconscious racism amongst them? I didn't fight these naysayers or engage in verbal battles. I just knew that I had to seek help elsewhere. There was something within telling me there was more for me in my life than they imagined. And those people were getting in the way. I had an inner knowingness that there were other opportunities for me. Sometimes, in the silence, we find the answers. Whether it was Spirit or those in spirit speaking to me, I am not certain—I just knew. Was this the beginning of my spiritual consciousness?

An inward knowingness? Guidance from Spirit, ancestors, and helpers? All of the above? Yet, I suspect, immaterial, because the message, for me, was to follow my inner guidance which was nurtured by the sense of myself as being "perfect" that I received from my family—the assurance "that I possessed/the Undeniable stamp/Of the right stuff!" In retrospect, how many people of color are separated from this inner knowingness? Is it a stretch to consider how different history might've been if people were in synch with their inner knowingness? Did George Floyd have this ability but lack the access to the quiet, where the voices of inner knowingness emerge?

And so, I turned to other people, whom I felt better understood my abilities and potential for success. This was, perhaps, not unexpected, as I have already chronicled how important self-help and mutual aid have been in my family and in African American communities more generally. From unofficial assistance, like the kind provided by Vera's family to Great-Grandfather Ceasar so long ago in Money, Mississippi, to the institutionalized grassroots aid from associations such as the Jackson Democratic Club and the Progressive Benevolent Association, black people have long known that if we are going to achieve anything in this country, we're gonna have to help ourselves.

Quite accidentally, I had two close friends who worked at an organization called the Harlem College Assistance Project, which was funded by the Ministerial Interfaith Organization. I believe there was some relationship with the Methodist Church. I cannot begin to tell you what a difference the director, Mr. Rufus Newlin, made in my life. Transcript in hand, I met with him and explained how I was being tracked into community college or trade school. He responded nonchalantly, "We will see about that." Shortly thereafter, I received a phone call to apply to what would become my alma mater, Drew University in Madison, New Jersey. After a visit, including an interview, I was offered and accepted on a nearly full scholarship.

It's been my experience that programs such as the Harlem College Assistance Program no longer exist. College assistance for young black people is often fragmented. Many students and families look to the schools to manage this effort. Sadly, it's often the students who need the most help are the ones coming from overextended schools without sufficient resources; often the schools themselves are the source of the problem. Today, I am struck by the current lack of mutual aid associations for black people. For example, what mutual aid organizations were available to Michael Brown, who was planning to attend trade school to become a heating and cooling technician? How different would his life have been if there had been a structured mentoring program for students interested in that work? How would his life have unfolded if there had been a strong democratic force in Ferguson, Missouri? What resources might've been available to him and his family?

Even though Drew was going to be very different from my previous experiences, I really looked forward to meeting new people and immersing myself in a learning environment. The weeks and months leading up to Move-In Day were a time of great excitement and expectation. I had contacted my soon-to-be roommate, Jane, and we had met for lunch around 42nd Street in New York City. Jane had taken the bus from Westfield, New Jersey to New York City to meet me, and this may have been her first trip on a public bus and her first trip to New York City. It was the first time Jane had ever had any contact with a black person. I remember her mother telling her that being my roommate would be "a good experience for her." Jane and I never really connected, and she left Drew University after her first semester.

Sunup to Sundown

When the big day to move on campus finally arrived, I was up early. I had all my lists prepared and had even been assigned a Big Sister peer-mentor to help me through the transition. My stepfather arranged for his best friend to move me in during freshman orientation. His friend had gone through the college admissions with his own daughter, and therefore helped immensely in translating the process. I suspect, although no one said a word, that there may have been concerns about a black family visiting Madison, New Jersey—a conservative, predominantly white town. These types of concerns, misgivings, apprehensions, and preoccupations were never outwardly discussed in many black families, and my family was no exception. Like many others, I had to listen for the metacommunications—the unspoken, secret messages—in the discussions happening around me. Years before, black male students at Drew University were refused haircuts in the town, a discriminatory practice that led to mass demonstrations. I believe Alex called upon this friend because he needed support and back-up while navigating this difficult racial terrain. As a black man visiting an all-white community, he wanted as much security as possible for himself and the family.

His fears were not unfounded. Even while the legislative effects of the Civil Rights Movement were officially desegregating the nation, semi-official race-based policies and practices were still the norm. Certain municipalities even within the New York Metro area, including parts of the Bronx, were "sundown towns"—towns where it was illegal for African Americans to be present after sundown. Violations of "sundown laws" could result in all kinds of punishment, including lynching. Far from being a thing of a Jim Crow past, "sundown" towns and anti-black violence were still common occurrences when I began college. In *Sundown Towns: A Hidden Dimension of American Racism*, author and historian James William Loewen writes of the thousands of towns across the country that were effectively able to keep such practices alive, one way or another, even after the passing of the Equal Rights Amendment and other acts of Civil Rights legislature. In fact, as recently as the mid-1980s and 1990s, Black Americans still avoided places known as "sundown towns." When I was a staff member at a psychiatric center near Pearl River, New York, many of the black staff refused to attend a holiday party because of the town's reputation as a "sundown town." I was clueless at the time and went to the party. When I asked where my fellow black coworkers were, I remember being told, "Don't you know why they didn't come? This is a sundown town." When realization dawned, I was frightened. I needed to get out of there—fast. Periodically, when I would drive up that way and take the local roads, even in the daytime, I was very, very careful, fearful of being profiled and stopped.

I think about the reality that no specific information for black people about sundown towns existed other than the Green Book, a mid-century guide for African Americans in the U.S. (North and South), as well as parts of Canada, Mexico, and the Caribbean, which listed the motels, restaurants and gas stations where they could receive service. Word of mouth was the only way to spread information about which places should be avoided, and, as a result, many people of color had the terrifying experience of finding themselves in the wrong place at the wrong time. It's sobering to remember how, twenty years after the day my stepfather called up his friend to help him navigate a white college town, 16-year-old Yusef Hawkins was shot and killed in Bensonhurst, Brooklyn in 1989. Yusef and his friends had gone to the predominantly Italian American community to meet a girl they knew when they were attacked by a white mob carrying baseball bats. One man shot Yusef twice in the chest. In the subsequent protests and outcry surrounding the killing, Revered Al Sharpton was stabbed.

Back in 1969, while my stepfather surrounded himself with a buddy in case something should go awry with my move-in, my mother was tearing down my Malcom X poster. Like so many young, black students, I supported Malcom X and was proud to hang up my poster in my dorm room. My mother, on the other hand, had different ideas.

"What are you doing?!" she said. "Do you want to lose your scholarship by being militant?!" Behind her words was fear. She was afraid that if I expressed myself too militantly, I would threaten the university's administration and they would cut off my scholarship. My mother and stepfather's careful planning and coordination around moving me into my freshman dorm are powerful examples of the mutual fear between whites and blacks simmering just the below the surface of desegregation and equality. But they are also indicative of my parents' care, even if it didn't always feel like care at the time. I may have resented my mother's tearing down of my poster (I put it back up when she left), but this was also the woman who rose before dawn on Parent's Weekend to cook all of my favorite dishes from home that I had been missing, took a long journey on multiple forms of public transportation, and showed up to support me with bags of still-warm, delicious food. Her presence at Parent's Weekend made me feel represented and validated. The tension between wanting to be independent and wanting to be cared for, or wanting to protect and wanting to indulge, are classic dimensions of parent-child relationships.

As Natural As Breathing

My years at Drew (1969—1973) were not all champagne and roses. My first year was especially challenging. Moving from a diverse, urban environment to a suburban, a largely white one, I often felt out of place. I was one of around five black students in a class of 1,600. There were times when I felt as if I was being swallowed whole by the sea of whiteness surrounding me. I felt choked and suffered from severe anxiety and fear. I would often run across campus in an effort to cope with these feelings. I recall simmering with fear, distrustful of whites whom I feared might treat me unfairly. I feared the informal execution of white supremacy, palpable to me in the unequal power dynamics on campus. I feared that the greater power wielded by white administrators, white professors, and white students might thrust me into a position of powerlessness.

I wasn't alone. It was 1969; many colleges and universities were experiencing the financial lucrativeness of federal dollars, and Drew was among them. They offered admission to many students without suitable advising and support. The result was that students of color often experienced academic difficulties and enormous emotional challenges as the result of being brown or black in a white university in the midst of the Civil Rights Movement and the Vietnam War. Indeed, there was a profound lack of black professors or black members of staff who would have been a source of support for students of color. At that time, the only black person in the administration was a staff member in charge of student housing. Help for black students was informal and took place largely through the black student group, Hyera, of which I was a member. Hyera organized events but was also a place where people could talk about their problems (for example, if they were struggling with a certain professor). As part of the group, I spoke with the black students facing academic probation (this was, sadly, at least half of the black student population). It was clear to me that they had poor or no academic advising from the university administration. For many, this was their first time away from home. These students were in the top of their high school graduating classes but had been thrown in with students coming from schools with much greater resources and opportunities. Nobody had prepared them for such disparity in background and training or for the emotional problems that came from being such a visible black minority. (This was before the development and implementation of the various opportunity programs designed to help students of color). Years later, when my own children went to prestigious universities, there was a marked improvement in representation amongst the faculty and staff. When I visited these universities, I could go to the black faculty and staff and say, "Please look out for my child." They understood my fears and uncertainties. But in my day, it was up to the students of color to help each other.

I served as informal "academic and personal issues counselor" from my sophomore year onwards. I remember talking to my peers about our shock and sadness after a black student ended up in a coma after a medical emergency that could have been prevented if there were greater resources for black students on campus. As a group, Hyera organized to support her and her family. I don't recall that the university did anything substantial. I didn't understand the impact of my service efforts until years later when former students would come to me and say, "We could always come to Mama Lorna!" For my part, I never felt like I was *doing something*. It was as natural as breathing. As drinking a glass of water when thirsty. My passion for mental health and service was also cultivated by my part-time work in the Counseling Center during my college years. My experiences at Drew watered and nurtured those seeds, which soon grew shoots, and would eventually blossom into a career as a social worker with a graduate degree from Columbia University.

A Meal and a Conversation (Maybe a Polka) Can Change the World

Throughout my years at Drew, I was asked to participate and sit on certain boards where student activity funds were allocated. In this way, we funded and shared diverse events.

The relationship between the white students who ran student government, our Dean, and the black students, was friendly and productive. As I discussed in Chapter Two, we embodied many positive aspects of intersectionality in our approach to sharing power and resources. Dean Sawin, a white Republican and conservative, was a staunch advocate for students, including the black students. He did his best to help us get whatever we needed. Although he was no Great White Hope, he was a benevolent man in a time when institutional cross-racial benevolence was rare. And when I was nominated for an Alumni Achievement Award in 2003, the elderly Dean Sawin was there. Now, after being a top administrator myself, I understand Dean Sawin's great skill—the man really knew how to move the money around!

With the help of the student government and the ongoing support of Dean Sawin, we would host "Black Emphasis Week," a week-long event of culture, music, food, and education. We hosted many stellar individuals such as Ralph Ellison, Kenneth Gibson, jazz musician Lee Morgan, poets Amiri Baraka, Sonia Sanchez, and Askia Muhhamed Toure, and more. These programs were validating for African American students, and educational and enlightening for other students. It was also during these years that I had the opportunity to deepen my interest in African and African-American literature. We were fortunate to find a talented white professor, who not only loved the literature but also loved us! This professor has since passed, but I cherished the opportunity I had to explore many themes such as sexuality in Zora Neale Hurston's, *Their Eyes Were Watching God*.

Through my work in the Counseling Center, God connected me with my surrogate mother, Mrs. G., who worked as a secretary. She was originally from Wales, and, in part, I think she connected to my religious background as a fellow Episcopalian. Her husband and daughter adopted me into their family, where I was cared for and loved, and given the support that I needed. Mrs. G and her husband, a salesman, were Republicans in a conservative area, but politics never played a role in how they treated me. I remember when the family invited me over for a steak dinner, even though I knew money was often tight. After dinner, Mr. G., who was Polish, taught me how to dance the polka. When I graduated, Mrs. G made my graduation dress and went around to all the student services offices, collecting beautiful graduation gifts for me from her colleagues. In fact, Mrs. and Mr. G. even came out to the Bronx to attend my graduation party and celebrate with my family. Can you imagine a conservative white couple cutting the rug with a black family in the Bronx in the early 1970s? I put forward this vignette to show how race relations can change, beginning with a meal and a conversation.

Studying the subjects that I loved and nurtured by a number of talented professors and a surrogate white mom who did her best to offer me love and support, I recollect those years as some of the best years of my life. Unlike my high school teachers, some of my professors and college administrators recognized the abilities I had to offer, both to the community and the world. I was often chosen to represent our school in nation-wide events, focus groups, and diversity conferences. There were many professors who helped and guided me; but after deciding to major in sociology, it was Dr. Kane, Chair of the Sociology Department, who said on the eve of my senior year, "You are going to be a social worker; apply to the Columbia School of Social Work." He saw in me the capacity to be successful at one of the nation's most top-notch and leading institutions for the study of social work. And again, I received an acceptance and complete tuition for my two years of study (1973-75).

The Wise Woman in the Ivy League

In retrospect, many themes from my past repeated during my graduate school days. It was, as Charles Dickens wrote, "The best of times and the worst of times." The global socio-economic-political context loomed large: the Vietnam War, the rise of black consciousness, domestic unrest, racial tensions, and an economic crisis, all affected me and the often-suffocating world of graduate studies. At times, I was devalued and underestimated; I was stigmatized by my skin color and not seen as smart or having something to offer. Despite the eye-opening courses in African American literature that I had the privilege to attend at Drew, this was still a time when serious academic studies of black people in America were hard to come by. Most of what I knew about my communities at home and around the world had been self-taught, and I often found myself in the awkward position of knowing more about this topic than my professors. My debates and research papers, based on facts that I knew to be true, were unfamiliar to the people attempting to educate me. I was often challenged. I asked myself more than once if I should take the easy road—like my fellow students—and avoid subject matter that might set me up for conflict with my white professors. Something inside propelled me to keep following these interests and to keep questioning.

My determined inquisitiveness persists to this day!

Graduate school was where I studied non-verbal communication, Transactional Analysis, Community Organization, and Casework. It was also the place where one white casework professor pointed her arthritic finger in my face and said, "You will never become a social worker 'cause you people can't write'." She also told me that I was an "intuitive" social worker and that intuitive social workers are "useless." Perhaps I heard the echo of Rufus Newlin, the man who helped me get my scholarship to Drew, and countless others who told me to not listen to the naysayers, but I also heard my own voice of inner knowingness that assured me of my potential. Instead of fulfilling this woman's hateful prophecy, I turned around and left the office, vowing that, indeed, I would be a social worker!

However, I would be less than honest if I did not admit that her words stabbed me, mind, body and spirit. Her words did affect me, even while I succeeded in my various pursuits. Shortly after this encounter, I was fortunate to find a job at a medical center covering for social workers on vacation. There, I met a wonderful social work professional, familiar with the curriculum and requirements of my graduate program, who reviewed the paper I was going to submit and that my professor had denigrated. She felt the paper definitely deserved an A. However, when I submitted it, I received a B-. I believe the adage that our worst critics can be our best teachers, but how much can a person of color withstand?

Yet, it was during this time that I honed and developed many of my skills as a mental health clinician, especially during my internship at Harlem Hospital. In the Department of Psychiatry at Harlem Hospital, I saw black psychiatrists and clinicians all providing state-of-the-art treatment to people in the community. There, I nurtured my ambition to become a mental health professional. By seeing the culturally competent care black mental health professionals provided to individuals in the Harlem community, I saw potential within myself. In my clinical work, I truly integrated my clinical and cultural understanding of psychotherapy, both individual and group.

The Wise Woman Launches Her Career

Shortly after graduating from Columbia, I needed employment and found myself being offered a job to direct a group home for girls. My youthful enthusiasm, strength, and stamina encouraged me to tackle a near impossible job. I was given the responsibility of managing adolescent girls who exhibited a plethora of symptoms and behaviors. The organizational and programmatic structure was all mixed-up, and the therapeutic environment could not meet all their needs. Quite frankly, a number of the girls needed psychiatric hospitalization; others could have benefitted from a structured setting where they would not leave the confines of the program, while others could have been placed in loving foster care settings. My resolve to counteract these issues was to work harder, put in longer hours, counsel and support the staff, organize countless activities for the girls, and also work with their families. There were continual physical assaults both between the girls and with the caring staff. But the ultimate challenge occurred when one resident attempted to set another on fire and ended up burning the building and destroying the house. After the home was rebuilt, the physical violence to staff continued. Eventually, I found myself, beaten and bruised, lying on a stretcher in Bellevue Hospital. I felt defeated and completely disempowered. I no longer had the strength, stamina, and zeal to continue this impossible work and resigned without having another job.

This was an exciting time in my life. The mental health movement making great progress and innovations in terms of medication, interventions, and the opportunity to work with families. New ideas and concepts were being developed to address mental health challenges. A mental health diagnosis no longer served as an end to life's possibilities. I was among those who developed new ideas and interventions. Despite what felt like new horizons of progress, I continued to face similar experiences of powerlessness. By now, I was working in a mental health setting also focused on the needs of children and adolescents. I served as a clinical supervisor with a number of staff reporting to me, and I was part of the senior leadership. I would often write scientific papers and lead workshops and educational forums. Quite by accident, I learned some of my work was being plagiarized by a program director who took credit for its development and implementation. When I discussed my concerns, I was told this was something that occurred in most settings and there was nothing I could do about it. I knew if I complained, this would be the end of any opportunities for me at this setting.

As I progressed through my professional career, some of my more glaring experiences with race and gender-based powerlessness had to do with pay and issues of sexual harassment. Early on in my professional career, I was paid less than men with similar qualifications and backgrounds. This information was often veiled in secrecy; it was difficult to prove. Now and then a budget or personnel report would cross my desk, and I would be confronted with the reality. I entered the workforce during a time when sexual harassment was openly expressed. I had my fair share of it, but I was also counseling women who daily faced dehumanizing workplace cultures. One of my clients had to perform sexual favors for her boss in order to maintain her livelihood as a New York City parks employee. During a workplace event, one of my colleagues (a young female social worker) pitched in by handing out dinner rolls, ensuring safety and hygiene by wearing rubber gloves. As one of the VPs walked by, he asked her if she provided proctology exams. We were horrified and unsure what recourse was open (besides punching the guy in the month—which, I must admit, I thought about and think of to this day!).

However, federal law can provide a solid avenue by which women can pursue justice for workplace and sexual harassment, even if some of us (myself, included) worry about the intense attack these protections may be under. I have been inspired by the #MeToo movement, which has galvanized women, who have experienced devaluation and humiliating circumstances, to utilize legal recourse to respond to these attacks. Although the law is not the only answer to these circumstances of powerlessness, costly lawsuits hurt the finances of corporations and entities that hurt women. And, in these circumstances, some change happens.

Such experiences of powerlessness in the workforce ultimately prepared me for what could've been a devastating blow to the career and professional reputation that I had fought for. I was dismissed from a very important job without warning despite a stellar performance over many years. I did not realize that I was a pawn in a political struggle, like so many people of color working in civil service systems. When the tides of politics change, there is too often little to no attention paid to the casualties of silent political battles between Republicans and Democrats. And so, in the midst of many financial and personal responsibilities, I was told to ship out without a lifeboat. Unfortunately, yet perhaps fortunately, I had these ample experiences of powerlessness in the workplace to guide me.

During these times of turmoil and experiences of powerlessness, I closely aligned myself with the nurture and direction of my higher power—Mother/Father God (I will share more about the healing potential of divine connection later!). By then, I had become a regular member of a nearby Episcopalian Church where I felt called to offer healing and be active in ministry. What I am about to share is an absolutely true and factual experience: During the installation of our Priest, I served as one of the chalice bearers on the altar. During the singing of a hymn entitled "I Am the Bread of Life," those of us in attendance raised our hands in praise. As I raised my hands, closing my eyes, I felt a tremendous surge of energy and power enter my body through my hands. At that very moment, I felt intensely blessed and knew all my troubles would be resolved. This moment remains life-changing.

Casting off the Stigma of "Less Than": The Wise Woman Matures

As we age, it's not always clear to what extent the harmful messages that we've received from others have impacted our minds, bodies, and spirits. Although the poem, "You Are Perfect," that opens this chapter is filled with passion, conviction, and gratitude for my family who tried hard to affirm me and nurture my self-esteem, at times, negative feelings and perceptions of difference have impacted my family and myself. I have surrendered, at this epoch in my life, to the reality that difference and intersectionality are intrinsic to who I am. There are constellations of characteristics, especially from a physical standpoint, that mark me out as different from the norm. But these same characteristics that I have re-learned how to love and appreciate are now the standards that others are striving for! From the vantage point of wisdom, I can chuckle about how, on today's current scene, many of the once-devalued characteristics I tried hard to modify are now valued. Large hips and buttocks are all the rage! Luscious lips and thick, curly hair that can be styled in a variety of ways are in advertisements for beauty products, high-end fashion, and music videos. Who would have known the once disparaged characteristics are now of such value that people who are different from me now seek to mimic them through surgery, lasers, and other medical interventions? Today's so-called defects will be the stars of the tomorrow's red-carpet specials. Now that I understand how beauty standards are social constructs that change over time, they have less power over me.

However, just because society's standards for success, beauty and legitimacy are artificial doesn't mean that they don't have real effects on real people. We now live in a society when a black Congressional Representative can speak openly about her baldness. Representative Ayanna Pressley's frank remarks on the impact of baldness on other people's perceptions of her femininity reminds us how much a woman's worth is still tied to certain expectations around her physical appearance. Ms. Pressley's willingness to converse openly on these topics is an inspiration, certainly. And yet, not all of us navigate the politics of appearance and identity with such self-assuredness and poise. Too many women and girls still look in the mirror and see a catalogue of problems, faces and bodies that will never live up to the standards of beauty set by the world around them. Too many of us are terrorized by feelings of low self-worth. And I have to wonder…had George Floyd been dressed in a three-piece suite carrying an attaché case, would his fate have been substantially different?

It's a painful question to consider.

I pray that this sojourn through my family's recent and distant past, guided by my on-going reckoning with the death of George Floyd, may catalyze your own straightforward insight, strengthening and validating you, and offering a clear way to understand and appreciate your life circumstances, family, and personal history. In going to the "dark places" in my narrative, my hope is to empower you to confront any trauma that may be affecting you or someone you love. So, as you begin to join together all of the various pieces that contribute to our existence and lived experiences, I urge you to consider all of the factors (even ones that may seem unrelated) that contribute to how we see and feel the world. These are the things that **Fill and Topple** our buckets.

Chapter 5

The Faces of Trauma

Filling the Bucket…again (and again, and again…)

4/20/21, 12pm-5pm: The jury is sequestered and has been deliberating since yesterday. There's electricity in the air as the various states within the U.S. begin to prepare for the possibility of rioting and destruction of property if, in fact, the jury returns a not guilty verdict in the trial of Derek Chauvin, the alleged murderer of George Floyd. I think pensively on the day's events. I marvel that the National Guard will be deployed in many major cities but muse quietly, introspectively, on why the same actions were not initiated on January 6th, when an insurrection took place in the nation's capital. Questions and conundrums go around and around in my head like a never-ceasing merry-go-round.

4/20/21, 4:15pm, somewhere in the neighborhood: My politically astute husband informs us that the verdict will be announced at 4:30pm. I stop working and look at the "breaking news report." Derek Chauvin: guilty on all counts. My reaction is mixed. I need silence to ground myself and focus on the myriad of emotions I am feeling. There's relief—hurt and pain will perhaps cease, albeit momentarily. But I am ill-prepared to deal with the onslaught of sadness and despair that follows. I find myself completely unable to join in with the joyous sounds of "justice was served!" Quite frankly, for me, the verdict reminds me of just how much evidence the world needs to see, hear, and examine, before a black person's lived experiences can be fully believed and validated. Today, there are no real winners; there are no prizes, no opportunities for joy, nothing to tell me—reassure me—that all is well.

The fact remains that Mr. Floyd is dead.

My complicated emotions around the verdict against Derek Chauvin are more than my body's physiological responses to external events. They are even more complex than "feelings." My response to trauma is, and always has been, connected to my intersectional identity. My reactions reflect the ways in which my emotions are engaged across many fronts: as a woman, as an African American, as a citizen of the United States, as a mental health professional, as a spiritual practitioner, to name a few… the deluge of feelings invoked by traumatic events result from how interconnected all the aspects of my identity are. Pull on one loose thread, and the whole quilt begins to unravel.

We call these multiple psycho-spiritual-emotional experiences *feeling states*. The various intersections of our identities have *feeling states* associated with them. We have discussed some of these feeling states in terms of powerlessness, confusion, turmoil, low self-worth (feeling "less than"). Each one of these feeling states can interact and intersect with others; for example, feelings of powerlessness because of our race and/or gender can perhaps intersect with our disability status and other sources of stigma, such as a felony conviction. When that white lady called me a "n-word bitch" on the highway, my urge to scream was the result of multiple negative feeling states firing up as my racial, ethnic, and gender identities (as well as my competence as a licensed driver of a car!) were attacked. While being a black woman is always foremost in the constellations of my identity and intersections, multiple and simultaneous feeling states precipitated the *drip drip drip* of water filling up the symbolic bucket of my soul, until it ultimately spilled, overflowing. On the day when Derek Chauvin's verdict was announced, I experienced multiple feeling states based on my multiple, intersectional identities. Unshielded and unprotected, I felt as if a machine gun was being aimed at my soul over and over again, without stopping.

As the story of George Floyd and the treatment of black people around the world unfolds, I continue to work through the vicissitudes of my own soul's traumas. I gain new wisdom. Part of this work, this wisdom, involves sharing with you, dear Reader, what I can on the intersecting and multifaceted nature of trauma.

Our Trauma—Our Worldview

I have devoted a significant part of my career to studying trauma. It is important for me to begin by emphasizing that trauma is intersectional—many factors create experiences and circumstances of trauma, and behind one form of trauma, there are almost always others. The teenager who self-harms may have been sexually abused by a close family member, and her community may lack the social, economic, and political resources to guarantee her basic welfare, let alone provide her with psycho-spiritual healing. Poverty, drug addiction, isolation, sexual and physical violence may all be at play in any given situation.

Our experiences of layered trauma have much to do with our worldviews. In my experience, I have seen how worldviews can intersect and produce emotional and psychological experiences of powerlessness, hopelessness, pain and wounding.

What do I mean by worldview? My working definition of this term is intersectional. Understanding how intersectionality shapes, and is shaped by, worldview increases our empathy and helps us recognize the value of examining worldview within others and ourselves. Worldview is a sociological, sociocultural, psychological, cognitive concept that helps to articulate our identity and philosophy of life. It includes every conceivable aspect of our selves, including race, ethnicity, religious and political affiliation, education and educational experience, group memberships, social class, gender, important beliefs and values, marital status, family background, economic class, nationality, regional traditions, occupation/career, and so much more. Our worldview is the interplay between our philosophy and psychology—the attitudes, values, opinions, and concepts which affect how we make decisions, behave, define events.

Forms of trauma are unique and specific to individuals and their experiences. Excellent research proves that "adverse childhood experiences"—including sexual, physical, and other types of abuse and maltreatment—exert a profound impact on our physical, mental and spiritual wellbeing and our capacity for good health. You may wish to explore this research further in "The ACE Study," expertly chronicled by Dr. Vincent Felitti and Robert Anda, MD. Closely related to this study, although not as well-known, is my wonderful friend and colleague Dr. Kristina Muenzenmaier's work on understanding the effects of trauma among women who battle the effects of mental illness. She found an inextricable linkage between different types of abuse, proving that many people experience multiple forms of abuse, although only one type gets reported initially. Such linkages are dramatized in a training film I once watched, many years ago, that depicted a woman in Canada whose psychosis was ultimately found to be rooted in a history of sexual abuse. In the film, the protagonist explains that while being abused, she would imagine herself in the flowers on the wallpaper in her room. While in the throes of her mental illness, she would scream "flowers, flowers, flowers" as she tried to give voice to her experiences of abuse. In the same film, a man shared the story of his sexual victimization and his reluctance to discuss it because of stereotypes and expectations around masculinity. Lastly, the work of Bessel van der Kolk, MD and many, many others have helped me to understand the psychosocial, cultural and biological impact of trauma.

My professional life has placed me in the nexus of many instances of multidimensional, intersectional trauma. As a licensed clinical social worker and mental health professional, I have worked with children, adolescents, and adults, as a clinician, supervisor, researcher, and administrator. My experience while working in major psychiatric facilities has been that most of the men and women receiving treatment had histories of abuse (even if the abuse was not the reason for which they originally sought help). By sharing the stories that follow in this chapter, I hope to shed light on the effects of sexual violence on my own life and the lives of others that I've known or treated. For reasons of confidentiality and ethics, names and situations have been thoroughly disguised. The scenarios I share are only a few examples of the hundreds I was challenged to care for and treat. There were just so many instances of harm.

Some forms of trauma are obvious. Murder, rape, war, loss, for example. Can you imagine the terror that might impact you because you belonged to the "wrong" ethnic group? Films such as Hotel Rwanda are brutal testimonies to the trauma of ethnic-cleansing and large-scale race-based violence. War's casualties include those who survive physically but whose souls and psyches are battered and traumatized. In my years of private practice, I met a war veteran suffering from symptoms of PTSD. This gentleman was trying hard to care for his family, working more than one job. During the day he was a teacher, and, at night, he served as a security guard at a used car lot. His PTSD resurfaced after armed assailants robbed the car lot—twice. He was frightened and cowered in his small, security booth, fearing he would be shot. I also worked with another war veteran experiencing ongoing PTSD after 9/11, when he found himself in the thick of things as a police officer.

Other forms of trauma are less visible. Corporal punishment—what some would call whippings—were a significant part of my mother's and my own upbringing. As a child, my mother was punished with outright verbal abuse and an occasional plate thrown at her head. Although she would later boast about not using the same forms of punishment on her own children, like many African American mothers, she disciplined us with a belt, which left scars and welts. I remember those instances with a sense of trauma, powerlessness, hurt and emotional turmoil. I often did not fully understand why I was being beaten; however, I knew when it was coming. I was often told I was "fresh" or "rude" when I expressed anger. Years later, I wonder if the real lesson I was being taught was that expressing one's feelings wasn't appropriate and could even lead to violence. In retrospect, I can understand that some of the beatings I received were, in fact, during the time my mother was experiencing extensive marital and financial problems; certainly, the intensity and length of my beatings related to those circumstances. It's quite common for parents to take out frustrations in other parts of their lives on their children. I also believe that, at times, my mother felt the need to reinforce the power dynamic between adult and child through the power of physical beating. I suspect this was an intergenerational coping strategy, passed on from my grandmother. My mother was simply repeating what had been done to her. I am pleased that my generation has sought other ways to address the behavior of children. Corporal punishment and verbal and emotional abuse are not within my child-raising repertoire. Thus far, our own children have adopted the use of non-corporal means to correct behavior, and I feel this is a wonderful example of intrafamilial change. Regardless of the intention or circumstances, my childhood experiences with corporal punishment traumatized me.

I have also been traumatized by witnessing unbelievable instances of child abuse in public. I have overheard a mother or father verbally abusing a child using the foulest profanity. Recently, while walking in New York City, I witnessed a mother verbally abusing her school-aged son because he dropped his hamburger. I sincerely wanted to intervene and offer to pay for another sandwich, but I was worried that I might make matters worse. I often go over that incident in my mind's eye...

Although child abuse and the use of corporal punishment happen within all kinds of families, from all different backgrounds, there is a cultural aspect to corporal punishment in African American communities. I am alarmed and beset with worry as I often hear older African American people who bemoan the efforts of child protective organizations which, in their opinion, prevent parents from exercising their right to corporal punishment. I have been told that the right for parents to beat their children is part of Biblical teachings. Perhaps so; however, the Bible also tells slaves to obey their masters! There are others who argue corporal punishment is more humane than other forms of emotional maltreatment and other interventions which test the borders of neglect. This was not my experience. Now, I am not here to sit in judgment of parents, elders, and even some helping professionals, who believe in whippings, spankings, and other forms of corporal punishment. All I will say is that, in my own life, corporal punishment was not a helpful process. My mother would have made a more long-standing impact if she had spoken to me about my behavior in a calm and effective manner.

As a professional, I have seen too many instances of violence between family members. And when it comes to child abuse or the use of physical force to discipline children, the physicality is the least of it. There is a more intangible process which occurs in the process of an adult beating a child. Their beautiful divine light is dimmed. It impacts the child's soul and personality in ways that can have adverse implications later in life. In some cases, such practices may teach a child that violence is the way to solve problems. I am also alarmed when parents decide to turn over their childcare responsibility to the "state," since they no longer feel they can exercise their right to corporal punishment. I am visibly saddened when confronted with these situations, because I truly believe there must be some middle ground where we can teach, educate, and counsel children in behaving and acting in socially and culturally acceptable ways. Perhaps we need to start much earlier in the lives of children, utilizing problem-solving approaches focused on logic and a sense of right and wrong. I will admit my suggestion takes time, effort, patience and resolve—often not readily available to the busy parent who works more than one job, frustrated by fatigue and powerlessness.

There are no easy answers to this problem. We want to raise healthy children (in mind, body, and spirit); we want to demonstrate the senselessness of violence and model alternative methods for our next generations. Indeed, we have learned that violence produces violence…I wonder, dear Reader, to what extent habitual violence was a part of the senseless murder of George Floyd? I leave it to you to discern…

Soul Murder

In addition to physical and mental trauma, I have experienced and witnessed how vulnerable our souls are to sexual trauma. But what do I mean by "soul," anyway? There are many definitions and understandings of "the soul," depending on your religious and/or spiritual beliefs. There are those who believe we all have the spirit of God within us and that spirit or God force, light, and energy resides within our soul. Many spiritually oriented folks often talk about our "soul's journey"—a belief that our life's purpose on earth begins even before our birth. Shall we all agree that our soul represents the innermost parts of ourselves—the very private parts of our mind, body, and spirit? Yet even our innermost self can, and will be, affected by external and internal experiences. In the most severe circumstances of trauma, we may feel as if aspects of our soul have been killed.

The rest of this chapter focuses on rape, incest, and other forms of the sexual victimization. In doing so, I hope to show how sexual trauma rarely happens in a vacuum. Beneath the surface, there are almost always layers of pain and trauma, intersecting negative feeling states, multiplied and intensified to such a degree that the very soul feels violated, harmed, even murdered. Although we may not see the pain, hurt, and suffering experienced by sexually violated individuals, the intensity of the violence placed upon them is so severe that, indeed, we can say that aspects of their souls are murdered. Yet just as our souls' wounds are intersectional and interwoven, so too, are the opportunities for healing. Holistic healing is possible, even for the most unthinkable of soul murders.

Healing Soul Murder

Much to my surprise,
my soul mate and twin flame,
uttered these important words
at a woman's group enterprise.

This was not the first time
she uttered these words which made me quake.
I first heard them from her
in books, interviews, and even on tape.

I continue to thank her, send love during my nightly prayers
for her courage, fortitude and strength
which has provided the impetus
for countless others to share.

She said she stopped talking after her attack.
There are so many among us who also lost their voice,
fears of shame, further attacks, and all kinds of abuse
erected a plaque that said, "you better get back, jack!"

It might be hard for you to believe
that many under my care, as their helper and healer,
had also shared similar words,
all focused on their attempt at ease.

This treatise is an attempt
to describe and share
a horrific experience
that my divine sisters helped to define
in the course of our mutual prayer.

I thanked and gave her love at the time,
not realizing at that point
that I would seize a moment
to share a tale that was mine.

The numbers only tell a part of the story.
When they say one in three,
what does that really mean
to you and to me?

I can't tell you how many times I have heard the story.
The countless tales of mothers' boyfriends, husband,
and so-called friends,
all pretending that soul murder
was an attempt at love's amends.

In the course of my many years,
I have heard men, women, and many children
recount stories that would
surely bring you to tears.
There were so many among them
who cowered, awaiting the coming of night,
begging Mom to stay at home,
for they surely knew
the scary stranger would come after her flight.

In my own life, it was no stranger at all.
He was a large brutish soul,
who himself had probably been brutalized
in the course of the army's treatment mall.

*He served in the military police far away in 'Nam.
There were so many like him
who returned home
with unseen scars of harm.*

*I didn't know better at the time,
I thought he was a decent fellow,
looking for a Black Sister
to spend time and be mellow.
I will not beat up myself any longer
cause what he did was no good.
He used his power and muscle,
And got what he could.*

*I remember quite vividly that afternoon day
when he forced himself upon me,
and I did not
have any say.*

*I told myself you have to get through this.
Because surely this monster can and would kill you.
So I asked Spirit and my guides to help me.
And oh they came through.*

*They lifted me up with ease,
my mind, body and spirit,
just as sure as you please.*

I did not feel a thing

through this terrible ordeal.
I guess that is how a lot of people get through it,
I have heard some even sing.

I baptized and cleansed myself after.
Water and spirituality can cure lots of things.
But until now,
I had not fully taken the time
to really heal my broken wings.

Like so many among us,
I thought masterful forgetting
was the only way to go
But it took a lot of years for me to finally realize, no.

This is a poem designed to help me,
and a lot of others,
to find their individualized way to heal.
Cause I know God has a special place
for us all to be.
Please heed my advice to take time to heal
these horrific soul murders,
as they are too much to feel.

The message here is clear:
What was done to you was the problem,
not what you feel,
my dear.
Challenge and assuage yourself
with people, places, and things

that shout
and surround you up and down,
in and out,
with love's gentle healing,
which guarantees a fertile ground.

The Vicissitudes of Soul Murder

One of life's most horrific challenges involves the exertion of power to initiate sexual abuse, incest, or rape. We must fully understand that these crimes have little to do with sex and so much more to do with exercising power over the powerless. Such disrespect and dishonor to the mind, body, and spirit often have lasting effects and have been shown to lead to major mental and physical health problems. The effects of soul trauma cascade like a waterfall; we must navigate these churning emotional waters from childhood into adulthood, flowing and falling, flowing and falling. And because the violation runs deep, sexual powerlessness impacts many aspects of victims' lives, including their relationships, careers, and so much more. This is what I mean by "the vicissitudes of soul trauma."

Years ago, studies claimed that 1 in 3 women and 1 in 6 men would experience some type of sexual abuse, from non-touching abuse to touching abuse. Was I one of those one in three women? Unfortunately, yes. From my girlhood onwards, I would experience and learn of a variety of sexual assaults, ranging from creepy to rape, each circumstance veiled in secrecy.

In junior high school, my close male friend, Sam, shared the truth behind his sister's pregnancy, a dark family secret that he swore I must keep. His father had impregnated his sister and his sister had subsequently been sent away to a "home." He cried painful tears, feeling guilt, shame, and powerlessness. His shame was amplified by his mother's decision to remain with the abusive, incestuous father in their home. I suspect his father was also physically and emotionally abusive. In retrospect, I wonder in amazement how both Sam and his family continued to function.

While walking home one winter's afternoon when I was around twelve years old, a well-known member of our neighborhood followed me home, touching himself. I arrived safely at home but to this day I remember what he looked like. I was thirteen when, while purchasing school supplies in a nearby store, the store owner grabbed me by the waist, unexpectedly pulling me close to him. In return, I grabbed his throat, squeezing it with all my might. I doubt he was expecting that! Although he was laughing, I am quite sure he got the message.

Later on, when I was fourteen, I was riding the train to Coney Island with friends and cousins when I noticed that a man kept moving closer and closer to me, trying to touch my leg. I am sure if the man had been confronted, he would have denied doing anything. However, our adult companion noticed the situation and moved me out of potential harm's way. As a much older graduate student en route to my internship in the morning, a man began masturbating in front of me and followed me as I left the train. He somehow managed to ejaculate on my coat. I could not find a law enforcement officer in the vicinity, but I received much support from my colleagues at Harlem Hospital.

In the times since these events, I often reflect the impact

they've had on my life. Perhaps my work in the field of sexual abuse, incest and rape were prompted by my many such experiences? Perhaps I rewrote my own personal narrative as a way to empower myself in the face of so many circumstances of powerlessness? I know from my personal and professional experiences that women in these situations often think, "maybe we're making it up, maybe it was an accident, maybe he didn't mean it…" We second-guess ourselves. I certainly did. Our self-doubt wraps the veil of secrecy even tighter around us. Many of us stay silent, fearing retribution for speaking out. Our own denial challenges the validity of the experience and impacts our whole self. Thus, secrecy, shame, and fear bolster the power of abusers while traumatizing our body, mind, and spirit. Our body remembers trauma, and it's possible that we may repeatedly re-experience our trauma throughout the course of our life.

These are but a few of the personal stories that have stirred compassion, caring, and concern in my soul, urging me to take part in the prevention and treatment of trauma and abuse. From these experiences, as well as my training and professional experiences, I began to understand the sociological and emotional toll that multiple forms of trauma and oppressions had on the people I worked with. In the 80s, I worked in a Community Mental Health Center in the Bronx, where the indices of poverty, HIV/AIDS, crack and drug epidemic, TB, asthma, and other problems associated with being poor, including the working poor, were quite high. These astronomical numbers among the people in this community also reflected the national statistics around socio-economic and political disparities among people of color. As a Clinical Supervisor in a Child and Adolescent Program, I was designated to provide care, services, and treatment to a wide range of challenging situations. In order to understand the different worldviews I encountered in the people I treated, it was essential to understand the various feeling states they were experiencing. The communities, families, and individuals in my care had high indices of poverty; crime, drug abuse, substandard housing, and even pest infestation, were all common themes. Add to these scenarios sexual violence. What I saw on a daily basis was the severe impact of soul trauma on adults and youngsters as they transitioned from childhood into adolescence and adulthood.

All In the Family

For a time, I served as a Clinical Supervisor at Bronx Community Mental Health Center in the Child and Adolescent Mental Health Clinic. It was my job to be the point person for the children, adolescents, and families referred to our Center from the Pediatric Emergency Room. As a seasoned clinician, it was my job to manage their care, ensuring youngsters and their families got the assistance they needed, from the Emergency Room to the Mental Health Center. This is how I met Cassie and her mother…

At 11 years old, Cassie is the picture of innocence and all of the wonderful things of childhood. She has smooth, chestnut-colored skin, long, wavy black hair plaited in two braids, and dark brown eyes. She's dressed in a Catholic school uniform: a white shirt and a plaid jumper adorned with pleats. Her Buster Brown Mary Jane's are so clean that they shine, and her dark knee socks rise exactly to her knees. Standing beside her, Cassie's mother, a slightly overweight, brown-skinned Latina, toys with her long, wavy black hair as she speaks. She cannot believe or fully comprehend what has happened to her daughter.

I look again at Cassie. Despite her picture-perfect appearance, the tell-tale signs of emotional upheaval are present in her luminous, haunting brown eyes. Eyes that I will not forget. Years later, as I write this book, I remember those eyes. I wonder how to explain what's written on the medical records in my hands. How can I explain to this mother that Cassie's gynecological system has been completely torn apart and her doctors are doubtful if she will ever be able to have children?

When I encountered Cassie for the first time, all I knew was that she had been seen in the Pediatric Emergency Room over the weekend and was found to be severely sexually abused. The father had been arrested. During our first meeting, Cassie's mother talked incessantly, not allowing Cassie to say a word (although I doubted whether the girl would, if given the opportunity). I wondered if the constant chatter stemmed from anxiety, guilt, or both. Throughout our work together, Cassie's mother continued to echo a sense of disbelief that this horrific abuse had gone on in her house without her knowledge. Yet, over the course of my intervention and treatment, I learned there had been many signs of abuse. During play therapy sessions, Cassie's drawings were honest and vulnerable, depicting open, watchful eyes that never closed, awaiting the arrival of her brutal attacker. She begged to accompany her mother during errands or shopping, crying that she didn't want to be left alone with her father. At night, Cassie's father would come to her bedroom.

Cassie's traumatic experience of repeated incest and sexual

abuse is a horrific example of the vicissitudes of soul trauma. Cassie and her family's external circumstances presented their own set of intersecting challenges. The family lived in the South Bronx where crime rates were high and most people lived with poverty, poor housing, a neglected educational system, and limited access to medical and mental health care, amongst other disparities. To this context, we now add the psycho-emotional consequences of profound violation and violence. Cassie's father, who was supposed to keep her safe and secure, was, in fact, her tormentor and abuser. Her mother, who was also charged with the protection and safety of her daughter, was unable to stop the soul murder that Cassie experienced. Such psychological damage, combined with the social-economic stresses of poverty, limited access to resources, and coming from a racialized minority group, all contributed to the intersectional and multidimensional nature of the traumas Cassie faced.

So, how do we understand and conceptualize how such intersecting trauma might present itself in Cassie's life—both as a school-aged youngster and as she moves into adulthood? What are the various feeling states Cassie experienced as a girl, and what feeling states might follow her into adulthood? Over time, the intensity of feeling states can dissipate but layers of pain, shame, and a sense of being damaged remain. And while, as a psychotherapist, I absolutely believe in the opportunity for healing, I have seen and treated women well into adulthood who are still suffering from the effects of childhood soul murder. These women struggle with the inability to confront their abusers, including their mothers who did not believe or protect them. They mourn the loss of a childhood innocence that can never be re-captured. With this knowledge, I often wonder with prayer and optimism about Cassie's whereabouts, hoping her healing and recovery have continued.

My experiences with families were equally disturbing. We treated a family of twenty or thirty people where many of the children had severe sexually transmitted diseases, due to incest and sexual abuse. We had several clinicians working on this emergency situation in conjunction with Child Protective Services. We also tried hard to obtain assistance from other public health agencies, as we felt this situation represented a clear public health emergency.

One of the most meaningful and therapeutic exchanges occurred in a series of multifamily groups facilitated by me and other clinicians. During a discussion on incest and sexual abuse, an adult female survivor and a pre-teen boy shared themes of their own sexual abuse and shame. They had similar experiences, feelings and emotions; they cried and hugged one another. I was so moved by the genuineness of this human-to-human experience that I also cried! The universal challenges of sexual abuse transcend the boundaries of age, ethnicity, and cultural context.

I treated many teens who were sexually abused and, in some cases, also physically abused, neglected and mistreated. I remember a young Latina woman who was fondled and abused by a medical resident, while awaiting treatment on a stretcher in an emergency. Another young woman, a beautiful school-aged African American girl, was repeatedly abused by her therapist while receiving so-called treatment. I even heard a Latine teenager say, with utmost conviction, that she thought all young women were sexually abused, raped or victims of incest, and this was a normal part of growing up!

While working in the Psychiatric Emergency Room, I was called to care for Jenalda, a single mother who was assaulted on her way to buy milk for her children. I recall her tearful lament, "I was only going to buy some milk for my kids." She was taken to the rooftop of her apartment building, threatened, and forcibly raped. She suffered from Post-Traumatic Stress Disorder, experiencing intense fear, anxiety and flashbacks, all exacerbated by living in the same environment where she had been victimized. My colleague and I worked tirelessly with the NYC Housing Authority to initiate an emergency move. I am still impacted by her tears, sadness, and sense of powerlessness. The interplay of poverty, violence, lack of options, and the turmoil of trauma, impacted her ability and opportunity to heal. However, our vehement advocacy prevailed and were able to help her to move.

I also remember Anna from Guyana, her beautiful, middle-aged, dark-skinned face crowned by thick and wavy black hair. She was experiencing social phobia after being raped by a young man whom she described as young enough to be her son. Anna begged her attacker not to rape her because she had just suffered a miscarriage. He ignored her pleas. As we worked with her, Anna was violently attacked and raped a second time—again in the same building in which she lived in. After this second violent attack, her family initiated a quick move. She was so thankful for the care we administered to her that she would bring delicious dishes in thanks, demonstrating she still had the capacity for kindness and giving.

While I have recounted the stories of women, whom I was

honored to help and promote healing, I would be highly remiss if I did not mention that male children, adolescents, and adult males are also, all too often, victims of incest and rape. I am certain that many do not report these crimes out of shame and fear, afraid that no one would believe them.

Ownership of our bodies – Is The Handmaid's Tale a glimpse of our future?

All sexual violation and trauma involves being forced into a position of powerlessness over our own bodies. Sadly, it is not only sick individuals who can make us feel as if we don't have bodily autonomy or ownership over our physical selves. Governments and institutions can also participate in soul murder when they challenge a person's fundamental right to make their own decisions about their bodies.

As you've just read in Chapter Four, my high school years saw the historical movements of Civil, Women's, and Gay Rights emerge and grow, forcing those in leadership to respond to the growing demands of both men and women. Like many, I, too, was impacted by the seeds of social change that were sowed during this period. Like many moving from adolescence to young adulthood, my worldview began to crystalize.

In my high school social studies class, we were asked to debate a woman's right to choose to terminate a pregnancy or carry a baby to term. I was assigned the "pro-choice" debate and diligently went to work researching the pros and cons, including the number of illegal abortions that led to death. For example, in the

1960s and 70s, Cook Country Hospital in inner-city Chicago had a special 40-bed "Septic Abortion Ward" for women who underwent abortions and became critically ill.

I recall the day I presented my pro-choice argument. I was intensely prepared academically, with facts, data, and vignettes of the experiences of women seeking abortions. I was also armed with passion and a sense that I was advocating for the yet unseen needs of women. My opponents did not stand a chance. Needless to say, I walked away the winner of that particular debate, with an inward sense I had done the right thing.

Later on in 1974, I served as the covering Social Worker in an acute care hospital in New York City. One of the services I covered was the Termination of Pregnancy Service. By then, the Roe vs. Wade Supreme Court decision had been finalized. Many care professionals celebrated what they saw as a progressive move towards protecting women's health and longevity. Nonetheless, I continued to serve a variety of women (most of whom spoke only Spanish) who would tearfully explain their shame, ambivalence and conflict around terminating their pregnancies. Many felt torn between their religious values and the reality of their social-economic position, knowing they didn't have the resources to accommodate another child. In one situation, a young woman of 18 or 19 had not disclosed to her parents she was pregnant, although she was visibly pregnant—somewhere between 20 to 25 weeks. The entire family was present, including the father of the child, when we discussed her options. My intervention, assessment, and care lasted the entire day. In this case, the young woman decided that she wanted to continue the pregnancy.

In the 1980s, I was asked to join a team of medical, nursing and administrative staff providing care to women seeking abortions in New York City. My coworkers and I were often heckled and accosted by "Pro-Life" advocates waving placards and calling us "baby killers." Our focus was not on babies, however. Our mission was to provide compassionate and skillful care to these women, some of whom were quite young. We facilitated a particular niche for Portuguese women in the community. During our counseling sessions, they, too, explained they were unable to manage additional children. These women were so grateful to have someone provide support and validation that they would press upon me gifts (which I could not accept). Yet their warm gestures reinforced the extent to which women in these circumstances needed compassion and care. I remember a young girl of Afro-Caribbean descent who came in with her mother. Both tearfully explained that the girl, who was only 11 years old, had been repeatedly raped by a family friend who volunteered to "look out" for her while her mother worked, ultimately burdening this beautiful child with an unwanted pregnancy. Like Cassie, this lovely and innocent child was frightened and unsure. I held her hand throughout her examination and procedure and was there when she awoke in recovery.

Given these experiences, when I learned that the Supreme Court overturned Roe v. Wade on June 24, 2022, not only was I personally impacted, sadden, depressed, and disempowered, I couldn't help but see the faces of the women I had cared for over the years. I also recalled how valid and critical their needs were. Surely, things have not so drastically changed over the last forty years? I knew they hadn't. I continue to hear reports of young girls who have been repeatedly raped, forced to go across state lines to avoid giving birth to the children of their rapists.

The writing is on the wall, and plain to see. Indeed, Chief Justice Thomas's ominous remarks in the days and weeks, leading up to and following June 24th, 2022, foreshadow more change to come. In the vision within my mind's eye I wonder…if any of those Supreme Court justices, or perhaps those in political leadership, had the opportunity to speak with any one of the beautiful women I had cared for, would their decision change?

The Wise Woman Succumbs

It may be convenient or tempting for us to look away from so many instances of violation. To inundate ourselves with others' pain is to risk our own health and well-being. During the last years of my tenure, the relenting stories of physical and sexual abuse, neglect, coupled with the high indices of poverty, poor housing, lack of educational equity, high indices of substance abuse with insufficient treatment services, began to weigh heavily on my mind body and spirit. While I was always ready to seek creative solutions to problems—my ability began to decrease. I found myself struggling to come to work, and, once there, I lacked motivation. I suffered extreme fatigue and felt that I was alone and alienated.

As it turns out, my experience was not unique. Current statistics suggest that burnout affects more that 39% of social workers and a lifetime rate of 75%. In situations where clinicians and/or helping professionals may feel powerless and traumatized due to the lack of meaningful interventions for their patients, they may begin to feel emotionally and physically exhausted and unable to muster the strength to offer much-needed care. This is known as Compassion Fatigue. It is now understood as a bona fide mental health condition necessitating some type of intervention.

Compassion Fatigue often happens when a social work professional doesn't recognize the extent to which they are devoting extensive time and attention to their clients, while ignoring the tell-tale signs of stress. According to the American Psychological Association, such behavior can culminate in one or more of the following symptoms: "[…] depression and anxiety, physical and emotional exhaustion, less enjoyment of work […] Another component of compassion fatigue is secondary traumatic stress, or indirect exposure to trauma via helping others." One symptom may be much more severe than others.

For me, the straw that broke the camel's back occurred during my last assignment in the Child and Adolescent Program. We had been working tirelessly with the Bureau of Child Welfare to intervene in the situation of a young mother who suffered years of abuse from her children's father. The mother had just returned home from the hospital after undergoing a C-section surgery to deliver her last child. The father of the children, who was no longer living in the home, returned unexpectedly, enraged, and threw the still-recovering mother out of a window. There was something about this situation that was so hopeless that I realized it was time for me to do something else. My Compassion Fatigue had reached critical capacity.

Sadly, despite its prevalence, we, as a society, do not talk openly enough about Compassion Fatigue and burnout, how such conditions can create their own kind of trauma. In my own professional career, burnout was not openly discussed or acknowledged. During my twelve-year tenure I worked in a variety of clinical capacities, including line worker, supervisor, manager and program developer in the Psychiatric Emergency Room, Mobile Outreach, In-Patient Psychiatric and Out-Patient

Mental Health Clinics. However, in none of those capacities or organizations can I recall an open discussion of Compassion Fatigue. During my supervisory conferences, we focused on the needs of the patients and their families, and I do not recall an opportunity to discuss self-care strategies for staff, although we were involved in various celebrations such as baby showers, retirements, and sometimes birthdays.

Interwoven through each of these challenging and draining work scenarios were the constant and persistent presence of the isms I was navigating as a Black woman. You must understand that by the time of George Floyd's murder, I was already bearing the tremendous challenge of trying to provide compassionate care and treatment to those facing and experiencing trauma. Compassion Fatigue was yet another of the *drip drip drip* filling up my overflowing bucket.

As we leave our discussion of the many faces of trauma, I want to re-emphasize its multidimensional impact. Individuals who experience one kind of trauma may also undergo other forms, including challenging environments and a lack of access to resources and many of the support systems that can intervene and heal abuse. We must understand how the many aspects of worldview, as well as the intersections of identity and experience, contribute to the variety of feeling states that shape how victims and survivors see the world and how the world sees them.

I've shared these true stories with the hope that they may help readers—perhaps you—to acknowledge your history of trauma, or that of a friend or loved one. In my on-going work as a psychotherapist in private practice, I continue to find many instances of sexual violence and other forms of trauma that manifest under seemingly unrelated symptoms and concerns. Yet the scars of victimization, dehumanization, and powerlessness are there.

Still We Rise

This chapter's focus has been heavy, daunting, and challenging. It's normal if you felt like disengaging your empathy or shutting down entirely in the face of such uncomfortable topics. An important component in our capacity as humans is a fundamental belief in faith and hope as fundamental for change and healing. Faith and hope can heal us! Many diverse groups have relied on the cultural, religious, and spiritual beliefs around the power of faith and hope in order to make it through dark times, impossible challenges. Was it not faith and hope that motivated and inspired my 15-year-old maternal grandmother to leave the comfort and security of her home on a beautiful island for the opportunities of Dobbs Ferry, New York? Was it not faith and hope that drove my grandfather, with limited resources, to also leave behind what was known and secure in Enfield, North Carolina, and board a train to New York? Our capacity for faith and hope is a potentially powerful resource available to all.

Even in the midst of my on-going sadness over the death of George Floyd and racial violence, I return to the wisdom and inner knowingness I've accumulated over many years. Throughout my life, I have had to seek and learn patience and understanding in order to manage my anger and despair in response to powerlessness. Perhaps only relatively recently have I fully understood how my journeys into my family's past (and my own) have provided a pathway to healing and reconciliation. As I came to understand and reckon with my ancestors' choices, I began to achieve the wisdom that would guide me through my own life's challenges.

I hope and pray that by now you have seen that healing is possible, even for the most horrific soul murders, and that you have not abandoned your belief in positive change. I often recite the poem "Still I Rise," by the literary icon, Dr. Maya Angelou, drawing its energy and inspiration into my own being.

She reminds each and every one of us that we have the capacity to rise, again and again, from our troubles. So let us call upon the wonderful and attainable energies so powerfully described by Dr. Maya:

> *"Leaving behind nights of terror and fear*
> *I rise*
> *Into a daybreak that's wondrously clear*
> *I rise*
> *Bringing the gifts that my ancestors gave,*
> *I am the dream and the hope of the slave.*
> *I rise*
> *I rise*
> *I rise."*

Mary Oma Hines Moses—my paternal aunt (deceased)

Gwendolyn Esme Pilgrim Hines McCord—my mother (deceased)

Edith Mary Hines—my sister (deceased)

Edith Amanda Hoyte Pilgrim—maternal grandmother (deceased)

Joseph Ceasar Hines—father (deceased)

*Joseph Ceasar Hines and Gwendolyn Esme Pilgrim Hines McCord—
my parents on their wedding day (both deceased)*

Above: Dr. Betty Lorraine Hines Miller— my paternal aunt (deceased)

To the right: (Top) Gwendolyn Esme Pilgrim Hines McCord—my mother—at a club (deceased); (Middle left) Edith Amanda Hoyte Pilgrim—my maternal grandmother—outside of our house (deceased); (Middle right) mother at a party; (Bottom left) my mother vacationing in the Caribbean; (Bottom right) me, my mother, and my paternal great uncle, McKinley Pilgrim at a family event (deceased).

TEARS, TRAUMA AND A HEALING PATH | 203

(Top) Joseph Ceasar Hines and Gwendolyn Esme Pilgrim Hines McCord—my parents—and me at home in my parents' apartment.

(Bottom) my mother and me at a dance recital.

Edith Amanda Hoyte Pilgrim—maternal grandmother at a family picnic (deceased)

Jane Harris—paternal great-grandmother, born in Ise of Mann (deceased)

Mary Booker Hall Hines—paternal grandmother (deceased)

Joseph Cesar Hines—paternal grandfather (deceased) and Frances Williams Hines—paternal grandmother (deceased)

Chapter 6

Death is Not Final: The Opportunities and Potential in Loss

Dearest Reader,

Is death the end?

Chapter Six of this book is significantly important. Up to this point, I have sculpted this narrative as both a memoir and a revolutionary psycho-social self-help narration focused on my reaction to and coping with the murder of George Floyd and many others. This chapter focuses on the conflicting aspects of death and loss that we encounter as part of our human existence.

The horrific experience of watching the murder and passing of George Floyd, right before our eyes, has brought us to a crucial moment where we can either embrace or turn away from an opportunity for profound growth and change—as individuals, families, communities, nations, and a species.

This chapter offers you the opportunity to explore the indefinite and begin to live with the uncertainties around death. It offers the opportunity to chart a course to a place of comfort with respect to life's major conflict—death. Please accept, with an open mind, body and spirit.

I am absolutely committed to the continued existence of human soul, but I am a human being and I work with other human beings. I often ask, how do we begin to find some sense of resolve between knowledge of a spirit world and our physical essence which grieves and hurts and pines for the people we have lost? Is it even necessary to find resolve?

As you read the pages in this chapter, keep in mind that I am inviting you to an open-ended and exploratory journey. Perhaps you will search and explore your own opportunities for closure. What are your beliefs regarding the finality of death? Is death the end? What happens when we die, and are there avenues to prove one perspective or another? If you do believe that death is not the end, do you prevent yourself from grieving, knowing you will meet your loved one upon your death? And yet, if you believe death is the end, do you plunge yourself into a never-ending sea of despair when facing loss? And are your beliefs around death impacted by whether or not a death occurs by murder, suicide, accident, or illness? Is the impact for loved ones the same? Does your grief change? For our loved ones who will be impacted by our death, how will they cope? Is it with the knowledge that we will see them after our own death? But how, then, do we deal with the loss of the physical person in our current physical life? How do we begin to manage the loss while believing that one day we will meet again? What about things left unresolved between us and our loved ones in spirit? What about things left unresolved on the earth plane?

As you read this chapter, dear Reader, do not seek finality in my words, even if you are swayed by any of the perspectives that I present. I do not seek to offer a conclusion or hard evidence on the finality (or not) of death. Let the conflicting ideas and lack of conclusion reign, as sometimes allowing conflict to live is the only alternative.

Death is both final and not final. For those of us who believe in an afterworld or spirit life, death's inherent contradiction can be difficult to navigate. On the one hand, the physical body does have its limits. At some point, all of us will face the death of our physical body and experience and feel the loss of loved ones' physical presence. On the other hand, we know and believe that death is not the ultimate end—it is simply the passing over from our physical realm to the realm of spirit. There is sadness and grief over the loss, but there can also be relief and even joy in the knowledge that someone has been released from pain or suffering and is at peace. Death and loss are like those classic staples of any New York deli—the black and white cookie. Chocolate-coated on one half and vanilla-coated on the other, the black and white cookie contains two equal but opposite sensations. There's conflict, but also sweetness and harmony. What might our experience of loss be like, dear Reader, if we did not feel forced to choose between sadness or joy? What if we could embrace death's conflicting message and find the sweetness in both? The following poem imagines and embraces the sweetness of death, even in the midst of loss's most painful moments.

Holy Glory Dancing and Singing Beyond Death

Among many erudite and spiritual folks
Much smarter than I
In the like of Chopra, Tolle, Beckwith, and many others
Even Matthew, Mark, Luke and Paul
Perhaps others beyond my mind's eye

The issue of our transition to death
Has met much pontification, discourse, discussion and
Alas I must sigh
Cause I've struggled with more questions than answers
Since I was knee-high

I have read with much admiration and glee
These spiritual men and women who I think
Are much smarter than me

I have not missed an Easter celebration
Since the day I was born
The shouting of Alleluia
At the rising of the Messiah

Was a significant event
After 40 days of mourn

In the course of my years upon this beautiful earth
I, like so many
Have faced life's circles
The ins and outs, ups and downs
Which have surely engendered my uncertainties

I, like many others
Screamed amen at the thought of resurrection
Never fully understanding
The multidimensionality of ascension

It was only a recent day or so
That I fully came to terms
With the truth and the light
That death is no longer a foe

Now let me be clear
I am not acting in blaspheme
Or urging bad things to happen
Among those whose souls and hearts
Make an inner gleam

What I am saying is more prophetic than not
And I truly hope it helps
Many among us
Who have found that in death
That's when it all stops

Some of the smart folks
I have referenced before
Have guided and focused me
Towards the gifts God had in store

I speak truly when I say
I did not know I had them
Till an inner voice repeated
Lorna, let's get started
Whatever come may

I say with humility at best
That I was fortunate to find out
That Spirit wanted me to channel
The thoughts feelings and ideas
Of those who live in other dimensions
As honored guests

And so that spiritual group of Goddesses
Whose paths I was fortunate to cross
Told me it was time
To put my feet to the pedal
And own what Spirit has given me
Without an overwrought

Please believe me when I say
I have learned so much
On many a given day
But what has happened this past week
Surely can be told
Much easier than you think

The veil between life and death is
Much thinner than you think
Why else would it be so easy
For a Black girl like me to speak

Death is surely not the end
And perhaps we have been sold
A bunch of garbage
Thinking sadly of what was
And what will not be
Oh Lord
What have we been told?

So let's give power to the continuation
The Soul's Spirit
That surely does not end
When the body is no more
And there is no possibility of mend

I need to continue to live my life
Find joy, singing, dancing
And shouting
Cause the spirit is eternal

Now I don't want you to think
That with these words I have uttered
I have figured out how not to be sad
When folks that I love
Have crossed over without a mutter

But surely I will try to prepare myself
For the time will surely come
But we all must remember
That life is eternal, joyous, and fine
And that I'm sure is a feeling that's mine

The Highways and Byways of Grief: George Floyd and So Many Others

All of my astute and intelligent readers may appropriately ask at this point, what is the relevance of death and grieving with respect to the deaths of George Floyd and so many others? Around the world, billions, with me amongst them, have been impacted in some way by George Floyd's story. The reactions and emotions spiraled out from his most intimate family circles to his city, his state, his country, and across the globe. Has the murder of George Floyd and others been relevant to you and your life?

As a father, grandfather, boyfriend, son, brother, uncle (and more), George Floyd's death had a significant and immediate impact on his family. I imagine his sister, initially the family spokesperson, succumbing to grief, tears, and distress. His girlfriend, who spoke briefly on television, cried so incessantly that many cried with her, including me. His beautiful granddaughter talked about her granddad being in heaven. She spoke with love, conviction and courage. Those within his community who witnessed his murder, among them a young woman who videotaped his execution, will be forever impacted by the torturous scene, recollecting with trauma. So many of us in the United States and across nations throughout the world were saddened and grief-stricken, subjected to conflicting and intense emotions—tears motivated by despair, anger, and a sense of powerlessness at yet another murder of a black man by those in authority who abuse that authority and terrorize communities. Even in places where, perhaps, English is not spoken, many experienced emotional upheavals. The human-to-human connection of senseless murder speaks volumes among members of our extended human family.

Not only were people impacted, but they also felt as if they had to respond. We saw demonstrations around the world; diverse audiences were grief-stricken as they watched the real-time murder of Mr. Floyd. People needed to do something; they could not suffer in silence. We needed to express to our communities around the world that this was an untimely, horrific and preventable way for George Floyd to die.

For many there would have been a major difference had we learned George Floyd succumbed to the Covid-19 virus, or cancer or some other disease. Many of us have watched friends and loved ones lose the battle against cancer. We often hear of people who die suddenly of an aneurysm without warning. In my own life, I lost a favorite friend, colleague and mentor. I received a phone call one day that she was ill, and the next day she was dead.

However, I believe the dynamic of grief shifts when we consider circumstances of death. Our grief feels different in circumstances where we believe death was preventable, yet we feel powerless to prevent it. The concept and theme of powerlessness is, indeed, relevant here. I am referring to the feeling that perhaps if you had the power to institute changes, the murder would never have taken place.

I wonder, as a person impacted by his death, how the dynamics surrounding his murder impacted others' own experiences of traumatic or preventable deaths within their own families? Did others, possibly you, also experience powerlessness, and did George Floyd's murder remind them of past or current loss…did that intensify their need to act on their grief? To what extent did the murder of George Floyd impact people, such as myself, with generational trauma? And how did it impact people who were, and are still, at risk for murder because of being black?

George Floyd and the many others murders I mentioned in Chapter One were entirely preventable, yet no one on the earth realm had the power to prevent them. And, we have no assurance that such actions will not happen again and again. Therefore, our grief, sadness, and despair have a greater resonance because we understand that Mr. Floyd is only one among many. And perhaps, whether or not their death is final feels irrelevant in the face of on-going violence. Perhaps even the belief that we may meet again upon our death does nothing to soothe the profound sense of loss, anger, or powerlessness that we feel?

As we explore our conflicted feelings about death, let us also explore the extent to which intersectionality and compounding of feeling states may affect our feelings about death and grief.

In previous chapters, we explored feelings states as relevant to intersectionality. Intersectional feeling states related to death are also important. Death and loss can create feelings of depression, sadness, powerlessness, anger, and frustration—simultaneously. And when there are multiple losses, these feelings may intensify and overwhelm the human spirit and our capacity to heal. For example, let's consider the multiple feeling states experienced by a black mother who has lost multiple children to police brutality. In addition to loss and grief, she is likely feeling angry, helpless, victimized, and overwhelmingly sad. She may be suffering from depression, anxiety, or even PTSD. Is it possible that this mother, who loses a child to police violence, doesn't really care about whether or not she will meet her loved ones upon her death? And perhaps, when there are multiple losses, this mother's pain and sadness become significantly compounded, especially in circumstances where she feels powerlessness.

In my own family, I saw a distant cousin experience these overlapping feeling states when her son was murdered by the police. Her grief and trauma were so layered and complex that she felt her only recourse was to leave New York City and move to a small town in Georgia. Indeed, many black mothers have lost their children to police violence and other preventable situations.

I imagine there are many people who, after being impacted over and over by losses related to the intersections of race, ethnicity, class, gender, religion…are simply no longer able to feel. In my own life, after the loss of ten close friends and relatives from 2016 through 2017, I no longer felt anything. I found myself unable to cry. I was numb. It was as if I was a robot, walking from day to night with my feelings bottled up inside. I was impacted, yet unmoving.

This discussion of loss and grief is uncertain and, at times, unclear. It may even feel open-ended to you, lacking any kind of reassuring conclusion. Notice how you are feeling, dear Reader. It is essential for us to examine our thoughts, feelings and experiences regarding the loss of our loved ones.

We must also understand the extent to which African Americans and many people of color experience the uncertainty of death by police violence. Repeated acts of violence and associated loss can lead to horrific and unrelenting feeling states for which many feel they have no way to manage, treat, or relieve. Loss in the black community, including among individuals and families, has many layers and complexities of feelings. We must not view these losses as a singular event. Indeed, there is a strong correlation between other situations of trauma, loss and powerlessness. That is why we must examine the many intersections of black identities to see the presence of loss and trauma in so many aspects of our lives—employment, health care, political and economic circumstances, the criminal justice system, media, religion and spirituality, and so much more. Let us journey into greater depth and understanding together.

One Journey in Grief

What we have been taught from childhood and onwards into adulthood impacts how we think about death and the grieving process. We pick up our cues about what to think, say, and even wear, when someone close to us from our surroundings and environment, dies. Our families and our cultures teach us when and where it's appropriate to show sadness and tears, and when and where it's not. As a result, many of us can go through life without having the opportunity to expand or revise our understanding of death, loss, and the grieving process. I certainly was among that group. My journey on the path towards understanding death's multidimensionality has been a long one. Like many others, my family's traditions and beliefs exerted a profound influence on my own conception of life and death. I was well into adulthood before I came to the full understanding that death is indeed not the end.

I was brought up to believe that death was the end, although it was possible for us to receive messages from our loved ones who had made their transition. My family's beliefs around death and the afterlife were not necessarily logical, scientific, or even fully imbedded in any one religious and spiritual philosophy. As I mentioned before, part of this resulted from my family's syncretic faith that merged "High Church" Episcopalian and folk practices. While issues of death were candidly discussed in our household it was always in the context of something else: "I had a dream of So-and-So…what is their house number?" Or: "So-and-So came to me in a dream. What is their birthday?" Or: "I dreamed about So-and-So doing such-and-such. Let's look at the dream book to see what that means." And so, while death represented the end, it also held the promise that the dead person's spirit could return to you in a dream, bringing possible good fortune. Occasionally, my mother would speak tangentially of the possibility that a dead relative could take a problem, such as a disease, with them. Therefore, at the time of death, we could ask the almost-deceased person to take the illness or problem away with them, allowing the living person to be free of the disease or problem. Yet, I was not privy to a full understanding of how this worked. But one message was clear—once you died, that was the end.

I can remember my first face-to-face experience with death as if it were yesterday. I was around six or seven when I viewed the body of a woman who had died in childbirth. While there were people in our family who had died prior, this was the first viewing and funeral I attended. The woman looked massive in my child's eye. I can see her swollen body wearing what I heard was a shroud but what looked like a fancy long-sleeved nightgown to me. I was scared and confused as I listened intently as my maternal aunt described what had happened: the woman's husband had been told that he could either save his wife or his baby. Although I am not clear whether he actually made the choice, my young mind struggled to comprehend how this man had chosen a baby over his wife. How was he—a man—going to care for and raise a baby?! This was my introduction to death.

Some years after this experience, closer relatives made their transition. I was able to fully experience our family traditions regarding not only the process of death but also the way my family marked the passage of their loved ones. When my dear Aunt Lorraine died, I participated in her wake/viewing at the funeral home, the formal funeral service at church, and, of course, the post-burial family get-together (what we call a "repast"). While I understood that it was acceptable and appropriate to experience and express grief openly in a funeral home, church, or at the burial ground, I was not exactly sure how to behave when we communed at our family's home. My uncle who had lost the love of his life (they were indeed soulmates) sat by himself on a chair in the living room. I felt unsure, awkward, and out of place. My family did not clearly communicate to me how I might navigate the emotional and psychological impact of death on the living. I did not know what to say, how to be, and ended up following the old saying, "children should be seen and not heard."

Another part of our ethnocultural tradition was to prepare the foods the deceased person enjoyed. During my adult years, I lost Grandma Edith, who had helped to rear me from age five onwards. During the process of her failing health I was no longer living with her; however, the closeness between us continued. A few days prior to one of her hospitalizations, where eventually she died, I sat with her in her bedroom, just holding her hand. She was breathing but unresponsive. Once she made her transition, we spent little time in actual grief and reminiscing. We set upon the massive tasks of cleaning and cooking. This was no small undertaking because my grandmother liked most foods and was an outstanding cook. She was an expert in cooking main dishes such as shrimp and rice, baked ham, fried chicken and an island favorite called *cou cou*, consisting of seasoned fish served over cooked yellow corn meal. Some island people call this *fungi*. And so I joined the small army of female relatives who produced mountains of delicious full-course meals to be served after the wake at the funeral home and then again after the burial. There were pounds of potato and macaroni salads, heaps of coleslaw, tables piled high with hams, turkeys, chicken and pork. We prepared giant bowls of greens, string beans and green salad, as well as enormous amounts of cakes, pies, cookies, and other sweet and savory offerings. I should also mention the cases of wine, liquor, and beer that were readily available for these festivities. Relatives, family, friends and perhaps a few funeral crashers, all ate and drank themselves into a blissful state. So much so that once the funeral process was over, we fell into the oblivion of exhaustion, and the much-needed grieving process would eventually occur in bits and pieces.

At the time, I didn't let myself feel anything about Grandma Edith's death. Like my relatives, I threw myself into the preparations for the various services and celebrations to mark her passing. If I felt anything, it was a sense of duty and obligation. It wasn't until much later, well after her passing, when I allowed myself to grieve. In retrospect, I have learned the importance of allowing oneself the time to grieve and to pay less attention to the exterior aspects of the funeral arrangements, church services and wakes. While those rituals are important, they should not take up so much time and space that we feel unable to stop, feel, and grieve our losses in ways that are healthy.

Given my chosen career in care work, it was inevitable that I would continue to encounter death as I matured. While the death of my patients was not an everyday occurrence, it did happen on multiple occasions as a result of suicide by hanging, accidents, or medical complications. I have also had the unfortunate experience of losing staff, who were under my supervision, to death by accident or medical complications. Due to my misunderstanding and perhaps fear associated with death, I never ventured to work in hospice, cancer wards, or other places where people were destined to die. At no time did I feel like I could see or talk to my patients or coworkers after they had died. In fact, the relationship felt like it was over.

Then, in 1994, I unexpectedly lost my one and only baby biological sister. Despite our 8-year age difference, there had always been an intense bond between us. Indeed, before her arrival, I had longed for a sibling for love and companionship. Our subsequent relationship gave me the opportunity to experience an understanding of unconditional love and acceptance. One particular incident from our childhood stands out as an example of our special bond. As children (unlike today's youngsters), we spent hours of play outdoors, on the street in front of our house, or at the local park. One day, my sister fell victim to the whims of the "Park Man," who locked up the park with a dozen or more children still inside. I don't remember how I heard that my sister was one of the "park prisoners," but I do remember running as fast I could to find her, screaming and crying to get out. A wire fence enclosed the park, separating us, ringed with dangerous barbed wire across the top. But I was not deterred. With passion and skill, I climbed the fence and showed my sister how to climb and get out. I do not remember whether it was while climbing in to get her or while climbing out, but a piece of barbed wire got hold of my right thigh and would not let go. It took out a big chunk of my skin and caused profuse bleeding. But I didn't care. My little sister was safe and sound, albeit a bit shaken up.

We never shared this incident with parents, but it cemented a lifelong close knit bond. Although she suffered from a number of personal challenges, my sister was always there for me. After a severe running accident, I fractured my ankle, leaving me disabled in a cast. I had no friends or relatives nearby to go to the store, help me to bathe, take care of myself, and live my life. It was my sister who tended to me, including the arduous task of trying to bathe with a heavy cast. She dutifully helped me both before and after the birth of my first child. This was an extremely difficult time for me as I suffered from Pre-eclampsia and also Post-Partum Depression. Like many new parents, we took extra care for our new baby. My husband, providing expert details regarding germs and infection control, was convinced that her clothes could not be washed in our washing machine. He felt the only way to circumvent infection was to wash the baby's clothes by hand. My dutiful and helpful sister joined us in this lunacy until another older and wiser cousin told us we must stop.

On the morning that my sister died, and before I was informed of her untimely death, my sister came to me in a dream. I thought the dream was so odd because she asked me to give her a dollar. Soon after that dream, I received a call from my husband to come home from the vacation I had taken with our kids in the Poconos. My sister had been called home to God, leaving a two-month old beautiful child behind. That drive was the longest in my life. For many years thereafter, I could not drive on Route 80.

Somehow, we all got through it. However, I was left feeling alienated from, and angry towards, God. I often walked aimlessly and without direction. Like so many people with tremendous loss, I blamed myself with the "should of's, would of's, could of's". I replayed our last time together and searched for an explanation and someone or something to blame for this loss. My anger grew so intense that I began to feel like acting it out on myself—I was not suicidal, but I did not take my usual care over my appearance and other relevant aspects of myself. God was nowhere to be found. I could find no balm to soothe my aching mind, body and soul. In retrospect, this was the exact moment when I needed to draw closer for religious and/or spiritual guidance. If, in fact, we are unable to turn to our Higher Power in times of challenges and difficulties, what prevents us from seeking trusted friends and relatives who also may be in the position to offer a listening ear and wise counsel? In my case, I didn't share my pain with those closest to me since…they, too, were suffering. Neither did I seek professional intervention or help. Instead, I drew into myself.

I believe my story is similar to many. I told myself that I was too busy, I had no time, I had no idea who I would go to, etc., etc., etc. It was not until many years later, after my father's death, that I received much needed professional help. By that time, as you can imagine, I evidenced all of the major signs and symptoms of Major Depression. For me, short-term psychotherapeutic interventions were extremely helpful. The combination of anti-depressants and psychotherapy was exactly what I needed to give me the energy to obtain insight into my thoughts and feelings.

I later spent much time considering my own journey through grief. I reconsidered and reframed my experiences within my personal losses, and also those of my community. I went to my experience with Pre-eclampsia during the birth of my daughter. At the time, my doctor told me, "You know you could've died." And thinking about that brush with death, I wonder if the woman whose dead body impacted me so greatly had perhaps also suffered from Eclampsia or Pre-eclampsia. These two conditions are especially significant for African American women in the United States. These serious medical problems can be life-threatening. In fact, the incidence of both Eclampsia and Pre-eclampsia is quite high among cross sections of African American women, much higher than they are in white women. The rates of infant mortality are also highest in our African American communities. We can't explain away these statistics by blaming poverty and a lack of proper health insurance, although it is true that many poor women do not have or receive adequate health care in the United States. The problem goes much deeper and has its roots in racism, discrimination, and forms of powerlessness disproportionately experienced by black women. Studies have shown that Eclampsia, Pre-eclampsia and even conditions related to infant mortality are directly related to the levels of stress brought on by racism and experienced among African American. The message is clear: being a pregnant African American woman is dangerous to your health. The loss of any one black woman is never just one loss. Every death is part of the on-going struggle for human dignity and the right to life within our communities.

As I continued to process my own journey with loss, I asked myself questions that would have great relevance for my personal and professional life: What inclines us to draw within ourselves during times of grief, nearly drowning ourselves in a sea of unhappiness without a badly needed lifeline to pull us to safety? How is it that it feels better in despair than the possibility of hope, peace and resolve? Are we afraid that we have committed some awful sin that withdraws the possibility of grace? Have we forgotten that God provides grace without conditions for his/her children including you and me? In the following chapters, I offer some of my multidimensional strategies for navigating grief's uneven path. In my own journey, each of these experiences with death brought me closer to re-evaluating the messages that I had received from my family around death's finality, on the one hand, but the permeability of the border between the realm of the living and the realm of the dead. I began to reframe and re-contextualize memories and experiences that challenged the conviction that death was the end.

Death Is Not The End

Grandma Edith was a highly religious and spiritual individual who relied on her sense of intuition in a number of instances. My mother and her sisters often told the story of a dance they had yearned to attend. They prepared for weeks, planning their outfits, designing attractive hairstyles and ensuring all of their accessories highlighted their lovely outfits. On the night of the dance, they bathed and perfumed their bodies, took time to straighten, curl and style their hair, until, at last, all four sophisticated and beautiful ladies were ready to light the light fantastic. According to the story, as they prepared to sashay out of the house, my grandmother spoke in an intense voice saying, "You all are not going anywhere. Pull off your clothes and go to bed!" My mother and aunts cried in utter disbelief, but their whining and questioning were to no avail. After several minutes, they relented in sadness. The very next day, the family learned there had been a terrible fight at the dance, causing people to run in fear, and someone may have lost their life. Eventually, I believe my grandmother told her daughters that she had had a vision about the dance and had followed her intuitive sense telling them they could not attend.

Indeed, my upbringing was filled with stories of ghosts, prophetic dreams, lucky numbers, and fortune-telling. My mother was always interested in astrology, and I often read her books. Some extended family members would organize "tea parties" where a woman was invited to "read" tea leaves, tell fortunes and give lucky numbers. I went to one of these parties when I was in junior high school and the woman suggested a few things that were spot on.

A few days after Grandma Edith's funeral, as I was falling asleep or had awaken in the dark, I recall seeing some type of entity wearing a Mexican-styled hat hanging on my closet. There was no strong emotion connected to it, either positive or negative—it was just there. During my formative years, I dabbled in "alternative or New Age" kind of stuff. During my professional career, I relied on a strong intuitive sense as an essential clinical support in difficult situations, especially when I performed crisis interventions and dealt with psychiatric emergencies, including suicidal and homicidal situations.

These instances of intuition, visions, and fortune-telling suggested to me that there was a world beyond our own and that it was possible to communicate with that world. I began to suspect that death was not the foe we've been taught to believe it is. The belief that death is not the end was strengthened into knowledge during my spiritual journey to mediumship. Please understand I am respectful and understand the impact of loss and grief. However, I know that as a result of my intensive studies and lived experience as a medium that life indeed does continue. My conviction is not just based on my observations of others but also on my own experience of love's ability to continue beyond death.

Ava's Passing

The story of Ava's passing illustrates what I would come to understand as the profound experience of lovingly transitioning our body, mind, and spirit to what awaits us all.

When my dear, 53-years-young cousin Ava's cancer diagnosis was shared with us, I did not fully shudder with fear. As an African American youngster growing up in the 50's and 60's, cancer was a known death sentence. However, I was certain this was no longer the case and that there must be many options to explore. After all, were there not clinical trials, pharmaceuticals from other countries, and a host of alternative interventions? Had not Suzanne Somers and lots of other celebrities recovered? Yes indeed, my beautiful and loving cousin would recover!

Her husband, sons, and a host of others set to work researching all of the possibilities to challenge the deadly brain tumor. No stone was left unturned; we pumped the Internet for all available information. There was a dynamic and multi-talented support team who searched relentlessly to the very end, seeking a cure to the disease that cut short Ava's life. In the meantime, there were treatments of chemo, radiation and steroids (to stop and prevent seizures and brain swelling) and a plethora of drugs whose names I do not know or recall. All of them rendered my beautiful Ava bald, with cheeks the size of cantaloupes. When she spoke to me, it was without emotion. In her monotone voice, I could not detect any emotion; I could not sense what she may have been feeling. It was heartbreaking to see my beloved Ava rendered so flat.

Nonetheless, her care in a number of institutions was noteworthy. The staff had no choice given the enormity of her immediate family and friends. What the staff refused or were unwilling to perform, her loved ones did without a moment's hesitation. Her sons and husband were at her bedside morning, noon, and night, responding to, and constantly anticipating, her every whim. The armies of helpers were valiant; their duties were completed diligently and completely, searching for additional ways to prove their dedication, love, and affections. Were there clothes to wash? What would she like to eat? Could they wipe down a table or chair? Could they run to the store for something she might like—as if their ministrations and efforts were absolutely crucial to her recovery. How was it possible for one woman to earn such devotion, you ask?

I am related to Ava from her paternal side. Her parents' marriage can be easily described as "brilliant." Her father was my mother's only living brother. Carlton Terrence Pilgrim, whose handsomeness and social skills were remarkable, was a smooth, brown-skinned wavy-haired gentleman who flowed easily between multiple languages in the course of providing meat and poultry or while dancing a tango or waltz. He was the one who assumed the paternal role in the family after the untimely death of his father. If you recall from Chapter 3, he was the one who helped my mother complete college and gave up his own education when Grandma Edith was widowed at age 36 with five children to raise during the Depression. Ava's mother, Ruth Cunningham, whose beauty and charm was infectious, was also my Godmother. Ruth was masterful in interior design. I am certain she could turn several hovels into palaces with less than one thousand dollars. Ruth's parents, Ava's maternal grandparents, were opposites who attracted—her Grandma "Beau" was vivacious and outgoing, while her grandfather was quiet, yet intensely loving, referring to us as his "baby dolls."

Ava's birth was cherished by the entire family—one of the best within the African Diaspora across the Caribbean and the Americas ;). As an only child, Ava grew up with a host of first cousins, including yours truly, who were treated like brothers and sisters. Indeed, there was enormous love for children in our families. We were reared in love; affection was poured out without hesitation. It helped to prepare us for the rigors of isms and powerlessness we were sure to encounter in our lives. Ruth and Carlton were a fun-loving couple who enjoyed all sorts of festive events; but true to their ancestral roots, they knew how to save and eventually obtained property in the North Bronx, where Ava was reared and educated. Seeing private parochial school as an advantageous opportunity for their daughter, Ava attended a number of prestigious Catholic schools and ironically made her transition in a Catholic hospice institution. Besides intense family loyalty (which spanned to non-bloodline kin) the importance of education was foremost in the minds of our elders within both sides of Ava's family. During holidays and other celebrations, adults took time to talk with us about school, future plans, and the importance of education. Our parents were not focused on just good grades, but proof beyond a shadow of a doubt that we did our best. And they did not hesitate to advocate for us or go up against our mighty teachers. All of this was done with love and care, even though our parents could be harsh and often used corporal punishments. Back talk, anger, getting "fresh" or "womanish" was never to be tolerated. Of the two of us, I believe I was the more assertive. Ava avoided trouble and beatings at all costs. Perhaps her religious education and background helped to inculcate her. I, on the other hand, would push the envelope.

Those who knew and loved Ava were unquestionably in awe of her. She inherited her mother's beauty and stylishness and both her parents' penchant for celebrations. During her eulogy, her fellow teachers talked about her unconditional love and availability as a friend. Many others talked about the brunches and cook-outs she hosted. Her loving second husband spoke of losing his best friend. They had shared so very much in common, including being avid shoppers, and had planned to retire in South Carolina. And so, many people, including myself, were called to the Catholic hospice on July 23, 2011, where committed and loving nuns cared for Ava.

Earlier on that hot day, I hurriedly tried to complete the menu of Saturday errands. We knew the potential for her passing was near, so my focus was to get to the hospice as soon as humanly possible. My last errand led me to Target Department Store, where I was trying hard to complete the camp "needs" list for my son, who would be attending camp the following week. As I walked into the store, the lights and colors seemed much brighter than usual. I typically didn't pay attention to things like that, chalking up any changes in the lights and colors around me to changes in my blood sugar (maybe I had not eaten) or because of rushing. However, once I secured a shopping cart and started pushing it, I distinctly heard a familiar whistle. Now, since the advent of iPods, cellphones, and lots of other ways to communicate, you rarely hear whistling. However, Ava's father, who made his transition in 1976, had a distinct whistle that was his alone. When he was alive and made that whistle, you were supposed to whistle back the same tune in order to confirm you knew it was him and you were you. We all knew the sound as distinctively Carlton's. Not wanting to miss an opportunity, and following my intuitive feelings, I whistled back only to "hear it" once again. This continued for at least a third of my shopping trip. Honestly I was filled with glee at the thought my uncle was some place nearby. Had you been in Target that day you might have thought or said, "surely this woman is hearing voices or is mentally ill!"

After completing my tasks at Target, I made my way to the hospice with my husband and daughter. Ava's two sons were already in constant vigil. The room remained essentially as it was on previous visits to the Catholic Hospice. Everything was immaculate and in its place with no hint of "hospital" and/or body function malodors. During previous visits, I had often wondered how the nuns, who cared for the patients day in and day out, managed this immaculate smell. Ava was in the bed closest to the door with multiple pillows strategically placed for comfort. During the course of her treatment, she had lost mobility of one side of her arm and leg, needing lots of pillows to achieve comfort. In spite of being in a coma for several days, Ava did not appear appreciably deteriorated. Owing to her care at the hospice, there had not been a breakdown in her skin, rashes, or other types of discomfort. Her skin did not seem dry or haggard, her cheeks remained enormous, and her eyes were shut. She was receiving oxygen and being fed water periodically through droplets from a straw. At this point, no other nourishment was being provided, in line with her expressed wishes. Ava had put her talents in planning and organization to use in planning for her eventual transition so that her immediate family did not have to make difficult decisions. She planned for it.

I shared my experience at Target with our family and spoke with them about my uncle and other family members who had transitioned. I wanted to thank them for their love and care for Ava and for all of us during this difficult time. As I walked over to Ava's bedside, I took her hand and spoke quietly in her ear, letting her know we were there and loved her. Later, when her eldest son was nearby, she began to murmur something which sounded like "no." She moved her mobile hand up and down as if seeking our attention or speaking to an unseen spirit or guide. In retrospect, I wonder if this was the last of her resistance to an all-too-short life.

As time passed I noticed her breathing was becoming more labored. A year before, I had been with a friend who was making her crossing, and difficulty in breathing was the prelude to complete transition. I thought it important to update her condition with the nurse overseeing her care. The nurse came hurriedly, checked her pulse, and agreed there were changes in her breathing. I continued to hold her hand and lightly touch her face. I knew that the end was approaching, and that prayer was a likely balm in this tremendously difficult situation. As I had been taught by my ancestors, I led us in the Lord's Prayer—a prayer that crosses all religious affiliations. Those assembled joined me without hesitation. We prayed in unison as if we were in church, just before communion. As we prayed, her breathing became increasingly labored and, at times, would stop. As we continued holy murmurings, sounding like my personal recollections of Monks or Buddhists chanting their various mantras, our group of family and loving friends encircled Ava with love, intense spirituality, and comfort. This sacred circle and its energies were strong and forceful. The strong energies of love and spirituality, combined with continued and unceasing prayer, made me feel, at times, as if myself and others in the room were levitating. Yet, I felt neither fear nor uncertainty. I am certain the room was filled with a sacred presence again, crossing all boundaries of Muslim, Jew, and Christian. As we encircled Ava with comfort and love, we, too, were surrounded by the manifestation of the Holiest of Spirit, as well as important members of our loving family who had already made their transition, assuring us that this was a sacred time. At times, I took a step outside of myself to watch and feel this beautiful assembly. I am sure that this circle of prayers and love helped Ava to detach herself from loving family and friends and move on to the next scheduled dimension. And then, without warning, there was no more breathing. Her transition was complete.

As you can imagine, many tears and much sorrow ensued. Although I was amongst them, I was also struck by the simplicity, beauty and love of her passing. It was then that I recalled my Uncle Carlton's whistle and understood that he had been with me earlier, bringing the message that this was Ava's time. I whispered silently to him, thanking him and all other family members for their love that continued beyond death.

Several weeks after Ava's passing, she came to me in a dream. All remnants of the disfigurement of her disease were gone. She presented as her beautiful and loving self, stylishly dressed in a pink suit. She let me know she was well and feeling ok. And I am so very thankful I received this reassurance.

The Wise Woman Develops Her Philosophy on Life and Death

Were there lessons I learned from Ava's passing? Yes, absolutely and unequivocally. It is challenging to live and to die, and individuals need support—even if they wish to die. Foundational elements of strong spirituality, loving family and friends, as well a therapeutic environment, are all essential elements in life's inevitable transitions. I am assured Spirit and loving family and friends who have already transitioned are with us and loving us during these painful moments. In addition, if we remain in peaceful quietude, we will receive important messages from loving spirit persons communicating love and healing. And lastly, that love continues.

The lessons of Ava's passing reinforced knowledge, convictions, and experiences that had already begun to impact my spiritual development and, consequently, my understanding of life and death. You may recall from Chapter 4 that I had already felt myself called to a higher purpose during the singing of a hymn at my Episcopalian church. I felt guided towards healing practices such as the laying of hands and other tactile approaches. And, as I previously mentioned, ever since I was a youngster, I had dabbled in New Age subjects including astrology, numerology and developing intuition. Prior to Ava's passing, I had participated for many years in a group led by a wonderful medium, healer, shaman, and teacher named Kerrie O'Connor. Kerrie's groups were focused on developing spiritual gifts—whatever they may be. It was there I learned to take risks with my feelings, thoughts and emotions about things that were seen and unseen. She introduced us to exercises that improved and enhanced our spiritual abilities. However, I believe it was the strong sense of community and self-help which helped me to thrive. It was there that I experienced the full meaning of unconditional love and acceptance.

Although I had been receiving messages from my guides that I needed to do more with my spiritual gifts before I joined Kerrie's class, it was through my work with her and subsequent connections and networks that resulted from our community that I began to formally practice as a medium. However, Kerrie's groups were multidimensional and wide-ranging in topic, and after some years, I felt called to take the plunge and sign up for more structured workshops and training in mediumship. And so, in the summer of 2010, I found myself in a workshop with the world-renowned teacher and medium, James Van Praagh. James is well-known throughout the world for his mediumship and mediumship training, and it was through work with James that my inherent abilities and nascent training fully came together.

I immediately felt synergy between myself and James. On the first day of our meeting, I got delayed in traffic and was the last person to arrive to the workshop. As I tip-toed in, trying not to make a disturbance, James came off the stage and walked right over to me. To my surprise and terror he said, "You have something special—what beautiful energy—you will be transformed this weekend." He was right.

Although the workshop was what I would call a mega-class composed of perhaps 150 people, James individualized his approach and his energy. He paired us up in groups of two, and I was fortunate to be paired with a lovely, dark-haired woman. After meditative exercises, which I enjoyed, he instructed us in how to read another's energy. When I reached my partner's heart and lung energetic areas, both of us burst into tears. Her sadness and despair overwhelmed me, but I did not know what lay behind the feeling. James then showed us how to connect with a spirit person. I could see my partner's husband and felt an enormous pain in my head—so severe I thought I might be having a stroke. However, I continued to describe all that I felt. I later learned that my partner had recently lost her husband from cancer that had metastasized, perhaps to his brain. He was aware of her sadness and despair but did say with love and understanding that she would definitely love again. Years later, I saw her and, indeed, she had found love again!

In 2004, it was my honor to share the platform with the stellar medium, Mavis Pattilla, Janet Nohavec, and other outstanding mediums, while at Lily Dale in upstate New York (near Niagara Falls). Mavis was a pupil of the world-renowned medium Gordon Higginson, and it was a joy to hear her recount the stories of his teachings. While sharing the platform with Mavis and others, I was able to share my visions of the runaway slaves I saw as clear as day. I saw them running through the forest, trying to get to Canada, I would imagine. Later, I was told that there were secret tunnels in the area which were "stops" in the Underground Railroad.

The Wise Woman Embraces the Seven Principles of Spiritualism

As my work as a medium developed, and I continued to develop and grow in my religious, spiritual, and ethnocultural understanding of the universe, so did my affiliation with the Spiritualist church and Spiritualism. I should point out that while the Spiritualist National Union is headquartered in England, I follow the particular teachings of the Journey Within Spiritualist Church located in Pompton Lakes, New Jersey, and founded by the Reverend Janet Nohavec. Although my purpose here is not to proselytize, I will offer a brief explanation of the Seven Principles that guide and inform my understanding and practice of Spiritualism, in order for you, dear Reader, to better understand my spiritual journey, particularly how I came to believe in the continuous existence of the human soul. To enhance your understanding, it's important to place the continuous existence of the human soul, Principle Four of Spiritualism, in context with the other guiding principles of Spiritualism.

Principle One: The Fatherhood/Motherhood of God

Principle One provides the foundation for the other important Principles. This principle teaches us that everything begins with God—that loving force and light that lies within us and outside of us. Indeed, there exists for us a father/mother figure from whom we, as the children of our Father/Mother God, can seek comfort and nurturing, as well as share our joys and triumphs. We can resonate and relate to that Spirit at any time, any place, and any hour. Incredibly, we can feel the response, the light and the love of our Mother/Father God. And, therefore, an ongoing and intense relationship with God is possible and important.

Principle Two: The Brother and Sisterhood of Man

The second Principle offers us an understanding of who we are to each other, in thought, word and deed. As children of an extraordinary God, our role as children is to conceive of humanity as one, related and interrelated. The Brother and Sisterhood of Man teaches us that we are all part of one human family, as closely aligned to one another as brother and sister. In the course of this divine and spiritual relationship, we rely on one another for support, mutual aid, and, of course, important spiritual resources and upliftment. We must expect to give as well as receive, as does our Father/Mother God. We must also remain holistically connected to ourselves. Without self-reflection and self-knowledge, we may unknowingly harbor thoughts and feelings that impact our relationship with others (particularly those who may be different from us). However, if we intend to live our lives within the understanding of this Principle, we are challenged to develop self-knowledge and come to terms with our shortcomings, even in the face of stress and trauma.

Principle Three: The Communion of Spirit and the Ministry of Angels

The Third Principle states that life is eternal, despite our inevitable transition to death. It also substantiates that the presence and assistance of beings of higher intelligence and energy exist and also offer hope, inspiration and support to those on the earth realm. It is fundamental to the understanding and practice of Spiritualism as religion, philosophy, and science. The science is revealed in our ability as mediums to demonstrate through evidence our ability to communicate with those in the spirit world. As a philosophy, Spiritualism places great importance on love. The Third Principle affirms the power of love to continue beyond the death of our physical body. It is through the process of mediumship that a loving reunion can take place between those of us on the earth plane and those in spirit. The purpose of this communication is to share hope, comfort and inspiration to those receiving communication. Indeed, we are often taught that our loved ones meet us as we make our transition to death.

This Principle also informs us that the energy we are made of cannot be destroyed, but only modified, due to the spark of divinity that is infused within us. The Communion of Spirit and the Ministry of Angels also establishes the categories of discarnate higher beings—Angels, Archangels, Ascended Masters, and perhaps others. In some non-Western countries, these beings may be referred to by other names. For example, in Africa and the Caribbean, these discarnate individuals may be referred to as Orishas. Regardless of what we call them, these beings have a higher intelligence, and their role and responsibility is to offer inspiration, assistance and love to all humankind.

Principle Four: The Continuous Existence of the Human Soul

The Fourth Principle is closely related to this chapter's focus—it confirms and affirms the existence of our human souls after we transition from life to death, from the earth realm to the realm of spirit. I will tell you more about this principle further on, but first—the remaining three Principles!

Principle Five: Personal Responsibility

By virtue of this Principle, we understand and accept that through the spark of divinity that lies within us, we are empowered to accept responsibility for our spiritual evolvement and development. That we cannot blame others is key to understanding Personal Responsibility. Nor can we hold others accountable for our spiritual development, including the choices we make. We are called to live our lives in acceptance of the role of Fatherhood/Motherhood of God and our relationship with others in our human family. We must accept the understanding that we have the opportunity to exercise free will, but, at the same time, our choices impact our actions and the progress of our spiritual evolvement and growth. For many, it would seem that this Principle only relates to personal or one-on-one situations. But we must also examine the impact and implications of our decisions on our family, community, nation and world. Our ultimate opportunity for spiritual evolvement is dependent upon our personal choices, and only we are responsible for those choices.

Principle Six: Compensation and Retribution for all the Good and Evil Deeds Done

The Sixth Principle reminds us that we reap what we sow, underscoring the importance of cause and effect. Much like the concept of karma, the Sixth Principle teaches us that through our thoughts, behaviors and treatment of others, we plant the seeds for how we will be treated by others. It suggests that those who harm will eventually be harmed, not out of vengeance or retribution, but as part of a spiritual process of balance. This Principle empowers us to significantly modify the way we live our lives by reminding us that our thoughts and behavior impact our spiritual growth (or lack of growth). Further, as Spiritualist, we do not believe in the concept of heaven or hell; instead, we are personally responsible for reaping the harvest of our loving or cruel behavior during our earthly existence. The extent to which we take steps to grow in learning and love intensifies the vibration in our soul and helps us to evolve and develop.

Principle Seven: Eternal Progress Open to Every Human Soul

This Principle is closely related to Personal Responsibility. It reminds us that the opportunity exists for us to develop our spiritual qualities, both qualitatively and quantitatively. We should always aim for higher spiritual achievement. It suggests progress is open to promote our souls' growth, and sacrifice may be necessary. It is important to understand that our blessings are in proportion to the effort we exert, and we should always do our best during our earthly life.

The Continuous Existence of the Human Soul

As we near the end of our journey through this chapter, allow me to return to Principle Four. Spiritualists are taught to believe that humans are made up of trillions (perhaps even more than trillions) of energetic matter; in fact, even upon death, we are not destroyed, but are modified. Upon physical death, our divine, indestructible spirit enters a spirit world where our physical, mental, emotional characteristics, including memory and relationships with loved ones, remain and can be accessed through the mind-to-mind communication between a spirit person and a medium.

In Spiritualism, we are taught to believe that our loved ones in spirit are with us, providing love, support, and guidance in the course of our daily lives. And, with the help of a medium, we are able to access evidence of their survival through mediumship. The evidence of their survival includes specific information only understood by the loved one on Earth. Information may take the form of physical description, work, hobbies, relationship(s), personality, and perhaps memories only known to their loved one. That communication can be pivotal in the lives of those on the earth realm. This is Principle Four.

White Eagle, a spirit communicator who came through the mediumship of Grace Cooke, validates and expresses the major thesis of Principal Four in the course of his philosophic writings. His philosophy operates from the premise that our energy cannot be created or destroyed—human life is infinite and eternal, as is that of our Father/Mother God. Yes, indeed, at death, our physical body dies; however, our spirit force continues, albeit in another dimension. And if we believe that we are part of a human family led and organized by and flourishing under a mighty Father/Mother God whose spirit is also indestructible, death is not the end. White Eagle writes:

> Establish in your mind that human life is essentially infinite and eternal; that there has never been a time when you were not, and there never will be. At this, you will ask, "shall we not get tired of this ceaseless round of incarnation? Even now, life is a burden!" This is why God has limited your days in the flesh; you live on earth only for a few short years which you call an incarnation, and then you leave your body as an outworn dress and go for refreshment to your true home in the spirit.

White Eagle paints a vivid picture of those in the spirit world for. He describes this eternal spirit world as he sees it:

> There is a vast concourse all with wills perfectly attuned with minds in harmony, with souls all at one [...] The vast concourse belongs to all peoples and nations, to present and to the past. There are prophets, seers, sages, wise men of the East and West of high and low estate, philosopher of Greece, and Rome, Syria, Chaldea, Persia, and Babylon, mingled with those of later generations from Italy, France and Germany. They exchange their knowledge and focus it all so that it shall be at your service.

If I am fully able to understand White Eagle's conception, the spirit persons in the heavenly realm have found a way to get along with one another, communicating energetically, yet at the same time have not found it necessary to disregard their ethnic and cultural backgrounds. It sounds like a "United Nations," however, there is no evidence of the isms, powerlessness, oppressions and stigma that presently plague our existence on the earth. Further, their careers, roles and responsibilities are also intact. This continuous existence is obviously a higher intelligence and operating at a higher vibration in comparison to our own. Those of us on the earth realm have so much to learn from those in spirit.

For example, in my own life, early on in the development of my mediumship faculty, I was providing psychotherapy to a long-term client. The client was a young black woman who had suffered emotional abuse from her husband and was trying hard to raise her son in a positive and productive manner. Her husband was a difficult man, refusing to provide child support even though my client's salary as a teacher was insufficient and they were living in inadequate conditions which affected her son's asthma. During our session, I began to feel the presence of someone on the ceiling of my office. The more I asked this spirit person to go away, the clearer her presence became. The spirit person was an older black woman who appeared to be sitting in a chair. She, the person in spirit, was quite insistent, letting me know this was a battle of wills, and she was not going away. Finally, because I had a trusting relationship with this client, I explained what was going on. The client was extremely interested, her body language changed dramatically, and she asked me to describe the spirit person and what they wanted to communicate. The energy, vibration, and words communicated by the spirit person, who was her great-aunt and matriarch of the family, ushered in a tremendous change for my client. The knowledge, experience, and feeling of the continuous existence of her great-aunt propelled her from a space of sadness and despair to one of problem solving (including challenging her husband for support). She eventually divorced and returned to school, gaining a PhD, and is now a school Principal.

And so, you can readily see that over the years I have begun to understand that death is not our enemy. Although mediumship focuses on the experiences and messages from the so-called "dead," I have learned so much about living. I have been afforded the opportunity to gain a closer relationship to God, Jesus, Angels and other Spirit entities. My personal relationship with God has grown quantitatively and qualitatively, and I have begun to understand the oneness we have with humans and other species, as well as the beauty of nature.

And now, dear Reader, you've had the opportunity to join me in a personal exploration of death, grief and loss. We know that the finality of death exists. Yet, perhaps with respect to Mr. Floyd and the many African Americans who have been killed without cause, the question of whether or not their deaths are final is irrelevant. What matters is that their deaths were preventable, and their deaths affected millions, including people who never knew the deceased during their lives. What matters are the multiple feeling states experienced by those in grief. Whether or not we believe their deaths are final, we know that their deaths were not necessary; and for this reason, we grieve and we grieve… without foreseeable resolve.

Chapter 7

What is Healing to This Wise Woman?

All Aboard! Gettin' on the healing bus

Dear Reader,

Please accept my profound gratitude for your commitment to read on! I thank you for your continued interest in understanding the many aspects of my personal journey as I reflect on the murder of George Floyd and others. I suggest at this point that we take a short respite as you prepare for the second half of my book, which introduces a different perspective, tone, and focus.

My recommendation comes from experience. In the Prologue, I described feeling like a tattered and worn bucket. As it filled, drip-by-drip, with waters I could not drink, I found myself searching for a life jacket in a sea of despair. When my bucket tumbled over, I was seized by the need to search for an individualized healing path to find solace from the intense and overwhelming feelings I experienced. What I found saved my life. And so, I want to offer you the same chance to take a break, to slow down, perhaps review where you've been on this journey with me and gear up for the remaining chapters. Let us seize the opportunity dear Reader, to seek and find a path that offers both of us a chance for respite and restoration.

When you're ready to continue this journey with me, our focus will be on our individual and collective healing. When we think about healing, we often think about doctors, medicines, psychology, rehab, therapy, and other situations in which we turn ourselves over to the knowledge and expertise of professionals. For the longest time early in my career in mental health, we promoted healing and recovery in a very circumscribed way, leaving out the wishes and desires of our patients. The power dynamic was clear—the physicians, nurses, therapists, etc., were the ones in charge. Most of us didn't know that prescription medications were only one avenue for treating major psychiatric disorders. It was so unfortunate; during the early part of my career, a diagnosis of schizophrenia was, in many ways, a death sentence. We were condemning patients to an unfulfilled or half of a life. Thankfully, things have changed. We now have multiple strategies, including and beyond medication, for people with difficult diagnoses. We are able to empower those patients to plan and design their treatment, facilitating much fuller lives. We routinely see people, who, even a decade or two ago, would have been confined to institutions or unable to lead normal lives, now enjoying careers, relationships, hobbies, and more. It is possible to have a fulfilling life.

In the following chapters, I will share with you a wide range of healing modalities. Some may be familiar to you, others less so. I will endeavor to use all the tools in my personal and professional toolbox to offer a variety of perspectives in the hope that you may find something of use, a way forward that feels right for you and whatever tough stuff you're facing.

I am particularly called to guide us through healing the trauma of isms amongst myself and other Black, Indigenous, and people of color. As we have seen, isms is a useful shorthand for capturing the feelings of powerlessness that come with racism, sexism, ableism, homophobia, xenophobia, classism, transphobia, religious intolerance, etc. But my wisdom and intuition assure me that there is something for everyone here, regardless of who you are! In particular, I am excited to include healing paths that heretofore you might not have considered.

As my wisdom has grown, I have come to understand that most problems have some sort of solution, even if our decision is to hold off from making a decision or taking any action at the moment. I am certain you will agree that even in the darkness of night, when things seem so utterly bleak, we know the sun will rise, inviting new possibilities and paths. And so, as you read and review the many pages that follow, you will encounter history, facts, statistics, and data. I put on my researcher's hat, appealing to our collective intelligence, our cognitive strengths, and our ability to think critically and logically, to interpret facts. It is my hope this information will lead to a greater understanding of the history of racism and how it is built into the entire fabric of our nation (and many nations). A renewed understanding of these demeaning narratives can lead to healing. For readers who have not been exposed to these facts, I pray this indeed will engender multiple "aha!" moments.

I pray you will find some ideas for coping and thriving in many of the horrific situations of trauma, violence, and abuse. I pray you may find some answers to the questions my previous chapters may have raised for you, your family, your communities, and our society at large. I am duty bound and motivated to continue the legacy of so many of my family members, on whose shoulders I stand, to share the avenues of relief that have provided a balm of caring and inspiration in my lifetime.

So, as you seize the opportunity for this brief interlude, please continue to read and journey on with me as we explore the paths and possibilities of resolution and healing, as we seek moments of peace in the midst of the ups and downs, and joy amidst the sadness and despair of this time we call our lives.

Love,

Lorna

Surrender to Healing

To My Sisters and Me, Who Need To Read This

I write this poem
Not only for Betty
John, Mary, and Bee
But specially for folks
Just like you and me!

There are many
Loving and compassionate folks
Who refuse to take a moment to spend
The time it takes
Their body and spirit to mend

They may be put off
By the term surrender
It may cause Mary or Sue
To have a fender bender

But I have learned a thing or two
Bout the urgency of humility
In the face of almost fatality

There is no harm in submission
Even if it deters us from our mission

There is something that evolves amongst us womenfolk
That has convinced us
That we are eternally made of oak
This poem is for those among my sisterhood
Who have been intensely convinced
That they should do
So much more than they could

Not heeding to the pleas
Of their bodies, minds and souls
That they should
No longer be among the worker bees

Now I'm not one
Who supports lazy sloven ways
I've been taught a clean house and hot meals are better
Than laying by St. Lucia's Bay

So there are multiple challenges here
We must try to effect
Balancing this or that
Here or there
That we must try harder to get

Let's take time to
De-program
Find solace
And stop the test

When our bodies, mind and spirit
Tell us it is time to rest

Sankofa: Or Healing Starts With Knowing

There may be some of my readers who ask, what made you decide to include historical information as part of healing? Dr. Maya Angelou once said, "History, despite its wrenching pain, cannot be unlived, but if faced with courage, need not be lived again" (wisdomquotes.co). What she means is that if we know and understand our history and can face the atrocities of our past with courage, we are that much closer to healing ourselves, while also ensuring that future generations need not experience the same trauma.

In the Akan language, and the Twi and Fante dialects spoken in Ghana, the word, "Sankofa," means you must know where you have gone to know where you are going, a going back to that which you have forgotten. The direct translation is more like "it is not taboo to fetch what is at risk of being left behind." The symbol for the word is based on a mythical bird. You can find the symbol in weaving and textiles, sculptures, photos and paintings. It depicts a mythical bird whose feet are securely planted on the ground while its head is turned backwards. The beautiful and graphic image is meant to remind us that we must examine the past as we design, research and implement the future. The Akans, an ethnic group that makes up part of the larger group of West African Ashanti, known for their tremendous cultural, socio-political and economic systems, are a learned and intelligent people. Sankofa fosters a belief that learning is key to self-improvement, utilizing the lessons from the past to prevent ourselves from becoming enmeshed in ignorance fueled by prejudice, bias and hate. The wisdom here guides us to utilize the past as a guide, providing learnings and insight for future planning. This is a concept that I will return to throughout this book: In order to heal ourselves as nations, communities, and individuals, it's essential that we understand how our identities have been shaped and formed by our histories.

So much of the history of African Americans has been full of untruths, falsehoods and deceptions; our histories have been deleted, maligned, devalued, and modified to fit stereotypes and racial caricatures: the mammy, the pickaninny, the brute negro, the Uncle Tom, and many more. The reality is that African American history has not been taught, or has been taught incorrectly, and/or has reinforced negative stereotypes of African people as unhuman, subhuman, and having less worth. I recently heard an interview (recorded during the 1950s-60s) with a white southerner who exclaimed slavery was good for the "nigra" because they were like children who came from uncultured and savage places. These lies and erasures kept black people trapped in second-class citizenship. Systems of slavery, exploitative sharecropping, Jim Crow, and legal segregation and discrimination maintained systemic injustices which continue today through police brutality, struggles for voting rights, and the prison system (amongst many other social, economic, and political disparities). It can be hard not to come out unscathed. As a result of historical and current discrimination, many of us experience self-hate and self-loathing. In fact, rectifying these historical traumas is essential to the healing of non-black people as well. Until all of us, both people of African descent and others, can understand the intersectional relationship between history, identity, powerlessness, and social disparity, equal status will evade us. Our healing will be incomplete.

The Fundamental History aka the Real Story

Let us use the history of African people in the United States as an illustrative example. I am not a politician, historian, or government official; nor do I have a magic wand to wave and magically solve all our nation's problems, past and present. I am, however, an elder woman with wisdom who has studied and experienced many forms of racism and trauma. I draw from these experiences, as well as my education and training, to bring this history to life for you, dear Reader, and to show you how our past continues to impact our present. Remember: my ultimate goal in sharing is not to dwell on pain, but to promote healing. If we are indeed aiming to heal the rabid disease of racism and the traumas it causes in ourselves, our families, and our communities, we must examine and understand the historical truths and experience of African Americans. Later, I will discuss specific strategies for healing our individual and collective traumas. But first, it's important for us to share a working knowledge of the history that has impacted not only my identity and that of my family, but also many people of African descent in the United States.

As Critical Race Theory (CRT) and journalist Nikole Hannah Jones's Pulitzer-prize winning *1619 Project* have eloquently articulated, the history of Africans in America begins before 1619. Sadly, this history remains contested in our schools. At the time of this writing, there are places in this country where the entire history of African Americans in the United States is under threat and/or being obliterated.

In order to fully understand the many African ethnic, cultural, and linguistic groups who were brought to the American hemisphere, it's important to understand the historical aspects of

West Africa prior to 1619, including early kingdoms in Ghana, Mali, and the Songhai Empire. It was well-known and documented that the extraordinary empires of Africa were successful. They were places of great wealth and academic learning, with substantial earmarks of successful nations (characteristics which, by the way, were recognized by white travelers who visited and wrote accounts of their travels). For example, the Angolan kingdom of Kongo, a large territory that includes parts of present-day Angola, the Democratic Republic of Congo, and the Republic of Congo, was thriving by the time the first Portuguese slavers showed up.

So, what might a curriculum look like that begins, not with the slave trade, but with the life of Mansa Musa, a wealthy ruler of the Mali Empire during the 12th century. Musa was well known for expanding trade, which helped to fill his coffers with enormous amounts of gold, which he used, in part, to build grand palaces. He also recruited scholars and academics to Mali, establishing Timbuktu as a learning center. Scholars have designated him as "the wealthiest person in history." How, then, do you actively change the perception of Africa from a rich, civilized, diverse, and wealthy region to a "dark continent" of savage beasts? In order to justify the entrapment, transport, and enslavement of 12.5 million people, you have to change the narrative. The people captured and enslaved were no longer kings, princes, queens, princesses, doctors, scientists, academics, farmers, teachers, people of enormous wealth and success…they had to become objects in service of raising individual and collective wealth, status and success. This is especially important as we begin to understand how the identity and personhood of the enslaved African people was modified, demeaned and sculpted to meet the fervent demand for black labor to cultivate cotton, sugar cane, tobacco, and the other important cash crops grown in the American hemisphere.

Many things get lost during this process, not only the complex history of African civilizations, but also the multiple forms of exploitative labor practices in colonial America. Before, and alongside, the importation of African slaves, poor, white (mainly Irish) indentured servants were brought to the American colonies by the British in the 17th century. Both Irish and English servants were sold to work alongside African people in North America. Working conditions for all were extremely harsh and the opportunity to own land and being free did not materialize. But multiple political, economic, and social forces at home and abroad, in the European empires, were already at work to replace indentured servitude with a racial caste system and, ultimately, chattel slavery.

How many of us are taught that the first African slaves, although purchased by wealthy white elites in colonial Virginia where there were no laws or policies permitting slavery, were listed as "servants" in the historical records? Yet, in 1640, a black indentured servant, John Punch, was sentenced to serve his said master or his assigns for the time of his natural life. This is the first recorded evidence of an enslaved African in the English colonies, and many scholars date the beginning of slavery in America to this event.

Despite an emerging race-based caste system in the Americas, one of the first slave revolts in the hemisphere was carried out by a multi-racial force of indentured people in Virginia in 1676. It is known as the Bacon Rebellion because of Nathaniel Bacon, who led the protest. As a result of this rebellion, the British immediately enacted a number of laws to intensify and, ultimately, legalize the caste system between blacks and whites, driving a huge wedge between black and white indentured servants. As African chattel slavery replaced indentured servitude, attitudes towards black persons changed. According to the Trans-Atlantic Slave Trade Database, between 1525 and 1866, 12.5 million Africans were enslaved and shipped to the New World. Approximately 10.7 million were forcibly brought to North America, the Caribbean and South America, although these numbers are estimates and many historians believe the numbers are underestimated.

During the years between the 17th century and the U.S Civil War, we see a general cultural shift toward describing Africans and their descendants as beasts to be disciplined, lesser beasts designated by God to toil in the service of white Christianity and a global plantation economy. Because Africans were presumed to be fundamentally inferior to whites, they could be beaten, tortured, punished, and literally worked to death.

We only need to look to the practice of slavery. In addition to the grueling hours of hard labor without adequate food, water, and rest, even the rudimentary medical care that existed for white slave owners was not provided for slaves. Such treatment was more than simply neglect or the result of misguided individuals—it was backed by the science of the time. The misalignment of medical care, and a so-called scientific understanding of enslaved African Americans, validated a system of plantation slavery. For example, in a report for the Louisiana Medical Association in 1850, Dr. Samuel A. Cartwright presented his hypothesis that African Americans were fundamentally different from white people. He claimed their smaller brains, more sensitive skin, and overdeveloped nervous systems, gave black people a propensity for servitude. He used "scientific" evidence to diagnose "drapetomania," a disease that supposedly explained why enslaved people ran away. He went on to claim that "drapetomania" occurred when enslavers "attempted to unwisely treat their slaved as equals." And the treatment? Severe whippings, the amputation of toes, and various other forms of torture.

Dr. Cartwright also contended that slavery was good for black people, noting greater numbers of black people housed in asylums in the north than in the south. Researchers have since discovered that Cartwright manipulated his data to support his proslavery perspective and agenda.

Likewise, Dr. James Marion Sims performed various types of experimental gynecological surgeries on black enslaved women, often without anesthesia, under the racist notion that black people did not feel pain.

This objectification process itself was transnational, beginning even before enslaved Africans landed in the New World. During my visit to Ghana in 2014, I learned that more than 40 "slave castles," managed by Europe and North America, existed along the coast of Ghana. These "slave castles" also existed in other parts of West Africa such as Senegal. Here, in these "castles," the objectification and enslavement process of captured Africans began even prior to their transport off their home continent. Often, groups of captured Africans were forced to walk long distances from the interior to the coast. In one encampment in Ghana, those captured slept outside on rocks. In others, hundreds of

Africans were grouped together in cave-like structures, whose floors would quickly become caked in human excrement. Troublemakers were remanded to airless cells where their screams of slow strangulation could be heard throughout the so-called castle. Women were brought out routinely from their cells to provide sexual favors by rape by their captors. You can still view the whipping posts where difficult enslaved were beaten to serve as an example to others.

The horrors and humiliations on-board the ships of the "Middle Passage" are well-documented. The chains, darkness, brutalities, rape, deaths…If a ship was found to be too heavy, African people were routinely thrown overboard. So that insurrections did not occur, slavers separated families and ethnic-linguistic groups, chaining together people who did not share a common language. The hellish trip intensified the objectification process.

Upon arrival, the objectification process and socialization into chattel slavery continued. On the auction block, children were ripped from the arms of their mothers; and Africans, including my ancestors, were stripped of their clothes and their dignity, inspected as one inspects a cow or a horse. The objectification had to continue once Africans were sold and transported to their new "home." They were forced to change their names and beaten for speaking their mother tongues or practicing aspects of their culture, including religion. Education was forbidden. Physical, emotional, psychological, and sexual abuse was the norm. Even the invention of the cotton gun by Eli Whitney did not help. Slave masters turned to more brutal methods to keep blacks in bondage: forced breeding, increased whippings, and official and unofficial laws that created financial incentives for planters to maintain slaves.

Throughout the 19th century, before, during, and after the Civil War and emancipation of black slaves, demeaning stereotypes, drawn from plantation life and culture, proliferated in our society. Despite the success in ending legal slavery, the years after the Civil War and passage of the 14th Amendment soon birthed the era of Jim Crow, an informal (but formalized in practice) system designed to re-enslave, persecute, and dehumanize black people. The term Jim Crow comes from the 19th century white actor Thomas D. Rice's racially caricatured and stereotyped performances of a black man (a practice we now call "black face"). This laid the foundation for further objectification through racial caricaturing of people of African descent: the Pickaninny, Uncle Tom, Mammy, Brute Negro… Stereotypes and caricatures became social, economic, and political truths in the minds of many Americans. Jim Crow, both the racial appropriation and performance of black identity by white people and the series of laws and restrictions aimed toward preventing the full inclusion of black citizens in the social, political, and economic life of the nation, reinforced limiting notions of black identity in the imagination of white people throughout the United States—that we were and are a group that required continual re-enslavement. Slavery was at an end, but legal segregation continued through formalized and informal ways of enslaving black people. These ahistorical misconceptions and violent portrayals continued well into the 20th (and 21st century) and remained prevalent during my own formative years.

History Is More Than 'Just the Facts'

Knowing the "facts" of history, while important, is only the beginning. While history shows that racist systems may be interrupted with moments of change, systemic racism persists in shadowy and secret ways. Those of us who study systems understand that systems seek stability. Sustaining change is often difficult and perhaps impossible. Even while we feel aided and supported with systemic change aimed at dispelling the diseased system of racism, we can still find ourselves fooled by modified laws, policies and procedures. We may experience moments of hope, only to find the personal and institutional racisms we thought were healed still present in new and highly creative manners.

Perhaps this is why, as I take time to review history, I am struck with the fact that we, as a nation, have never truly gotten it "right." We have yet to fully understand our history. We have failed to adequately teach our youngsters how and why African Americans and people of color have had their identities changed, while being subverted, persecuted, and traumatized. The historical path towards removing the remnants of legal segregation, so that we could obtain the right to have a soda or hot chocolate at a Woolworth's counter or have a night's lodging in a hotel, has, in truth, merely stirred a pebble.

In our current century we are living through a new-old era of Jim Crow. A review of the major institutions in our country, as well as the personal and vivid experiences of African Americans, demonstrates how history repeats itself. Mountains of formidable challenges persist, affecting every aspect of our personhood. Social disparities and unequal access to resources perpetuate the process of objectifying and dehumanizing African American identities, compounding trauma on the social, familial-communal, and individual levels. Although I will focus on the United States, I am certain this is a global phenomenon. We have to confront these disparities as part of our own collective and individual healing. Again, I want to make clear that I believe this process of reckoning with a racism past and present is vital for ALL people. Non-black people also have stakes in the game; we cannot heal ourselves without each other. Effective and long-lasting social justice benefits everyone.

In the following pages, I address the following central question: **Where do we continue to see examples of powerlessness and inequality for African Americans, and how does that inhibit our individual and collective healing?** It is my hope and wish that by sharing my knowledge and expertise as an academic and researcher, I can illuminate a way forward, from trauma and pain towards true and lasting healing.

Willie McGee and Me

The reader of this personal and profound
Written expression
May wonder with incredulity
What lies in the relationship
Between a would-be poet
And a man in Laurel, Mississippi
Wherein they never made a face-to-face
Lasting impression

Mississippi is one of the infamous states
Within our Union
Boasting of multiple lynchings, castrations,
And so many forms of torture
Where many people of color
Were destined to meet their
Final fate

One day our own personal story
Will be retold
Because like the McGee Family
Our story remains untold

I would be remiss if I did not offer
That there remain many untold stories
Cloaked in the darkness of secrecy and shame
Their participants too frightened to utter
Not one word of distain

I hasten to add that I make a heartfelt promise
To spend the rest of my life's work
On uncovering the stories of Black and Brown
Ordinary folks throughout the US
Whose lives were unhappy and sometimes lost
Through the thoughts and whims of powerful folks
In many a town

I was captivated when I heard Willie's story
There was something that stirred within me
Hearing the details of his fate
Which had much to do with hate

His comely and intelligent granddaughter
Saw herself as powerful Isis, Cleopatra
And decided to challenge both history and authority
Without a care of what might happen to her

Willie was a handsome brown-skinned dude
Who obviously attracted the attention
Of a Caucasian woman's intentions
She could not stop her need for his love
And he in turn felt he could challenge
The ethos and mores of Mississippi's gov

Once their relationship was uncovered
The woman shouted RAPE
And you can vividly imagine that those
Infamous words sealed his fate

His initial so-called trial
Lasted only an afternoon in Laurel
Willie's so-called defense
Would surely be called immoral

You won't believe
When I tell you cats
That in 1946
A civil rights group
Made contact with a feisty white woman
By the name of Bella Abzug
Who sported a big hat

Bella rallied as many as she could
I am told that among them were the likes of
Faulkner, Robeson, Baker, and even
The brilliant Einstein
But all of them were not able
To overturn the injustice which turned out
To be as sour as a lime

Ultimately, dear Willie was sentenced
To a horrible fate
A traveling electric chair
Was his ultimate fate

There was an additional secret
That his Divine Goddess uncovered
She went in person and tracked down
The prosecutor who led the charge
Of Willie's illicit affair discovered
He, finally under pressure and duress,
Confessed and told the story
Before his ultimate put to rest

With urging and a need to purge
The prosecutor lamented
That dear Willie
Knowing his Fate
Sealed with premature death
Told the truth that the woman's story
Was all made-up and pretend

I share this important information with you
Because there is so much about us
Black and Brown folk
And a High Yalla's too
That's meaningful and important
To me and to you

So long, Willie
I guess I'll see you sometime.

Chapter 8

Creating Cultures of Healing

The yin and the yang. The alpha and the omega. The circle of life. These images and metaphors remind us that there will be challenges, conflict, and periods of chaos in our lives. We all will experience powerlessness, trauma, and isms that threaten to diminish our spirit. And we may feel—and act—estranged or alienated from our Higher Power. But we can make a conscious choice to seek healing for our beautiful, resilient souls with a fundamental belief in faith and hope as the foundation for change and healing—a resource we *all* share. And although we may not feel it, within our mind's eye and the recesses of our heart, the opportunity for that choice exists. Both well-researched data as well as personal experience has prompted me to share these thoughts about handling life challenges.

Reframing Our Societal Legacies and Identities

We begin our healing journey by addressing the harmful impact of certain societal legacies on our individual and collective identities. While it may seem, at times, that my focus here prioritizes the experiences of Black Americans and people of color over others, the truth is that disentangling fact from fiction is essential for ALL of us, regardless of our race, ethnicity, gender, sexuality, age, ability, class, religion, country of origin, etc. What I set out to do in this chapter is offer corrective data as a way to push back against the negative label society has given African Americans and to offer alternatives to misinformation, assumptions, or the complete erasure of our presence in dominant narratives. This is in service of our healing.

Understanding how societal legacies impact our identities matters for non-black people, too. First, access to a fuller picture of the social-economic-political contexts of African American life in the United States can increase understanding, awareness, and perhaps empathy. Second, and perhaps more importantly, such information also offers non-black people a way forward with their own healing. What I mean is that non-black people in the United States have gone through a socialization process which often left them with unexamined white privilege and misleading stories about their own opportunities and value to society. These stories have a negative impact on the identity and personhood of non-black people by inflating their sense of self in such a way that negates their true personhood and contributions as part of the population here in the United States and abroad. Therefore, the alternative versions of societal legacies illuminated in the following pages offer all people the opportunity for much-needed healing.

Far from being dry, facts are relevant. Facts, data, the historical record…a closer attention to the documented realities of our communities helps to dispel the toxic influence of harmful myths and violent stereotypes on our body, mind, and spirit. And so, as you peruse the following pages, please keep in mind that this information is about healing, because it is about casting off the oppressive stigmas that keep us from living our truest and best expressions of ourselves. And dear Reader, please also keep in mind that these examples are an expression of Willie McGee, Emmett Till, Medgar Wiley Evers, Michael Donald, Rodney King, Phillip Pannell, Amadou Diallo, Trayvon Martin, Tamir Rice, Eric Garner, Sandra Bland, Philando Castile, Botham Jean, Atatiana Jefferson, Michael Brown, Elijah McClain, Ahmaud Marquez Arbery, Breonna Taylor, Daniel Prude, Adam Toledo, Daunte Wright, Ma'Khia Bryant, Jacob Blake, Tyre Nichols, George Floyd, and the many others who will surely follow in the weeks and years to come.

Disparity, Or Modern-Day Slavery?

Racism rears its ugly face in every aspect of African American life. The few examples that I will discuss here fail to approximate all the ways in which racism is experienced among Black Americans. Take, for example, the sport of football. "In the NFL, 58 percent of players are Black and just a quarter are White. As recently as last decade, nearly 70 percent of the players were Black. But just 11 percent of full-time head coaches since 1990 have been Black. During that time, 154 White men have served as an NFL head coach, compared with 20 Black men." I have chosen to share a handful of examples that are particularly important to my own experience of "life, liberty and the pursuit of happiness." These include educational equity; health care, including mental health; income, debt and wealth; the employment gap; black voter suppression; and the justice system.

Challenges to Educational Equity

There are many ways to enslave a person, and not all of them involve physical bondage. Slavery is an intersectional experience that has taken many forms. Historically, slave owners denied their slaves opportunities to read and write. By controlling their literacy, they could prevent slaves from documenting their existence or offering narratives that might challenge or defy the status quo. An illiterate population was easier to control. Today, all American children enjoy the right to literacy. However, in practice, obstacles to equal education for African Americans (and all minorities) still exist. Consider the following:

- As of 2021, the U.S. Department of Health and Human Services, Office of Minority Health, indicates that 87.9% of non-Hispanic blacks earned a high school diploma compared to 93.5% whites; 24.7% of blacks go on to achieve a bachelor's degree compared to 38.3% of whites. And while we know advanced degrees are now necessary for most employment and/or careers, only 9.8% of blacks have graduate or advanced degrees compared to 15% of whites.

According to the United Negro College Fund (UNCF) website:

- African American students are often located in schools with less qualified teachers, novice teachers, and teachers who earn less than their white counterparts.

- Research demonstrates evidence of systematic bias in teacher expectations. White teachers were found to have lower expectations of black students, than black teachers had for them.

- Black students spend less time in the classroom due to punitive disciplinary actions.

- Black students are nearly two times as likely as white students to be suspended without educational services.

- Black and Latino students are under-represented in Honors or Advanced Placement courses.

- Black students spend less time in the classroom due to discipline, which further hinders their access to a quality education. Black students are nearly three times more likely to be suspended without educational services as white students. Black students are also 3.8 times as likely to receive one or more out-of-school suspensions as white students.

- Black children represent 19 percent of the nation's pre-school population, yet 47 percent of those receive more than one out-of-school suspension. In comparison, white students represent 41 percent of pre-school enrollment, but only 28 percent of those receive more than one out-of-school suspension. Even more troubling, black students are 2.3 times as likely to receive a referral to law enforcement or be subjected to a school-related arrest as white students. Is this an example of the school-to-prison pipeline?

- Schools with 90% or more students of color spend $733 less per student per year than schools with 90% or more white students.

- Students of color are concentrated in schools with fewer resources.

According to the U.S. Department of Education's Office for Civil Rights, in 2011-2012:

- Black and Latino students represented only 37% of students in schools that offered Advanced Placement courses; however, only 27% of those black students were enrolled in at least one Advanced Placement course.

- The same Office reports that Black and Latino students have less access to Gifted and Talented Education (GATE) programs than white students. In 2011-2012, white and Asian-American students made up 70% of those enrolled in GATE programs, compared to 26% of Black and Latinx students.

Meanwhile, a 2016 report by the Department of Education found that only 10% of school principals were black compared to 80% white principals. Overall, 82% of public-school educators are white compared to only 18% who identify as a person of color. Of that 18%, black male teachers only constitute 2% of the teaching workforce.

When we are confronted by data and statistics, it's easy to shake our heads and then quickly move on with our daily lives. However, I ask you to keep in mind the personal and, at times, tragic stories associated with data. For example, as a youngster, I had only one black teacher and not until high school. In graduate school, I had two. Being an inquisitive and self-motivated student, I avoided my teachers' low expectations because I always had my hand up. Yet, my own children faced immense challenges to being accepted in the Gifted and Talented programs at a suburban (supposedly) progressive school. One of my daughters was only admitted to the Gifted and Talented Program after numerous meetings and discussions regarding the criteria—which she very clearly met! In fact, a black elementary teacher told us that if our daughter was not allowed entrance into the Gifted Program, the program should be closed to everyone. Our other daughter met the same resistance. But this time we were prepared. Our son also faced severe discrimination in an elementary school run by a principal who spearheaded a "reign of terror" that targeted the black students and their parents. She (and others with numerous biases) believed that young black males, fueled by "rap music," had numerous behavioral problems. When one parent objected and admitted to playing rap music, she attempted to destroy him. The principal castigated and demeaned the black, male parent in a meeting with other staff. She singled him out and said, with conviction, "The problem is you are playing rap-music for your son, and this is directly impacting his success in school."

I do not believe that we can depend on the benevolence and honesty of teachers and administrators. All educators come with their biases, both explicit and implicit. My husband and I had to be ever vigilant to secure a sound educational plan for our children. It was time-consuming and often required time away from our jobs. But we found it was the only way to ensure our children had equal access educational opportunities. It is essential that parents review their children's progress and advocate for them when needed.

Disparities in Physical and Mental Health Care

African Americans have a long history of bodily neglect and mistreatment. Since their capture and enslavement, Africans and people of African descent in this country have lived out the painful consequences of, on the one hand, being valued for their labor and the potential profits such labor could provide; and, on the other hand, being regarded as less than human.

As far back as colonial America, people began to make connections between increased wealth (and responsibility) and threats to mental well-being. Early Americans hypothesized that symptoms of mental illness in white men were related to increased stress, particularly the strain of wealth management. *(Journal of Blacks in Higher Education, 2014)*. Yet, the same was not true for other groups of people, including those we now regularly treat for mental illnesses, such as women and children, whose mental sufferings were generally ignored until well into the 20th century. At a particular disadvantage, were African Americans. Due to racial ideologies that cast people of African descent as subhuman and/or capable of tolerating more pain than whites, the mental well-being of enslaved people was of little concern to the slaveholders, as long as they were healthy enough to work.

Nonetheless, enslaved people did suffer from mental illness.

We had no documentation on the status or treatment of their mental health until the 1840 census. Essentially, prior to Emancipation and especially in the South, there was little need for mental health care for Black Americans because prevailing racist beliefs maintained black people depended on doing hard physical labor in order to be healthy. Nonetheless, in pre-Civil War Virginia, both free and enslaved black people could be admitted to state asylums, based on the discretion of the individual directors and the willingness of slave owners to pay for their care, even though most white doctors concurred that "race and skin color offered immunity from mental illness" for Black Americans.

The 1840 census data, drawn from erroneous and unethical research, refers only to increased rates of insanity among freed Blacks in the North. The inference drawn from the "data" suggested to those in power that as Black people migrated north, rates of insanity increased.

Enter Louisianan physician Dr. Samuel Cartwright, mentioned previously, who, in 1851, identified a mental disorder among enslaved Black Americans that he called "Drapetomania: a disease, causing Negroes to run away from their slave owners." The treatment for this so-called mental disease? Whipping.

Did things change for Black Americans after Emancipation? Yes and no. Dr. King Davis, Research Professor at UT Austin's the School of Information, together with a team, spent several years digging into the question. His work focused sifting through archival material from the first (segregated) mental health facility for Black Americans: The Central State Lunatic Asylum for the

Colored Insane, which opened its doors in 1868 in Virginia. His team unearthed and analyzed 36,000 photos, 5 to 7 million pages of materials, including admissions information, and 800,000 records.

What prompted the governmental leadership in Virginia to plan and implement a segregated psychiatric facility for African Americans post-Civil War? It was an initiative led by the Freedmen's Bureau, who felt the need to create and implement health care (including mental health care) for newly freed African Americans. Two Virginia psychiatrists, in charge of the existing psychiatric hospitals in Virginia, felt that segregated facilities were necessary so that the treatment of newly freed African Americans would not interfere with the treatment for whites.

The Central Lunatic Asylum for the Colored Insane was housed in the Howard's Grove Hospital for the Confederacy outside of Richmond, Virginia, and operated until 1968 when segregation was deemed unlawful by the federal government. During its years of segregated service, the hospital's numbers grew steadily—from 373 patients in 1885 to a startling 5,000 patients in 1950.

In its initial decades, black families faced the involuntary commitment of their loved ones. As illiteracy remained high amongst the formerly enslaved, there was little chance that a commitment order could be fought. Many families lacked the resources to visit and intervene on behalf of their loved ones. Conditions in the Asylum were described as highly unsanitary, making it harder to get well and return to one's family. Forced sterilizations and experimental surgeries, without informed consent and adequate medical facilities, were common practices. The prevailing belief among hospital leadership that mental health among Black Americans improved with hard labor, inpatients were required to engage in heavy farm work, various domestic chores, laundry, cleaning, etc., basically performing all the physical labor in the hospital.

The reasons for hospitalization were confusing and based upon circumstances that had little to do with psychopathology. According to research conducted by the Washington Post, "women could be admitted because they were upset about their husband's desertion or because they had intense menstrual pain."

The commitment system was such a sham that admission could be based on the testimony of a white employer or simple hearsay. People were admitted for "talking back to a white person or refusing to step aside when a white person was walking." Davis's research found examples of black men being committed on the basis of anger and potential violence.

According to Davis, social, economic and political circumstances, such as a need for medical care, economic and dire financial circumstances, housing needs, old age, unemployment, poverty, fear, and continuous trauma drove people to the Asylum. Some patients may have suffered from some form of psychosis, alcoholism, and mania; however, the diagnostic criteria were unclear. In some of the clinical records that were reviewed, patients were hospitalized based on "mania" due to "religious excitement or being free". He also discovered a peculiar trend: the diagnosis of mania was disproportionately applied to blacks.

While some of the patients attempted to escape these horrific conditions, many died due to illness contracted onsite. Sadly, many African Americans who died in this facility were placed in unmarked graves, leaving families and loved ones without an opportunity for a funeral and closure. Additionally, some of the bodies of former patients were stolen by grave robbers seeking cadavers to be used at the local medical college.

Similar institutions in the American South opened segregated doors for formerly enslaved people during this time, including the Alabama Insane Hospital, South Carolina State Hospital, and North Carolina's Asylum for the Colored Insane. Similar to the so-called treatment approach at Central State, hospitalized in-patients were required to engage in ongoing and relentless physical labor. Again, similar psychiatric care was also provided at the Eastern North Carolina Hospital, where Black in-patients, both male and female were required to engage in hard labor. Over time, the North Carolina facility went through several name changes and was the site of Cherry Hospital until 2016, when it moved into a new facility. The name Cherry Hospital is infamous for locals with a long memory. Until the Civil Rights Act of 1964, the Hospital was known for many unfortunate and horrific experiences. One example is Junius, who, deaf and mute, was admitted at age 17 on accusations of rape. He was castrated. Although the rape charges were eventually dropped, Junius remained a patient at the hospital until his death in 2001.

Unfortunately, the extensive, detailed research Davis and his team were able to provide on Central State has not been performed on these, or any of the country's other early mental care facilities for African Americans. What we do know is that they shared at least two things in common—a practice of admitting patients on dubious conditions and the requirement that black patients engage in heavy and demanding physical labor as part of their "rehabilitation."

Conditions facing African Americans were no rosier on the medical side of things. A pattern of medical neglect, performing procedures without informed consent, and utilizing black bodies for experimentation continued well after slavery ended. The Tuskegee Study of Untreated Syphilis in the Negro Male, conducted by the United States Public Health Service, began in 1932. The intent of the study was to record the natural history of syphilis in Black people, and the participants were told they were being treated for 'bad blood.' A total of 600 poor and illiterate men were enrolled in the study. Of this group, 399 had syphilis and 201 were control subjects. By 1947, penicillin became the recommended treatment for syphilis, but the researchers didn't provide penicillin, so they could continue to track the disease's full progression, as the men went blind or insane or developed other serious health issues.

A similar experiment was conducted on Henrietta Lack in 1951 at Johns Hopkins Hospital in Baltimore, Maryland. Mrs. Lack sought care at the hospital for a uterine tumor. While a biopsy was being performed, the patient's cells were also taken without her consent and utilized nationally and internationally for medical research and experiments until quite recently.

Some scholars refer to such experiences as "medical genocide." Hopefully, as a nation, we have moved beyond pseudo-scientific justifications for the torture and neglect of the bodies of our fellow citizens. Through research and scientific study, we have identified the key factors that determine good health. We know what works. The U.S. Department of Health and Human Services identifies the five social determinants of health:

1. Economic Stability: including employment status, level of poverty, level of housing and food insecurity.

2. Education Access and Quality: including, language and literacy, early childhood education and development, high school diploma, access to higher education.

3. Health Care Access and Quality: access to primary care and health care, and health literacy.

4. Neighborhood and Built Environment: access to food, quality of housing, level of crime and violence, and environmental conditions.

5. Social and Community Context: level of social cohesion, civic participation, experiences of discrimination and incarceration.

So, if we know what works—if we can name it and quantify it—shouldn't that mean we've reached a point in our history where we are ensuring good health for all? Sadly, the answer is no. Despite knowing what we need to live healthfully and safely, whites and non-whites do not yet have equal experiences when it comes to the five social determinants of health. Gross disparities still exist and, as you might know or have guessed, African Americans are often on the losing end when it comes to achieving good health.

When we Know Better, but Aren't Doing Better

My mother and grandmothers were often full of poems and parables, sayings passed down through our family. The phrase above, in the subheading, is one of them. It perfectly encapsulates the idea that while we know what factors contribute to our health, we have not seized the opportunities for the vast institutional change required to ensure them for all. Let us examine the facts…

Evidence continues to document disparities in health care between Black Americans and white Americans. Consider the difference in life expectancy. Current life expectancy rates, based on the 2020 census, indicate that the overall life expectancy for Black Americans is 77.0 years: 79.8 years for women and 74.0 years for men. For whites, the current life expectancy is age 80.6 years; 82.7 years for white women and 78.4 years for men. The Office of Minority Health (OMH) also reports a higher death rate for blacks than for whites when it comes to the following conditions: heart diseases, diabetes, stroke, cancer, asthma, influenza, pneumonia, HIV/AIDS and homicide.

Private healthcare insurance is also an area of economic disparity. The 2019 OMH report shows 55.9% of blacks utilized private insurance compared to 74.7% for whites, and 43.5% of Black Americans relied on Medicaid or public health insurance compared to 34.3% of white Americans. The latter data is also related to access to health care and prescriptions. Lastly, 10.1% of blacks were uninsured vs 6.3% of whites. Remember, too, that alongside disparities and challenges in receiving care and living long, healthy lives, African Americans are simultaneously facing an array of challenges in other areas, all of which compound and affect our mental, physical, and spiritual health and well-being.

Environmental factors in the neighborhoods where we live can have adverse effects on our health. In my own family, asthma and respiratory ailments plague us. My mother, cousins, my children, and others all suffer or suffered from these diseases. More than genetic bad luck, could these illnesses be the direct result of our living conditions? I grew up in close proximity to the Cross Bronx Expressway, located in the Bronx, New York. Recent studies show that city planners and civil engineers designed this particular highway to cut the borough in half, based upon racial factors. Is it any coincidence, then, that the Bronx has the highest indices of asthma in comparison with the four other boroughs? In fact, I strongly suspect that my own respiratory illnesses, and those of my family, were caused by our proximity to the Expressway. At the time of this writing, it has been only a handful of months since the troubling past of the Cross Bronx Expressway has garnered national attention, thanks to efforts by Dem. Representative Ritchie Torres and Transportation Secretary Pete Buttigieg.

The intentional segregation of neighborhoods, which corrals minorities into less desirable areas, near major highways, power plants, waste treatment plants, industrial sites, etc., while securing more desirable areas for whites, is known as environmental racism. Environmental racism is backed by research that points to clear correlations between poor health and environmental conditions that differ across race (and class). Take asthma, for instance, a respiratory condition known to be caused by and/or exacerbated by environmental factors. In 2019, the OMH reports that black children had a death rate 7.6 times more than white children. Black adults were almost three times more likely to die from asthma-related causes than white people.

For Black Americans, challenges and obstacles to our good health begins even before birth. I had the enormous pleasure to meet Dr. Kenneth Clark, a social psychologist whose hallmark research propelled the 1954 Supreme Court decision Brown v. Board of Education. Dr. Clark claimed that you could assess the evolution of any society by how it cares for its most vulnerable members. When it comes to prenatal and infant care, sadly, the United States has a long way to go.

Black women are more than four times as likely than white women to die from pregnancy-related complications, regardless of class or private health insurance. But why? Research conducted by Linda Villarosa for the *New York Times Magazine* is clear:

> *For black women in America, an inescapable atmosphere of societal and systemic racism can create a kind of toxic physiological stress, resulting in conditions — including hypertension and pre-eclampsia — that lead directly to higher rates of infant and maternal death. And that societal racism is further expressed in a pervasive, longstanding racial bias in health care — including the dismissal of legitimate concerns and symptoms — that can help explain poor birth outcomes even in the case of black women with the most advantages.*

I understand this all too well. Although I am a privately insured, middle-class black woman, I, too, suffered from pre-eclampsia. At the birth our last child, my obstetrician told me that I should not have additional children.

Tragically, making it through pregnancy to a successful birth is just the beginning for black infants. Black infants have 2.4 times the infant mortality rate as non-Hispanic white infants. Black infants are four times more likely than non-Hispanic white infants to die from complications related to low birth weight. In fact, low birth weight remains the leading cause of infant mortality. Black infants have 2.9 times the rate of sudden infant death syndrome (aka SIDS) mortality rate, as compared to white infants.

Pain management for our children also reveals troubling disparities. In a 2015 article in the *Journal of the American Medical Association Pediatrics*, researchers described the results of a cross-sectional study of a million children's (defined as 21 and younger) medical charts for emergency rooms admissions for appendicitis between 2003-2010. When pain scores were reviewed by the researchers, black patients with moderate pain scores were less likely than white children to receive mild pain-relieving treatments. Those with severe pain among the black patients were less likely than white patients to receive opioids.

As I read the article, I had to wonder whether this was a remnant of the pseudo-scientific medical practices of Dr. Samuel Cartwright. Is this yet another example of the continued objectification and powerlessness for Black Americans? Are current disparities in the care of Black Americans based on past and present racism?

The Tragic Human Cost of Inadequate Care

We find disparities also when it comes to the mental health of Black Americans. Perhaps you won't be surprised to learn that Black Americans not only experience higher rates of certain mental illnesses but also have less access to appropriate care and help. Access to mental health treatment and the stigma associated with seeking treatment are essential factors in discussing the differences in mental health between blacks and whites. As a result of both poor access to help and social stigma, Black Americans suffer disproportionately.

For example, the Office of Minority Health reports that during 2020, 37.1% of black adults aged 18 and over received mental health services, as compared to 51.8% of white adults. While medication is not a panacea for mental health challenges, the efficacy of medication in combination with various mental health treatments and alternative interventions has been well-documented. Nonetheless, only 27.5% of black adults received prescription drugs for mental health services in 2020, compared to 44.5% of white adults. Lastly, 59.6% of black adults who experienced a major depressive episode received care for depression, compared to 70.2% of whites in similar distress.

And yet, Black Americans experience depression as much as, if not more than, white Americans. Consider the differences in how symptoms of depression are experienced across white and black Americans:

- Sadness: 4.2% of Black Americans vs. 2.6% of white Americans

- Hopelessness: 1.8% of Black Americans vs. 2.2% of white Americans

- Worthlessness: 1.8% of Black Americans vs. 2.3% white Americans

- Everything is an effort: 11.0% of Black Americans vs. 6.6% white Americans

Depression can often lead to suicide. In 2020, suicide was the third leading cause of death for blacks aged 15-24. Statistically, more whites commit suicide than blacks; however, the black suicide rate is steadily increasing in comparison to whites. This is a cause for concern.

I am particularly alarmed by the data around suicide in African American communities because of the misinformation and assumptions many people carry regarding suicide and black people. In the minds of some, including many healthcare providers, African Americans are less likely to commit suicide due to the strong cultural role that religion plays in many black communities. In my own extensive career, I have witnessed white health care and white mental health care providers often mistakenly assess suicide risk in an African American patient. This happens when white practitioners rely on assessment tools and processes that may not be culturally competent.

In 2018, the death rate from suicide for black men was four times greater than that of black women. Suicide was the third leading cause of death for Black Americans aged 15-24 in 2019. Black females in grades 9-12 were 60% more likely to attempt suicide compared to white females of the same age. These data should concern us. Why are so many young people, in the prime of their lives, feeling as if they have no other recourse but to take their own life?

The tragic experience of suicide within the black community was recently highlighted by two unfortunate and tragic deaths of vibrant, young Black Americans. Ian Alexander, Jr. son of award-winning actress Regina King, was 26 years old when he died of suicide on January 21, 2022. Only a week later, we learned of the suicide of former Miss America and practicing attorney, Cheslie Kryst, who jumped to her death at the young age of 30. While these two celebrity suicides captured the attention of the media, there are so many others, unnamed and unnoticed, whose lives were tragically ended because they saw no way out of their pain except by suicide.

Unfortunately, due to continued racial bias in our health care system and the stigmas associated with mental health diagnoses, we simply don't yet have sufficient data to link suicide rates for African Americans to possible mental health disorders.

When Money Doesn't Move: Racial Disparities in Income, Debt, and Wealth

Black Americans, who are descendants of enslaved ancestors, constitute about 12% of our nation's population; however, they own less than 2% of our nation's wealth. When it comes to wealth and economic status, Black Americans begin their lives far behind white Americans. And as a black person's life unfolds, they find themselves further and further behind. Why is this the case and how did this happen?

Because African Americans were enslaved and unable to earn money (let alone save it or amass wealth), for over two hundred years, they have had less opportunity to establish wealth than white Americans and other immigrant groups. Black Americans were not invited to participate in the benefits of the Homestead Act, which distributed land to citizens during the 19th century. Further, through redlining and exclusion from federal mortgages in the 20th century, Black Americans did not enjoy the opportunities for home ownership offered to white Americans. Many African Americans were excluded from New Deal programs, such as unemployment benefits, intended to help raise Americans out of the Great Depression of the 1930s. In fact, assistance to agricultural and domestic workers was specifically denied so as to purposefully exclude black laborers.

After centuries of one financial obstacle after another, it's unsurprising that present-day African Americans are far behind white Americans when it comes to income and wealth. Census data show that the median income for black households in 2019 was $45,438, compared to $76,057 for white households. In the same year, 18.8% of black households were living below poverty level, versus 9.1% white households. Unemployment rates are equally revealing. In 2019, the unemployment rate for whites was 3.3% versus 6.1% for Black Americans.

Why do Black Americans earn less than others? Again, the reasons lie not in a nation of evil-tempered racist bosses, but in measurable structural inequalities. A recent study by Northwestern University found that for every 1 dollar of accumulated wealth that white families have, black families have just one cent.

Black students take out larger student loans, amassing more debt than their white counterparts. The average black student leaves college with a debt of around $23,400 versus around $16,000 for white students. Research indicates 21% of black graduates with bachelor's degrees default on their loans, which has enormous consequences for wealth and financial health. That number is more than five times the rate of whites who default. On the graduate level, black degree holders have higher levels of graduate school borrowing and lower rates of repayment.

With more debt and less earning potential, many Black Americans find themselves in positions of financial precarity. In 2016, the *New York Times* reported, "Of black households with income between $50,000 and $85,000, 30% said they had been unable to pay a bill after a financial setback. By contrast, only white household with incomes below $25,000 reported similar challenges paying bills; 31% said they had fallen behind." Similarly, a survey conducted by the Pew Charitable Trust indicated that black households earning between $25,000 and $50,000 reported having emergency savings of only $400. Meanwhile, the average white household in the sample earning range had an emergency fund of $2,100. Debt collection and lawsuits also indicate a disparity. The rate of court judgments from debt collections suits was twice as high in most black communities versus white communities.

Home ownership has also long been considered the main path to financial stability; it forms a central part of "the American Dream." Still, when it comes to home ownership, data show that Black Americans are at a disadvantage. According to the U.S. Census Bureau, homeownership varies significantly according to race and ethnicity. In 2019, 73.3% of white households owned homes compared to only 42.1% of black households. We might expect to see an increase in the percentage of home ownership for Black Americans since the Civil Rights Movement. Alas, that's not the case. The numbers have not changed over time. Looking back to 1960, the rates are fairly consistent: 65% of whites owned homes while 38% of blacks were homeowners—a less than 4% increase over the course of more than 60 years.

Inheritance can decrease debt and/or facilitate home ownership. But whites are more likely to receive these boosts in wealth acquisition. According to the Brookings Institute, white households are 2.5 times more likely than black households to receive an inheritance; and the median amount of an inheritance for a black family is $38,224 vs. $456,217 for a white family!

Retirement is the long-awaited reward after many years of work. The Brookings Institute reports: "The median African American family aged 70 and older has a net worth of $36,900, which is markedly lower than the net worth of the median U.S. household." Furthermore, African American households are more likely than other American families to rely solely on pension plans for their retirement. One reason for an over-reliance on pension plans is because "income from assets represents a much smaller portion of total household income for African Americans than for other households (almost half as large)." The bottom-line: Black Americans have to work harder and longer in order to approximate white wealth. For these reasons, combined with the other setbacks of structural racism, many believe that the racial wealth gap for Black Americans is impossible to close.

Beyond Welfare Queens and Deadbeat Dads: The African American Employment Gap

While popular discourse continues to portray African Americans as lazy, drains on our social systems, and unable or unwilling to hold down jobs, the truth is more complicated. Black Americans do have higher unemployment rates than other groups, but the reasons are historical and structural, not cultural.

The gap in unemployment among African Americans has its roots in the historical period of Reconstruction. Former enslaved people faced high rates of unemployment and poverty as they struggled to integrate into hostile social and economic systems that were actively working to prevent their integration. Legal segregation, Jim Crow laws, and pervasive racial discrimination prevented African Americans from having the same employment opportunities as whites and other minority groups. And today, centuries since enslavement, and despite changes in laws, policies, and procedures and increased educational paths, Black Americans are still underemployed. As African Americans continue to struggle to accumulate wealth from their jobs, they still lag behind white Americans in home ownership, the pursuit of higher education, and even the possibility of better jobs.

According to data shared by the Center for American Progress, a non-profit and nonpartisan organization dedicated to improving the lives of Americans, Black Americans have higher unemployment rates than whites across all educational attainment levels and age cohorts. The organization's website states: "between January 1972 and December 2019, other than the during the aftermaths of recession, the African American unemployment rate has stayed at or above the white rate." Furthermore, unemployment is particularly high in places where Black Americans are the majority, such as Washington, DC. In the capital, unemployment rate for African Americans is a whooping six times higher than it is for whites.

Not only do Black Americans experience higher unemployment, when they are employed, they face inadequate and unstable jobs with poorer benefits than whites. They are often the "last hired and the first fired." Black Americans remain underrepresented in management and leadership positions, as well. At the corporate level, the United States has an alarming lack of black executives. A recent study by Fortune.com indicated that only 3.2% of executives and senior manager-level employees in the United States are black, and only five Fortune 500 CEOs are black. Of these few executives, black men are paid 13% less than white men, and black women are paid 39% less than white men and 21% less than white women. At Amazon, the second-largest corporate employer in the United States, only 12 of the 400 Vice-Presidents are black. The executive leadership (called the "S" team) hired their first black team member in 2020. The Fortune.com study also found that when equally qualified candidates apply for promotions, black candidates are less likely than their white peers to get promotions and salary raises. In a 2004 article in *The American Economic Review* titled, "Are Emily and Greg more employable than Lakisha and Jamal?" researchers conducted an experiment on labor market discrimination and found a significant racial gap along occupations, industry, and employer size. As part of the study, fictitious resumes were forwarded to help-wanted advertisements in the cities of Boston and Chicago. The false resumes were equal in qualifications but were randomly assigned "white-sounding" or "black-sounding" names. White sounding names (such as Emily or Greg) received 50% more callbacks for interviews, although the researchers indicated there was no evidence that employers were "drawing inferences from social class based on names." Their bias was based solely on assumptions around applicants' racial identity.

The continuing presence of a gendered "hiring bias" compounds the situation for black women. A study conducted at Yale University indicated male and female employers who had received anti-bias training "still preferred to hire men over women, viewed them as more skilled and were willing to offer $4,000 more per year in salary". In other words, women of all races already face employment biases that result in lower compensation. When you add in race, the situation worsens. Indeed, for black women, the fight for equal pay and equal employment can feel more daunting. 84.4% of black women work and are more likely than their white female counterparts to be the breadwinners in the family, increasing the stress and responsibilities associated with employment. However, despite working, black women occupy lower paying jobs than black men and white women: "Among those who worked full time all year in 2018, black women earned 61.9 cents for every dollar that white men earned". Black men on the other hand, "earned 70.2 cents for every dollar earned by white men and white women earned 78.6 cents." We must keep in mind the wider implications of these wage gaps, such as the added responsibilities of childcare and the care of elderly relatives, which often lands on the shoulders of women.

Across the gender spectrum, the lived experience of African American workers is fraught with discrimination, harassment, and unsafe working conditions. An investigation into the experiences of Black Americans employed with Amazon's Web Services found that Amazon failed "to create a corporate-wide environment where all black employees feel welcomed and respected." Further, the study found that black employees were hired at levels below their qualifications, experience and interests, part of an overall policy at Amazon described as "down-leveling." Black employees interviewed for the study reported that Amazon's employee review process (i.e., performance evaluation) and opportunities for promotion create few opportunities for black employees to excel. A review of performance evaluations found "large disparities" in performance review ratings between black and white employees. Black employees were given lower marks more often than other colleagues and were promoted at a lower rate than their non-black peers.

As is the case with many black employees in a variety of career settings, black Amazon employees discussed being on the receiving end of racial microaggressions in the workplace. Microaggression, a term popularized by Columbia University Professor Derald Sue but originally coined by Dr. Chester Pierce, a black psychiatrist, names: "brief and commonplace daily verbal, behavioral, or environmental indignities, whether intentional or unintentional, that communicate hostile, derogatory, or negative racial slights and insults towards people of color." At Amazon, a white manager told a black female employee, unprompted, that his ancestors "owned slaves but I'm pretty sure they were good to their slaves." These types of microaggressions in the workplace are insidious, and understanding the motivation behind them is essential for our healing. Microaggressions are often meant to restore white authority in situations where a black person or persons is perceived as having a power advantage. Consciously or unconsciously, their purpose is to disempower black people and put them in a subservient position. Other employees validated this experience, confessing they had "been called out by their managers and peers for not smiling or being friendly enough."

It may be hard to understand why such comments might cause harm. Consider the racial caricatures of African Americans as smiling and accommodating, always willing to serve and comply. Placed within a history of demeaning expectations around behavior and identity, it's easier to see why Black Americans might be troubled. The Amazon study reported that the employees affected had sought resolution through their Human Resource Department only to come to learn that the company had no policies or protocols in place for dealing with microaggressions.

Sometimes microaggressions are not so micro. Take the story of Michael, a colleague of mine who served as Vice-President in the corporate sector. One day, as he entered the elevator at his place of business, two white junior colleagues questioned his presence, asking, "Can we help you?" Another time, a coworker of mine found a noose on her desk. As you can imagine, she was extremely frightened. She felt as if she was being warned by her white, male employees. It can feel daunting and overwhelming to face pervasive racism and white supremacy so directly in the workplace. I also found myself in a professional situation where folks openly used a racial slur when talking about the Japanese and Japanese Americans. In my view, if one kind of slur becomes an acceptable part of the professional lexicon at your job, what's to stop people from using others? It sends a message that those types of words are acceptable in the workplace.

Other examples are less overt, but no less troubling. Black employees are often asked to take on the role and duties associated with diversity and equity, on top of their regular work, often without sufficient resources and with unreasonable expectations. Fortune.com conducted interviews of black executives, middle managers, and entry-level staff in a variety of corporate settings. They reveal the lack of a true commitment to diversity and equity. Additionally, the anecdotes and stories help put a face and identity on the statistics and data. I have included a few telling examples for you to consider. The following are excerpts from African Americans in non-profit and corporate settings, shared on Fortune.com website:

- Brian, 51: "As I slowly moved up the corporate ladder, I began to notice there were fewer black employees until I was the only one. […] I watched as the CEO of our company systematically forced out women and African Americans in leadership. Eventually, I myself resigned because I learned I was being paid less than half of what my white colleagues earned. When I confronted HR and my manager about it, they blatantly lied to me."

- Sanaa, 30: "The top of nonprofits is predominantly white and male; most worker bees are women (of color)."

- Another interviewee, Rachael, 36, addressed the difference between diversity and inclusiveness, pointing out that diversity does not necessarily mean being included in the decision-making process within the organization.

- Azizza, 30: "I have to work harder than my white counterparts just to get respect all while suppressing my big personality in order to dispel the 'angry black woman' stereotype or not be called 'sassy.' If you want to create a truly diverse and inclusive workspace, you have to stop thinking that a splash of color here and there is the best you can do."

- Kimani, 22: "People are simply not doing enough of the critical self-work to unpack their biases, (non-black people of color), so it makes it soul crushing to attempt to be friendly, beyond the fact that I have rarely seen coworkers care to befriend or mentor people who don't look like them."

- Bernard, 57: "I have hidden my black culture all my life because I thought it was the 'corporate' thing to do. The stress of being a black man in corporate America means we can't have the full range of emotions. We can only be happy—never angry."

- Adrienne, 50: "I'd like the white folks at my office to know: We see *you*. We see through all the insincere words that are never followed by action. We see that you talk the talk of 'diversity and inclusion,' but we know that you don't walk the walk. […] Stop trying to convince us that you are inclusive and just be inclusive. That would require you all to acknowledge your privilege and acknowledge the actions you've deliberately taken to elevate your white counterparts for no other reason than that they look like you. Ask yourself, what is it about black people that makes you so uncomfortable? Ask yourselves, why do you go out of your way to hold black people back—by paying them less than their white counterparts, by not promoting them?"

- Charlene, 37: "I overheard a racist conversation and was offended by what was said. First response of HR: 'I'm sure they didn't mean any harm'."

- Marion, 25: "If you're going to accept and give an equal chance to black women, please make sure it's not just the ones who conform to your standard when it comes to physical appearance—I shouldn't have to look like a model for you to respect me like you respect my white counterparts."

- Monica, 37: "A senior white male leader expressed his allyship after George Floyd's death. The irony is he previously made a joke about my being able to afford my luxury vehicle because I must be 'moving kilos.' That undertone that black people must be engaged in illegal activities to have nice things is the same way of thinking that led to George Floyd's and countless other murders by police."

- Christina, 24: "There are Amy Coopers everywhere, in male and female form. The passive-aggressive critiques, the whispers about 'tonal' and 'emotional' black women and men. The outward liberalism but actual fear and perceived threat of black professionals. They wield their power to stop growth, advancement and exposure of black talent. It feels like combat each day to do the dance while their bias goes unchecked."

And yet another poignant expression: "I want you to know how it feels to be the only one that that looks like you in a conference room, in a meeting, at a networking event or happy hour. I want you to know what it feels like to constantly have to assimilate and ingratiate yourself in to another group's culture and way of doing things even though you're citizens of the same country. I want you to know what it feels like to not be able to stand up for yourself or correct someone's assumption about you or your culture or community for fear of losing your job. […] I want you to know the pressure that comes with trying to be perfect and represent your race well because if you make a mistake, the odds of you being given another opportunity are slim. I want you to know what it feels like to live, work, and raise your children in a world where you don't have the complexion for the connection or the protection." Dee, 49.

When I read these thoughtful and courageous reflections, I felt as if I was coming home. Although I will never have the opportunity to meet and speak with these individuals, they were indeed articulating my own experiences. As my own career progressed from line worker to executive positions, I also found myself being the "only one". Upon reflection, it seems to me that, in most arenas, the line staff (worker bees) tend to be people of color and, by and large, female. This was my experience until I moved into my first executive position. During these times, it was always important to learn the culture of the group I was part of. I knew intuitively I had to work hard, especially in sharing verbal and written reports. I spent countless hours, perhaps more than my white counterparts, researching and documenting my recommendations, grounded in evidence-based practices and the latest research. To prepare for workplace interactions, I would often find myself trying to think like my white, male co-workers, adopting opinions that conflicted with my own in order to ready myself for their comments, questions, and debates. It was exhausting.

I particularly resonated with the experience of being seen as having a "big personality." Even recently, a white woman told me that she considered me to be a "formidable" person. In the past, this aspect of how others perceive me has not served me well amongst some of my white colleagues. In fact, in my last position, I believe my perceived "big personality" was the reason behind a downgrade in position and salary. In retrospect, I believe my white colleagues expected me to quietly accept opinions without question. And in circumstances where my data and argument were persuasive and correct, they resorted to personal attacks about my appearance, as my natural hair was atypical. I believe that others saw me as a braggart, prideful, and know-it-all, instead of knowledgeable, experienced, and confident. Over the years, I've learned to handle personal attacks by focusing more on what the attacker meant, specifically. In those situations, my strategy is to allow my attackers to dig their own holes as I watch without emotion but with curious attention.

For example, I was invited to a prestigious, international conference on the relationship between incest and sexual abuse and cultural competence. The conference was sponsored by the American Orthopsychiatric Association and was held in Toronto, Canada. As part of a panel (all white) of experts, I presented a paper on the cultural aspects of childhood sexual abuse and incest. The audience was also overwhelmingly white. At the end of the presentation, a rather average-looking white man, who identified himself as a psychologist, approached me and offered the following comment: "I am aware of different types of black people: either they're ones from the ghetto or others who are acting white." Although I was horrified at the way in which he attempted to stereotype African Americans, I asked him, with curiosity, "Where do I fit in in your framework?" He confidently responded that I was in the "acting white" category. Again, I asked for more information: "How is it that I am acting white?" I pointedly queried him for additional details about my supposed "acting white." As I continued to press him with my questions, he began to turn beet red and became flustered. My co-presenters joined our conversation and only then did our beet red "friend" begin to listen to the racism in his own words. He quickly excused himself, apologizing for his misinformation, and left. Approximately a month later, I received a letter of apology from him, confessing to his lack of insight and understanding of the experiences of Black Americans.

As we come to the end of our discussion of the employment gap, please keep in mind our on-going conversation about the relevance of intersectionality—both in terms of identities and feeling states. While I have focused on the many ways in which Black Americans are excluded from the workforce, we must remember all the traumas, the negative or challenging intersecting feeling states many endure as part of life as a black person in America.

African Americans and the Justice System: A Lesson in Disparate Treatment

Flashback to Wise Woman's pre-teen years. I was living in the projects in an apartment in the Bronx with my mother, sister, and father (who was occasionally absent). (In those years, the projects were full of families (with children) who needed affordable housing, and such neighborhoods lacked the stigma they currently have.

When not at school, I spent my days playing games with friends, reading comic books, playing cards, eating various snacks, and slurping down cold drinks. In many cases, it was quite idyllic.

As I mentioned earlier, my father completed tax returns as a successful side job. He had worked previously for the Internal Revenue Service and had a technically proficient mind; he was excellent in understanding the convoluted and sometimes unclear requests necessary to complete tax documents. For this work, he was often paid in-kind. Such was the case in 1962 when I was about eleven and my father was given a black and white photo essay featuring photographs of the infamous Tombs Prison in New York City. My father, in turn, gave it to me. The book left an indelible mark on my mind, body, and spirit. Although the faces of the women were hidden, most were African American in varying degrees of dress. The decayed atmosphere depicted by the photos was not fit for human beings. I wondered incessantly about the lives of these women. What had they done that merited this severe punishment? What about their families, their children? Did they work? Were they going to lose their jobs? Would they become ill in that awful jail? Were they being beaten and abused? I wondered if the men were treated the same way and suspected they were. I pored over the pictures and written descriptions for hours, trying to make sense of the horrors I viewed. Question after question rolled through my mind. My parents couldn't answer my questions; they, too, were horrified. Those images left an indelible stamp. I knew I must do something to be of help to these women and others who suffer from unseen pain. But how could I help?

Sixty years on, my questions are slightly different. In 1962, prison incarceration was inordinately higher for African Americans than for whites. And today? Prison incarceration is inordinately higher for African Americans than for whites. What makes this a reality? What do we make of the data that point to continued racial disparities in the criminal justice system? This section is my attempt to work through these questions with you, dear Reader, with our eyes on the prize—healing.

Please consider the following information from The Sentencing Project, a non-profit organization which "advocates for effective and humane responses to crime that minimize imprisonment and criminalization of youth and adults by promoting racial, ethnic, economic, and gender justice:"

- One of every 39 black women in prison is serving life without parole.

- In 12 states, more than half the prison population is black, and seven states maintain a black/white disparity larger than 9 to 1. This statistic represents the fact that "nationally, one in 81 Black adults in the US is serving time in state prison."

- Wisconsin has the dubious distinction of leading the nation in the imprisonment of Black Americans: one of every 36 Black citizens in that state is in prison.

- There are 12 states where more than half of those in prison are black including the following: Alabama, Delaware, Georgia, Illinois, Louisiana Maryland, Michigan, Mississippi, New Jersey, North Carolina, South Carolina, and Virginia.

- Black Americans are imprisoned at a rate that is roughly five times the rate of white Americans.

- In 2021, the imprisonment rate for Black women (62 per 100,000) was 1.6 times the rate of imprisonment for white women (38 per 100,000).

In her groundbreaking book, *The New Jim Crow*, Michelle Alexander shows how the school-to-prison pipeline for young people is an example of disparate treatment by our justice system. Between African American and white youngsters charged with the same offense, African Americans are more likely to be placed outside of their homes; given more lengthy sentences; more likely to be referred to adult court, and less likely to receive probation. In fact, in Cook County, Illinois ninety-nine percent of juvenile offenders were referred to adult court. "In ten years, the United States has cut youth incarceration in half. While the reduction is impressive, youth involvement in the juvenile justice system continues to impact youth of color disproportionately. [...] These disparities are not only caused by differences in offending but also by harsher enforcement and punishment of youth of color. White youth are less likely to be arrested than other teenagers, which is partly attributable to unequal policing and partly to differential involvement in crime".

In many cases, youth violence is precipitated by a number of factors including abuse, neglect, maltreatment and head trauma. In a path-breaking study published in the *American Journal of Psychiatry*, the brilliant advocate, Dr. Dorothy Otnow Lewis, found that violent white adolescents were placed in residential treatment settings while violent black adolescents were sent to jail. A very interesting and essential part of the research indicated that the black adolescents had high indices of undiagnosed and untreated head trauma.

Still, even when confronted with data and statistics, it can be hard to understand how our justice system could perpetuate such glaring disparity. How did this "new Jim Crow" system come about? Were black individuals simply rounded up and placed in jail? There is so much to the story. Let's take a long look at some of the history...

As I have mentioned before, the post-Reconstruction period was an intensely violent time for Black Americans. These were the years of the infamous "Black Codes." It was also during this era, in the late 1800s and early 1900s, when we saw the growth of the prison farm system. Although the 13th Amendment abolished the institution of slavery, prison farms became a "loophole" that allowed the exploitation of incarcerated people who were then (as they are now) disproportionately black. Under this system, men, women and children (as young as six or seven) could be "leased" to private farmers and business owners. Modeled after the environment of the slave plantation, prison farms were known for round-the-clock work, uninhabitable living condition, beatings, and unclear sentencing. Prison farms were places where disease, lack of sanitation, poor food, violence, and no medical care, led to death: in 1882, nearly 1 in 6 black prisoners died. In fact, "Working prisoners to literal death was so commonplace that not a single leased convict ever lived long enough to serve a sentence of ten years or more." In many cases, family members had no information regarding the passing of their loved ones, who were buried in prison cemeteries. At least one of every four convicts in the prison farm system was a child or adolescent.

These enslavement systems were a lucrative way to fill the coffers of individuals and local government. To increase revenue, while also targeting Black Americans, laws in many states that did not include imprisonment charges for white offenders (such as being unemployed, loitering, breaking curfew, insulting gestures, cohabitating with white people) sent thousands of free African American men and women into the prison farm system. Certain laws, known as "Pig Laws," were specifically modified for African American defendants to attach more serious sentences to relatively minor crimes. For example, to steal an animal or other property worth ten dollars was categorized as "grand larceny" and came with a 5-year prison sentence (one that could be extended on the whim of the judge and/or prosecution team). These conditions only applied when a black person was accused. Mississippi sent 272 Black Americans into the prison system in 1874. Yet by 1877, after the law defining what counted as "grand larceny" changed, the number of African Americans sent to prison farms increased to 1,072. Please keep in mind that high unemployment and poverty during this time often propelled a black person to steal in order to feed himself and his family.

As uproar and advocacy developed over the re-enslavement of black individuals, prison farms began to close. However, both the Parchment Farm in Mississippi (now known as the Mississippi State Penitentiary) and the infamous Angola Prison in Louisiana (now known as the Louisiana State Penitentiary) still exist, despite horrific and inhabitable conditions. But what about elsewhere in the United States? What propelled the high percentages of African Americans in prison? Are there historical antecedents?

To understand the current high incarceration rates for African Americans, we must look at the political climate in the United

States from the 1950s onward. During the years of the Nixon, Reagan, Bush, and Clinton administrations, policies focused on the "manufactured war on drugs" and the promotion of "law and order" proliferated. The so-called "War on Drugs" impacted the entire fabric of our nation. The Supreme Court, governmental agencies, states, local police, legislators, as well as all parts of our government, were swept up in fighting this war. Monies previously allocated for substance abuse treatment were transferred towards police departments to fight the war. There was tacit approval among prosecutors (who have extreme purview) regarding who gets charged and for what, as well as control over plea deals.

The efforts to fight crime and the sale and spread of illegal substances disproportionately targeted African Americans. The Anti-Drug Abuse Act of 1986 "established a racially discriminatory 100:1 sentencing disparity between crack and powder cocaine. As a result of this legislation, possession of 5 grams of crack cocaine, which was disproportionately consumed by African Americans, triggered an automatic five-year jail sentence—whereas 500 grams of powder cocaine, which was mostly consumed by richer, White demographics, merited the same punishment."

Furthermore, black adults were subject to racial profiling for a number of innocuous reasons, including "driving while black." Such was the case with this Wise Woman, who was stopped several times in New York City and New Jersey because I was driving an Acura, a type of car associated with drug dealing and illegal activities. I didn't know anything about that...I was looking for an attractive car with good mileage! One white police officer did not offer me any credible reason for the stop; although one young white male officer on the New Jersey Turnpike confessed that he had made "a mistake" in pulling me over. Still, that "mistake" led to extreme anxiety and distress, especially as I thought of other black females who had been stopped and never made it safely home.

Indeed, research shows that, once pulled over, people of color are more likely to be searched than whites, and blacks are more likely than whites to be arrested. Individuals found with small amounts of marijuana were encouraged to plead guilty and were sentenced to prison time and branded as "felons." Individual black men hold a disproportionately high number of multiple convictions, compared to white Americans. With more arrests and incarcerations, new prisons were needed. During this era, we saw the design, planning for and implementation of new prisons, particularly in areas where there was white poverty and unemployment, such as upstate New York. Prisons, of course, meant jobs and an economic boost for the community. Presently, prisons are big business for individuals, communities and corporation who specialize in providing essential services to prisons.

This so-called "war on drugs" continues. Minor infractions are handled with disproportionate force and violence. Readers may recall the use of tanks and other war-like machinery to quell the uprising after the murder of Michael Brown, who was stopped by police due to jaywalking. Meanwhile, police practices and policies such as broken windows, stop-question-frisk, mandatory minimums, and three strikes laws, place African Americans and other people of color in the hands of police officers at higher rates than whites. Such was the case of Eric Garner, who died at the hands of police in a chokehold due to selling cigarettes on the street. According to Dr. Nazgol Ghandnoosh, Ph.D., a Senior

Research Analyst at The Sentencing Project, other tremendous disparities include:

The availability of and funding for public defenders. The high caseloads of public defenders often do not encourage an adequate defense.

- Difficulties in posting bond among low-income individuals.
- The lack of support services for people on parole or probation.
- The lack of adequate drug treatment facilities and access.
- For those who develop mental illness in jail or are mentally ill upon admission, there are few treatment facilities. Management of inmates within prison and upon discharge are woefully inadequate. After-care services, including housing help and financial counseling, are inadequate.
- A felony conviction may prohibit an individual from voting, obtaining educational benefits, living in public housing, obtaining welfare assistance, food stamps (also known as SNAP).
- A felony conviction acts as a barrier to obtaining employment. Many leave prison owing tremendous fines, which cannot be repaid without adequate employment.
- Imprisonment of African American women and men exerts a tremendous impact on the well-being of their families and children.
- In places such as Ferguson, Missouri where African

Americans comprised 63% of the city's driving-age population in 2013, they accounted for 86% of drivers stopped. This accounted to almost one for every two black adults versus just over one stop for every eight white adults.

- Additionally, court fines and forfeitures accounted for 20% of Ferguson's operating budget in 2013.

Every statistic represents a personal story for Black Americans who are impacted by having a loved one in prison. This Wise Woman, whose great-grandfather was likely imprisoned in one of the prison farms in Florida, wonders what was it like for him... how did he finally escape and make his way to North Carolina where his wife and family resided? I often think about him and his incomplete story.

But, to end on a note of positivity and change, at some point after my encounter with the picture essay on The Tombs, and perhaps because of being exposed in such a shocking, public way, this horrible place was closed. Change is possible.

Black Voter Suppression: A Return to Jim Crowism

The ability for African Americans to vote remains an essential path to obtaining full citizenship and participation in the United States. Unlike other ethnic and racial groups, African American voting rights have been fraught with ambivalence, challenge, and negation. This may be because voting rights are a direct way for African Americans to exercise power and authority. As I write these words, the Republican Party in the United States is actively working towards thwarting legislation by Democrats that would make it easier for Black Americans to vote. Across all three branches of government, conservatives are working to block efforts to address voting disparity. Recently, I was alarmed to hear a key Republican leader indicate that Donald Trump, who has played a major role in voting suppression among Black Americans, would be integral to the upcoming 2024 election. The grim truth is that many in our leadership are more than willing to obstruct and prevent access to voting. It is now more important than ever for us to seize the opportunity to demand change to our voting system. I call on all African Americans to gain insight, understanding and knowledge regarding our importance and power. Such knowledge is organic to our capacity to be productive and effective citizens and offers us the opportunity to act and to heal. I call on all Americans to support our fight for the basic rights of any democratic society. How do we understand the history of voting suppression for African Americans?

The right to vote and education have always been powerful tools for African Americans. Both are among other important, life-sustaining tools which were denied to Black Americans during slavery. Yet even the end of legal slavery with the passage of the 13th Amendment did not secure the right to vote for former slaves. In July of 1868, the 14th Amendment was ratified "extending citizenship to all persons born or naturalized in the United States and also secured all citizens equal protection under the law." Good news? Yes and no.

Despite fundamental changes to our governing documents, not all Americans were thrilled at the possibility of black voters. Skepticism and outright racism persisted, even at the highest levels of government. In 1867, in his Third Annual Message to

Congress, President Andrew Johnson said: "Negroes have shown less capacity for government than any other race of people. No independent government of any form has ever been successful in their hands. On the contrary, whenever they have been left to their own devices, they have shown a constant tendency to relapse into barbarism." I am unable and perhaps unwilling to search for a history that would help us to understand Johnson's comments. My enslaved ancestors had not been given any opportunity to self-govern in this country, so where was Johnson getting his information? On what basis did President Johnson come to that conclusion? When had he ever witnessed a population of "Negroes" who had the right to self-govern and fully participate in a democratic society? Was this yet another example of political and social policies based on a racist belief system?

Given such an outright rejection of the capacity of blacks to be responsible citizens in a democratic society by the highest office in the land, it is perhaps unsurprising that no sooner than the 14th Amendment was ratified, attempts to suppress black voters emerged. One of the first of many violent actions aimed at black voter suppression occurred in September of 1868, in Louisiana, where 250 people were killed while attempting to vote, most of whom were African Americans.

Two years later, in 1870, the United States government ratified the 15th Amendment, "prohibiting states from taking away the right to vote on account of race, color, or previous condition of servitude." But this still wasn't enough to prevent states from trying to curtail the black vote. Only three years later, in April of 1873, again in Louisiana, between 60 and 150 blacks were killed to prevent them from exercising their political power. States were permitted to impose all sorts of conditions on voting, such as poll taxes, literacy tests, and other "creative" tactics that were only ever required of Black Americans. In the film, Selma, Oprah Winfrey brought these experiences to life when she dramatized what it took to pass the literacy test—her character was required to memorize pages and pages of history, a nearly impossible task that was not a requirement for white Americans to vote. Indeed, the Mississippi Convention of 1890 led the southern states to develop a number of implicit and explicit interventions denying the right to vote among Black Americans. One of the leaders of the convention, Circuit Judge James Graves Jr., quoted James K. Vardaman, who later became a governor and a senator: "Mississippi's constitutional convention of 1890 was held for no other purpose than to eliminate the n****r from politics". How were such practices allowed? We must understand that federal and state administrations were careful to hire people they knew would enforce immoral and illegal policies at the grassroots level. The parallels to our current political landscape are harrowing.

I want to emphasize how much violence, and how the threat of violence, has played a role in efforts to suppress black voting rights. During this post-Reconstructive period, historians have noted a tremendous rise in explicit race-based violence which carried over into the Jim Crow era. By the way, white people, who provided, or attempted to provide, assistance to black voters, were also subjected to violence and violent threats. In 1898, the year my grandmother was born in Barbados, as many as 60 black people were killed in Wilmington, North Carolina, when a group of white rebels joined forces with area militias to stage a coup against a duly elected biracial government. The day after the election, the "White Declaration of Independence" was published, which stated, "We will no longer be ruled and will never again be ruled by men of African origin." The courts joined in supporting the disenfranchisement of African Americans in June of 1915 in Guinn vs. the United States, and again in April of 1944 in Smith vs. Allwright. Both decisions, among others, signaled the Courts' alignment with illegal and immoral disenfranchisement of Black Americans.

I recently learned the unbelievable story of Ms. Fannie Lou Hamer, a former sharecropper who became a leading civil rights activist with the Southern Christian Leadership Conference in South Carolina. In August of 1962, Ms. Hamer led 17 volunteers to register to vote at the Indianola, Mississippi Courthouse. They were denied the chance to vote based on an unfair literacy test and harassed by police, "who stopped their bus and fined them $100 on a trumped-up charge that the bus was too yellow."

Ms. Hamer lost her job as a result of her attempt to vote, and much of her and her husband's property was confiscated. They moved to Mississippi. Less than a year later, after completing a voter registration program in South Carolina, Ms. Hamer was on a bus back to Mississippi with other activists. They had been practicing peaceful protests by sitting at "white-only" lunch counters and using white-only restrooms, testing compliance with recent de-segregation legislation. In Winona, Mississippi, Ms. Hamer and her friends were arrested by the local police (who had been alerted by their white bus driver) and thrown into jail, where they were tortured.

One of Fannie Lou's companions was June Johnson. When

June refused to give the police the answers they wanted to hear, they hit her in the face and beat her in the stomach. They tossed her onto the ground where they repeatedly kicked her, tore her clothes, and eventually cracked her skull with a blackjack. June was 15 years old.

But what awaited Fannie Lou was even worse. According to historian-writer David Dennis Jr.:

Then the cops dragged Mrs. Hamer into the cell with the incarcerated Black men, who reeked of alcohol. The officers made one of the men lash her until his arms gave out. Her booming voice, which had awakened the spirit in so many of us, was now a scream of terror. Then it was another imprisoned man's turn. He hesitated. Mrs. Hamer, her dress pulled up to expose her back and buttocks, blood soaking the sheets below her, looked back and, as she later told me, said to the man, "Now go on 'head and do what you gotta do, because they gonna do you worse than you do me if you don't." The man wept as he whipped her. He apologized through tears, but his crying didn't pause his swings.

Ms. Hamer survived and went on to co-found the Mississippi Democratic Freedom Party. She continued to fight tirelessly for African American rights until she died of breast cancer in 1977 at the young age of 59.

As is evident, if we examine the initiation of Constitutional Amendments, it is always necessary to develop amendment after amendment to seek redress for Black Americans. Such was the case in July of 1964 when the signing of the Civil Rights Act prohibited "employment discrimination based on race, color, religion, sex, and national origin." This Amendment was introduced in response to the relentless civil rights movement led by the renowned Rev. Dr. Martin Luther King, Jr. Shortly after this Amendment became law, protests regarding the right to vote continued. The memorable and most violent attack on unarmed and non-violent protestors occurred on March 7, 1965 (known as "Bloody Sunday"). As 600 multi-racial, multi-ethnic, and multi-religious leaders marched peacefully, they were attacked, beaten, and severely injured. John Lewis, the famous leader of the event and noted for his concept of "good trouble," famously made several remarks about fearing for his life during the violent attack. Following the televised assault and coverage by print media, the Voting Rights Act was signed into law in 1965.

Problem solved? Not really. In 2006, President George W. Bush signed legislation extending the Voting Right Act for an additional 25 years. However, following the 2013 Supreme Court case Shelby County vs. Holder, the Court again ushered in the opportunity for the disenfranchisement of Black Americans. Previously, U.S. law required certain jurisdictions with histories of voting discrimination had to seek federal "preclearance" before making changes to their election laws. In Shelby County v. Holder, the Court declared that the 40-year-old method for determining which jurisdictions needed preclearance was outdated and unconstitutional. Soon after the Court's decision, Shelby County, Alabama enacted new photo identification requirement laws that had previously been barred due to federal preclearance. Arizona, North Carolina, North Dakota, Ohio, Wisconsin, and Texas quickly responded with their own voting restrictions. According to a 2020 report by the Southern Poverty Law Center, "Across the Southern states, in fact, you see a litany of polling place closures and photo ID requirements, restrictions on early voting, and efforts to block voting by mail in the midst of the COVID-19 pandemic, with people being forced to choose between their health—and that of their loved ones—and their constitutional rights. We are seeing a disparate impact on people of color." In the 2021 legislative session, Arizona and Georgia held the dubious honor of introducing the highest number of bills restricting voting access.

However, more explicit acts further encroach on the right to vote for African Americans. In July of 2017, Georgia's Secretary of State Brian Kemp purged nearly 600,000 people—8% of the state's registered voters—from voting rolls. Of those, approximately 107,000 names were cut because they had not voted in a recent election. Writing for the *New Yorker*, Jelani Cobb described how Governor Kemp's manipulated voting laws to win the election against Stacey Abrams (a black woman). Kemp invoked what is known as the so-called Exact Match Law to suspend 53,000 voter registration applications for minor infractions, such as missing a hyphen. While African Americans are 32% of Georgia's population, they represented 70% of the suspended applications.

The ACLU (American Civil Liberties Union) chronicled another move to decrease black voter turnout—restrictions around early or absentee voting. On their website, the ACLU reports that ten states have introduced bills that would reduce early or absentee voting periods. These bills have already been passed in Florida, Georgia, Ohio, Tennessee and West Virginia, states with larger African American populations (according to U.S. census data). Coincidence? I think not. In fact, the data show just how many black voters utilize early voting.

A month after the 2013 Supreme Court decision, North Carolina passed a sweeping bill that would restrict African Americans' access to early voting. Legislators examined the voting patterns of Black Americans and decided to curtail early voting by seven days to exclude a Sunday when black churches in the state would typically bus voters in their congregations to the voting polls as part of what is called "Souls to the Polls Campaign."

In Georgia, where Black voters vote Democrat and make up roughly 1/3 of the state's population, new legislation will limit drop boxes for mail-in ballots, increase voter identification requirements for absentee balloting, and make it a crime to provide food or water to people waiting in line to vote. The bill contains measures to restrict early voting on the weekends. These measures disproportionately affect Black communities.

A poll conducted jointly by *The Atlantic* and Public Religion Research Institute is equally revealing. The poll documents "deep structural barriers to the ballot to Black and Latino voters, specifically for the 2018 election; restrictive election laws seem race neutral but they are not." The poll further revealed "voter suppression is commonplace and that voting is routinely harder for people of color than their white counterparts." Senator Warnock of Georgia agrees. In a speech in December of 2021, he said: "We are witnessing right now a massive and unabashed assault on voting rights unlike anything we've ever seen since the Jim Crow era". Indeed, attempts by Republicans to discredit President Joe Biden's election have been, in many respects, a move to discount the political power of Black Americans. Former President Trump's continual baseless claims of voter fraud were aimed at Black Americans. He targeted cities with a significant Black population, including Philadelphia, Atlanta, Detroit, Milwaukee, and Pittsburg. As you may well be aware, Trump and many others continue to contend he did not lose the election, despite a plethora of certifications and agreements by both Democrats and Republicans. Obviously, Trump hates to be a loser and has yet to concede.

There are those who perhaps will disagree; however, I truly believe the attack on the U.S Capital on January 6, 2021, also known as "The Insurrection," was also meant to send a message to Black Americans: this is a white country, and the Black vote and Black presence are not welcome. The sheer violence aimed at law enforcement, as well as the destruction of the physical representation of our democracy, will forever live in our minds as the manifestation of white supremacy. For many African Americans, such actions signaled a dangerous and frightening movement toward the destruction of a democratic system in which we are still fighting hard to fully participate. For us, January 6 was not about freedom; it was about tyranny, violence, and devastation.

The events of January 6 encouraged me to reflect on the U.S. history books my maternal grandmother studied in preparation for citizenship. Those who attempted to tear down our treasured democracy make a mockery of my grandmother's desires and treasured citizenship. She worked hard all her life and contributed to the building of our nation. Rain or shine, she never missed voting in an election. Neither did my other family members, who were active participants and leaders in the local Democratic Party. I looked forward to the day when I would be old enough to register to vote, and I marched with pride and enthusiasm to the polls. I also recall with pride when my weak and ailing mother, who was in her 80s, stood in a long line to vote for President Obama. These are the memories I recollect when I think about the concerted efforts to challenge African American voting rights. I am saddened beyond belief.

Senator Warnock's words have repeatedly echoed in my mind, reminding me that the path towards my own healing and that of my fellow Black Americans is not without obstacles, challenges, and confrontations. However, by the same token, it is incumbent upon us to seize, with urgency and care, the political power and authority afforded to us as citizens of this country. It is our democratic right, obligation, and necessity.

Dear Reader, please keep in mind that the historical and statistical information that I have presented had an enormous impact on the identities and experiences of Black Americans, including the lives of George Floyd and our ever-growing list of murdered Black people in this country. Understanding these disparities is essential to understanding their deaths and preventing future harm. As you process the amount of data this chapter has thrown at you, please keep in mind that these disparities are intersectional and overlapping experiences—they are connected to each other and, as such, exert a powerful influence on our identities. Multiple and intersectional feeling states are wrapped up in all of this as well. We aren't only talking about sociological realities—we are talking about the inner-worlds and emotions that Black Americans, such as George Floyd, experience as part of our intersectional identities.

The historical and statistical information I've recounted here substantiates the claim that we are witnessing the re-enslavement of African Americans. Our Justice System joins other systems in our country in a lengthy objectification process that continues to impact me and my ancestors. We are not seen worthy and valued as human beings. Why else would there be such ongoing and relentless disparities between the care and treatment of white versus Black Americans? When will we begin to understand that we must change our thoughts, words, and deeds, and embrace the multidimensionality that real and meaningful change demands?

However, before we can initiate and implement the urgent change necessary, we must pause. Focus. Breathe in. Breathe out. Breathe in. Breathe out. We need an in-breath to take in the vibration of healing and an out-breath to exhale the vibration of pain and hurt.

Chapter 9

Healing Our Communities, Healing Ourselves

    In previous chapters, we have explored historical, conceptual, and current disparities among the various institutions within the United States, in order to assess how societal legacies impact our identities. But is it possible there's more to the story of our healing? Indeed, there are a number of highways and byways yet to be discovered. After all, I am certain you will agree that healing is an individualized, multidimensional and personal experience. In this chapter, we will continue on our path towards holistic healing by exploring how we can promote healing within our immediate communities, our families, and even within ourselves.

Creating Communities of Care

To create environments of healing we must first create environments that are safe—and feel safe. What does this mean, exactly? Well, there are many dimensions to feeling safe. Some include individual feelings of internal and external safety, a sense of predictability in your life, and a general expectation that you will not come to harm. Being and feeling safe also includes the extent to which you are welcomed and respected within your community and protected by those who are empowered and authorized to maintain a safe environment.

Additionally, an essential aspect of feeling safe is the ability to know where, and from whom, to obtain help. This is especially difficult for those with language barriers or new to the specific community. There are many communities that are so large that it's difficult to know where to turn for help. The classic strategy of "knowing somebody who knows somebody" may not available. Historically, community help centers, or Settlement Houses, had places where people could obtain help. Centers where information and access are fully integrated and culturally and linguistically competent can contribute enormously to feeling helped and safe. Additionally, the offices of local politicians can be helpful, but only if we understand where and how to access and obtain these resources.

Sometimes, a feeling of safety and security may come from an unexpected source. For example, in a number of communities where there are gangs, older people feel safe because there is respect among gang members for the elderly. A gang member may be observed carrying groceries for an elderly person, who may, in turn, experience feelings of safety. However, the opposite may be true for other community members. We are aware that many gang members commit horrific crimes.

Sometimes, external conditions may cause or exacerbate feelings of being unsafe in our communities. For example, many of the women I've worked with, who were attacked and raped, felt unsafe in their communities; however, they did not have the choice of relocating, due to poverty. Large housing projects in many cities within the United States have become havens for violence, drug trafficking, and assaults. For many of the working poor, these residences are the only places they can afford. Perhaps you will recall the tragic story of Jenalda from Chapter 5, who was assaulted and raped when she left her apartment in the projects to get milk for her children. After her horrific assault, the police brought her to our hospital where she was seen by our mobile crisis staff and treated for Post-traumatic Stress Disorder. During that time, the entire Emergency Department underwent a comprehensive training initiative focused on the care of the rape victim. Our role was to provide her follow-up care. Through consistent and ongoing advocacy, we were able to help her move to another location. However, I am unsure if her experience and situation improved. Indeed, there is so much unchartered territory when it comes to creating positive and safe communities. However, it's essential that all of us advocate for safety and security within our communities in order to begin to heal some past ills and traumas.

Warriors or Protectors: Changing Perceptions of Police

Where to start…there is so much work to be done in the arena, especially when it comes to the relationship between many African Americans and a substantial number of members of the police. For many of us, the police represent terror and harm, a reminder of the armed slave catchers during enslavement. When we look at history (as we have attempted to do in this book), we find century after century of incorrect, ineffective, and reprehensible police practices. We find police occupying the role of warriors, and, in some instances, flexing the strong arm of institutions aimed at reinforcing a racial caste system. Is it reasonable to believe that if many members of our community, including physicians, teachers, academics, storeowners, and others, are guilty of bias, how can we expect police to feel and behave differently? Is it possible for police personnel to retain and maintain all the training and expectation of their roles, including issues around bias? In Ferguson, Missouri (and other communities), police were used to obtain revenue for the community by issuing violations for somewhat innocuous events. Did that role for police as de-facto tax collectors drive a wedge in the relationship between the police and people (Black) in the community?

I am reasonably certain that some police must be confused about their roles, and, at times, feel in conflict with courts, prosecutors, and their supervisors. Yet at present, our strategies for handling encounters with police are not consistently successful. Namely, many of us teach our youth the importance of remaining calm when stopped by a police officer. It has been ineffective in a number of circumstances, because there exist no consistent standards of and/or expectations for police behavior across communities and states. You never know how an officer may react.

Once, while en route to pick up our son from sleep-away camp on the border between upstate New York and Pennsylvania, my husband and I were stopped by a very young police officer who could have easily been our son. I believe we were going five to ten miles over the speed limit. While we remained polite and respectful, there was something within that particular officer that made him direct anger towards us. He had an incessant need to demean and scold us. We calmly explained that we needed to pick up our son, but he continued on and on. The take-away message for Black Americans is that we never know in what frame of mind a police officer may be. It's important to read any given situation intuitively, especially the needs of the officer—is this a warrior or someone truly committed to safety? A just "grin and bear it" attitude may not seem like the most helpful response; however, it may be the safest response under certain circumstances—we may need to employ this attitude to remain safe and sound. While we can all try hard not to be stopped by police, the truth is it's a crapshoot. We must prepare and manage situations in light of what makes sense for us at any given moment. To put it lightly, if we are going to provide an address to the Klan, we don't want to talk about the merits of Malcolm X! When it comes to keeping ourselves safe and out of harm's way (to the extent that we are able), we must do whatever it takes.

How do the police separate criminals and non-criminals? Some believe in instinct, while others may have an informal, unscientific criteria (such as racial profiling). I hope you will allow me to share my own experience of a powerful intuition that warned me that I was in close vicinity to a criminal. Once, while driving to New Jersey, I spotted a rather tall, white, heavyset gentleman in an older model Lincoln or Cadillac, who was trying to pass me. I let him pass, and the man moved ahead of me, but not before shooting me a sinister glare—it was truly menacing. His energy was so sinister that I could feel anxiety rising from my stomach and flowing throughout my body. I felt myself to be in danger. Why was he so angry? Because I did not move quickly enough to allow him to pass me? My very strong intuition told me he was certainly involved in organized crime. I had a gut feeling that this was not a person I wanted to cross paths with! Here was a man who did not fit the standard racial profile for a criminal and would probably not be targeted for a "routine" stop by the police. Profiling doesn't work. We need a new system for the identification and apprehension of the true criminals in our communities.

Changing police culture and our relationship with the police is a tremendously difficult undertaking. Demands among communities to dismantle the police force were based on examples of police violence that resulted in the murder of unarmed individuals such as George Floyd. Demands based on trauma and experiences of powerlessness are hard to fight against. Citizens such as I do not want to see effective and positive officers shot or injured by criminals. However, we must take a more strategic and multi-directional approach, perhaps starting on a small scale to build partnerships between the police and our communities. We need a number of approaches, including defining clear roles for police, and providing mental health assistance, education, training and meaningful employment for youth and adults seeking work. After-school programs and community centers are sorely needed. Smaller public housing that is more manageable with access to services for people who need them would go a long way as well. There is so much that needs to be done in this arena.

Strategies for Safety

Ask yourself: Do you give yourself choices in situations that may not serve to support your sense of self?

In the pain and heat of the moment, we can potentially do damage to ourselves. For example, maybe you've had a very stressful week. On top of that, several times you've experienced microaggressions from co-workers or members of your community (perhaps when opening the door to your spacious home in the suburbs that you've earned through talent, hard work and savings, only to be mistaken for the maid…). You may ask yourself:

- *What will serve me well in this situation?*
- *Are there ways I can get my point across without feeling my only recourse is to blow the place up?*

After the immediate threat has subsided, you may have to nurture yourself and seek a supportive individual to help you heal your immediate wounds and perhaps figure out next steps. You may consider ways in which the pain and hurt associated with feeling unsafe in your community may be lessened. Are there ways to increase our internal fortitude that help to lessen the pain of these encounters?

Reframing Our Familial Legacies and Identities

All too often people—the ordinary, average folk who make up most of the earth population—frame their family backgrounds either positively or negatively. And that particular mindset tends to color how we see ourselves and our families as either good or bad. We often inculcate either positive or negative feelings about ourselves that impact our opportunities to develop and evolve. It is through family, after all, that we are socialized and inculcated into living within ones' community. I often wonder the extent to which we may stunt our own growth and development by limiting our potential as a result of the mistakes and choices our family members may have made. We may deny or inflate the characteristics of family members so that they neatly fit in our mind's constellations of positive and negative.

So much of what we may have experienced might have been cloaked in secrecy and shame, especially in situations of incest, sexual abuse and other terrible secrets. We also limit ourselves when we inflate or overly glamourize our family members. I have witnessed situations in which people came up with narratives that bordered on delusional, as a way for them to cope with negative experiences in their family. We have a tendency to bind ourselves to identities of dysfunction, mired in negativity. Without guidance, we may perpetuate multidimensional dysfunction in mind, body, and spirit in our relationships with others, especially with our mates. So why does this happen? How is it that we come to see our families one-dimensionally, good or bad, happy or dysfunctional?

From a medical standpoint, we may feel doomed by genetic markers of diabetes, high blood pressure, and depression, for example, dismissing opportunities for preventative self-care that could address some of these potential problems. And yes, there are maybe those of us who believe, both from a career and lifestyle standpoint, that we must follow the path established by our foremothers and fathers. For some, this means following a safe path of civil or public service, teaching, nursing, social work, etc., when what we really want is to go to art school, act, take the risks of a Wall Street career, or stay home and raise a family. For others, it means achieving the same level of financial security as their parents, or numbly going to mass every Sunday when, in fact, our minds, bodies, and spirit soar at the thoughts of something else.

We have been deluged with media images of familial perfection. On TV and in the movies, we see families with sufficient housing and financial resources, mothers and fathers (heterosexual) who gleefully get along and love each other unconditionally. We see children who rarely have problems in school and dutifully complete their homework. And even when problems or challenges arise, there always seems to be cheerful, simplified solutions presented with a smile. Although youngsters today are growing up with a more diverse set of images, most Baby Boomers, Gen Xers, and Millennials got variations on the same themes of heteronormativity, prosperity, unconditional love and a problem-solving "can-do" spirit. And I am sure you also know that the degree to which you and your family "fit in" with society can create conflicts large and small in our lives. What was your family's relationship to society at large? And how did that relationship influence your family dynamics and sense of self?

Such was the case in my own life where Donna Reed, June Cleaver and other icons represented the fulfillment of the American familial dream—a dream I knew did not mirror my own family nor the possible family of my own that I might have in the future.

In reality, despite trends towards increasing diversity in the media, not much has changed since the days of the Cleavers (or even the Huxstables!). Consider the present icons of familial success. Whether in entertainment, athletics, or business, "successful" families are still largely portrayed as heterosexual couples with happy kids and few financial troubles. We are meant to believe that wealth solves the problems of family dysfunction, yet we all know this to be untrue. I needn't take the time to delineate the numerous famous families I've come into contact with where money has not solved the problems of substance abuse, communications, divorce, teen-age pregnancy, etc. (as I write this, Mary Trump has just released her memoir about her family's troubled relationships). Why are we fed spoonfuls of idealized families that do not exist, and we know this, yet we continue to move towards them with energy and zeal?

I would offer a hypothesis at this point: an essential step in reframing our family's context is to cast off images of success and failure. The truth is, most families, including my own, have elements of both the positive and the negative. Families are complex and messy. And while I do not want to minimize the past traumas you may have been dealt, I do want to assure you that healing is possible. Learning to truly "see" our families for both the good and the bad, the ugly and the beautiful, will help you heal.

Once we can let go of our attachment to the skewed versions of our familial pasts, we can shift our energy towards forgiving ourselves and others. All of us have been impacted in one way or another by a multitude of events, slights, neglect, hurtful words and attitudes acted out by parents and other members of our family. The extent to which we carry unresolved damage differs from individual to individual. Wherever you are in your journey of reconciling yourself with your family and your upbringing, an important element in the reframing process is forgiveness.

The process of forgiveness is far too important to gloss over, and there have been numerous books, studies, videos, and erudite lectures on this subject. I speak from my personal and professional experience of treating thousands of people who harbored anger, frustration, and hurt towards their parents and/or other family members. Their feelings were like an awful case of emotional constipation—they were unable to fully express and experience the full gamut of human emotions and authenticity in other relationships. When we choose to not forgive ourselves and/or someone who has hurt us, there seems to be a negative shift energetically. Aspects of our personal power remain with that person. That's power and energy that can be put to better use! For some people, the inability to forgive is related to feelings of depression, sadness, insomnia and anxiety. On the other side, practicing forgiveness has been aligned with wellness: improved sleep, lower blood pressure and relief from other medical ailments.

Please keep in mind that there is a significant difference between forgetting and forgiving. We do not have to forget the slight or hurt, but I do think it is helpful to remove the powerful emotional energy attached to whatever or whomever we can't forgive. This includes situations in which there is no opportunity to contact the person who has hurt us.

Many of us may find that we require help in the process of forgiving, especially ourselves. It may be difficult to come to terms and acknowledge the immense feelings we had/have for that person, i.e., "I always wanted my father to love me," or "I had the darkest skin in my family and was the scapegoat." Remember my own story of being told by a graduate school professor that I would never become a social worker because, "you people have a problem with writing"? Between a good therapist and a host of supportive friends, I began to acknowledge the hurt and pain this assessment of me caused, and how it related to past and present themes in my life overall. Not feeling good enough has been a life-long scenario that I have felt both outwardly and inwardly. This professor had power and authority over me, and her opinion mattered at that time. As I processed the hurt and pain she caused me, I gradually began to come to terms with the fact she really did not know me or my potential. Only then was I finally able to let go of that horrific experience.

While I'm not saying that you have to follow in my steps, I do believe that type of acknowledgement can take a great deal of strength and courage. Coming to terms with our vulnerabilities isn't easy. Therefore, you may need to seek help from a trusted mentor or counselor to help navigate these unchartered waters. There are also a number of workbooks, self-help books and other ways to begin this process. The first step is perhaps the hardest.

Another essential element in this important process of reframing is to candidly assess and review which unique characteristics of our family's legacy currently serves us, and which do not. To be more specific, *are we able to move towards the successful identity and legacy we wish to leave during our time on this earth?*

Straight Talk: Healing Our Familial Wounds

Only you can know the extent to which your family's legacy contributes to, or detracts from, your personal evolution. Family Therapy, one of the many tools utilized in the mental health treatment community, posits that most individual problems can be understood within the context of the family. Family Therapy works from the premise that changes within the individual can propel changes within the family. You may find this to be a useful perspective.

Take stock of what is working and not working towards the success you know you deserve. Often, this can be scary and daunting for people fraught with the dark steps of the unknown. To that end, you may enlist the support of a trusted mentor, counselor, or perhaps a mental health professional to join you in this important sojourn. Enlist and request assistance from whomever you recognize as your higher power—God, Allah, Buddha, a host of others immortalized in the world's spiritual and religious communities, or perhaps your higher power is your belief in your best self.

There is something intangible about the importance of calling out for support, reassurance, healing and grace from our higher power (I discuss this in greater detail later in this chapter). Tune into the spiritual inner-self that supports your ability to feel—whichever of your emotions, thoughts, or feelings. Your feelings and thoughts will help you unravel and discern some of the conflicts and challenges that may at times seem insurmountable. You may consider asking yourself:

1. *What are the things I received from my family that helped to promote my sense of satisfaction and progress?*

2. *Were there problem-solving approaches that were helpful to them and may be helpful to me?*

3. *Are there things that I have been inculcated with that will limit my development and success?*

4. *Have there been instances where the limiting self-scripts have prevented me from taking the risks that may open unchartered but potentially rich territory?*

Perhaps the focused and strategic intervention is to begin to reframe difference. We can reframe our family and societal legacies as neither positive nor negative but as opportunities for growth and healing. Equally important is the careful and thoughtful evaluation of what changes may be necessary. I will grant you, taking stock is a potentially difficult and fearful process. We are inviting ourselves to potentially critique a way of thinking or being supported by many years of tangible and intangible evidence of its existence. However, if we miss this necessary step and move forward to reframing, we may end up simply pasting enlightened information on top of damaging thoughts and ideas. Think of this process in terms of a cake: while the outside, covered in frosting, may seems luscious and inviting, beneath, the cake might be rancid and uncooked.

In addition, it is essential to concretely visualize your "new and improved" framework. Use your mind and senses to design and create the new picture you have developed. You are the creative genius in the process, and you must own the product from beginning to end. This is your masterpiece, and you are the artist!

While this may seem like the end point, it indeed is not. Once your masterpiece has been created, you must ensure your entire body, mind and spirit has fully bought into this "new and improved" perspective. This may be the time to test out this redesign to ensure you will not revert to old habits and perspectives, which is easy to do. I suggest you create reminders either visual, oral, or other methods to ensure you stick to these wonderful creations.

I truly believe we all have to own the reality that what we may need and desire is hard to accomplish and definitely harder to sustain. But that doesn't mean we should be hard on ourselves or become daunted by the challenge. Again, I suggest that mindfulness around the challenges associated with profound change can go a long way. It may take more than one try to succeed, and that's ok. Again, seeking a mentor, counselor, coach or therapist may also provide much-needed support and an objective viewpoint in initiating, developing and sustaining this process.

Further Paths Towards Familial Healing

It's essential to understand the concept of family has widely differentiated understanding among various ethnicities and nationalities. As we have seen, one version of the "perfect" "family" may not easily translate to other cultures. Many of us who grew up in a different model of family feel stigmatized for not being part of the norm. As a result, the potential confluences or conflicts between ourselves, our family, and our society have different ramifications for people who feel themselves to be somehow "different" from society's norm.

For example, among African Americans the term "family" extends beyond bloodlines to include "fictive kin." Fictive kin is an anthropological term used to describe a kinship relationship that is not based on blood relationship but is similar in commitment and intensity to a blood relationship. During our enslavement relationships, roles and responsibilities could change depending on the needs, aspirations and whims of the "owner;" therefore, the notion of what constitutes a familial relationship was much more malleable. To this day in many black households, your mother's best friend may be referred to as "Aunt," and her children may be called "brother," "sister," or "cousin." Godparents, too, play important roles and may be called upon for childcare, financial contributions, and, in some instances, childrearing. Personally, as I have expanded my understanding of these relationships, I have found understanding in our West African past, where older women are referred to by the honorific "Ma" or "Mama."

When we discuss paths towards healing, it's so important for us to include a frank and generous understanding of family and the extent to which family impacts the experience of trauma among individuals. We need to be attuned to how we may have come to internalize the "ideal family" and judged our families to be lacking.

As members of a wider community, we are naturally inculcated with the cultural values of that community. However, it's individuals who make up our communities, and each individual may have a different understanding or interpretation of their community's values. When we study and examine the experiences of a community, we must also explore the expansive and multidimensional experiences of the individual within the community. We must look to our individual inner-worlds, our psychological, biological, cognitive, and physical selves. So, let us explore the complex inner world of the individual, and let us gather the understanding we need to heal.

Unraveling Understanding

I struggled far and wide with a particular situation
Which at times caused medical and physical distress
Sadness, despair leading me to feel quite the mess

I searched far and wide for answers and resolve
Asking questions, reading, praying, and asking
Our Dear Father
In a manner some may say is bold

This is another personal situation
That through internal churning

Up and down, in and out
That at last I gave birth
To the following notation

These written ramblings of mine
In principle are sojourns
Healing resolve and peace
And a spiritual journey
To let conflict cease

I have spoken to many with pain
Of the very personal decision
One of my blood kin
Decided to make without gain

When I first learned of her transition
I cried both inside and out
Conflicted with powerlessness, horror, guilt and pain
Not understanding what she had to gain
I felt left out
Put out
Of circumstances I could not fully understand
I could not find solace in spite of the demand

At a later date I could not recall
That I did not fully
Grant myself
The opportunity to remember
The multiple blood kin losses
That occurred well before September

Please keep in mind
That if an individual might ask
Do you believe a person has the right
To live their life with all their might

I would be the first on line
To vote a resounding yes
Using a Nordstrom's-bought pen
That writes so very fine

And so, I think Our Dear Savior
Has taught me a lesson or two
In the importance of so many things
That I most sincerely must do

I pray you are healed
As you read these confusing words
As unraveling understanding
Is like the process
Of eating a fine meal
Take a lot of time
Enjoy the courses
Savor the tastes
The bitter and the sweet
And acknowledge and honor
Our loved ones' powerful choices

Unraveling the Senseless: Reframing Our Personal Pain and Legacies of Trauma

Life can be incomprehensible. It can take all of our internal and external resources to try and make sense out of the senseless. And still, the decisions and choices of others are often a mystery to us. Sometimes we try to understand the actions of others, based upon our perceptions of those people. Perhaps we engage our empathy when we try to follow the path of someone else's logic.

How is it that Derek Chauvin decided to seize Mr. Floyd? How is it he placed his weight on a handcuffed Mr. Floyd in broad daylight in the middle of a neighborhood street? Did he think his actions would have no consequences? Did he feel so empowered that he cared little for any consequences? Was he simply not thinking at all? Why didn't his colleagues intervene? What were their thoughts and perspectives? Did the officers consent to a tacit denial of Mr. Floyd's civil rights? Did they understand and agree to murder?

Questions like these reverberate through my mind as I think about the senselessness of all the murdered Blacks and people of color discussed in previous chapters—so seemingly senseless that I am unable to utilize my own logic to parse the events, to understand the rationale or mindset of the perpetrators. We can only speculate that the intersectional feeling states of privilege, anger, power, combined with an authoritarian personality style, all contributed to the inner worlds of the police officers who committed these murders.

Yet, the truth is that we don't have to look far outside our own lives to find questions and mysteries, behaviors and choices, which appear pointless, meaningless, and even irrational, yet are made by our loved ones. The inspiration for the poem above came from learning how my beloved cousin made the decision to keep her cancer a secret. It was extremely hurtful to learn, all at once, of her death, her prolonged suffering, and the vow of secrecy kept by her closest family members. I grieved the loss of someone I loved. And I grieved the lost opportunity to help her, to minister to her needs and offer respite to those around her who would have benefitted from added support. In a whirlwind of emotions, I sought explanations from her immediate circle as to why she chose not to disclose her condition. No one gave me a reasonable answer. I relived our moments together, remembering when I last saw her, dissecting my memories for clues to her condition in her appearance, her voice—what had I missed? I was left with a chaos that defied logic.

The same thing happened with a very close friend, a man I grew up with and was honored to call, "brother." I was only notified of his impending death when his bodily functions began to fail. And again, I found myself writhing in powerlessness, guilt, and pain—all rooted in my inability to understand their decision and my inability to be part of these dear people's transition.

You may notice the many I's in these paragraphs. Without the opportunity to process my loved ones' decisions, I was left with the I's. I felt similarly about trying to understand and process the murder of Mr. George Floyd and other murdered people of color. As I continued to struggle with the decisions of others, I began to see aspects of my self-absorption in my ruminations. So, I tried something. I began to focus less on my own feeling. And, as I thought less about myself—my hurts, my pain, my powerlessness, and my feelings of loss—I opened myself to the perspectives of others. I began to make sense out of the senseless. Both the officers who committed those crimes and my loved ones who chose not to confide in me had their own perspectives, their own choices, and their own need for self-determination—all things I fiercely believe in. And as I journeyed on this path, I began to see my quest for understanding shift from a focus on the choices of others to my own understanding of myself. What other people do, or don't do, does not need to make sense to me. Their decisions may come from multi-dimensional and intersecting feeling states. They may be complex and will likely always be incomprehensible to me. And that is ok. This was my "Aha!" moment.

I learned so much about myself and others from this realization. Indeed, sometimes the obvious is not obvious at all. Most importantly, taking the "I" out of situations, and accepting we may not fully understand the choices of others, paves the road to understanding. It doesn't make the pain and hurt disappear. I carry those heavy, weighty feelings in my mind, body, and spirit. But I can send a soothing message to comfort myself when the feelings seem overwhelming. I can remind myself of my inability to control and manage the behavior of others, whether they be family, friends or the police.

I hope these chapters have inspired you, dear Reader, to take the time to go inward and initiate a personal understanding of yourself, especially the extent to which you have been impacted by your external environment—your community, society, state and nation, as well as various forms of media. I hope that by now you have been, or are feeling, empowered to examine the extent to which this enculturation process began in your infancy and continues within your family context, molding, designing and modifying who you are. As we come to understand our inability to make sense out of the senseless actions of others, are there other aspects of our experiences that also seem quite senseless? Is it possible that, over time and unconsciously, the beautiful light that you were born with has grown dimmer and dimmer?

The *ISMs* That Dim Our Light

Let me explain. For me, the term "light" is an essential part of our personhood. We are all touched by the divine light of our Higher Power at birth. That light increases, decreases, or becomes dismantled, depending upon our circumstances. Our experience of isms can be one of those circumstances. You may recall our working definition of isms from Chapter 2: Racism, sexism, classism, ableism, ageism, antisemitism, homophobia, transphobia, xenophobia and discrimination of all types are isms. They objectify us and can make us feel powerless or "less than" because of who we are. As we have seen in Chapter 8, isms impact every aspect our lives, from our health and wealth to our ability to secure and retain jobs, and our life expectancy; isms take their toll on us, emotionally, mentally, physically, and spiritually.

Have you met individuals who seem lifeless? Have you seen emptiness in their eyes instead of life? Unfortunately, I have. I have met those who have been beaten down by the rigors of poverty, racism, sexism, homophobia, classism, privilege, xenophobia, and more. Sometimes these individuals do not even realize their light has been dimmed as a result of isms. They continue to live their lives as best as possible, seeking small moments of joy.

I recently viewed part of a television series describing the upper classes during the late 1800's in New York City. Although fictional, I suspect that what I am about to share rings true. The scene: a well-dressed and well-to-do African American man and woman are strolling the city streets and talking with one another when a well-dressed, well-to-do white couple approaches from the opposite direction. As the white couple nears the African American couple, they pause, glaring. Promptly, the black couple moves aside, granting the sidewalk to the white couple who walk away with an air of privileged determination, knowing that the conventions of that time have been respected, understood, and their rights observed. This scene aptly depicts how the racial hierarchies of the time dictated small social behaviors, even for free and middle-class African Americans. Sadly, watching this scene unfold, I wasn't congratulating my country on how far we've come since then, nearly 150 years later. I was thinking about the similarities between this scene and any number of experiences in my own life and the lives of people that I know.

I was reminded of a particular incident from my youth when I was walking through the Bronx with Aboagye, a Ghanaian friend, when we crossed paths with a white couple, walking in the opposite direction. My inclination was to move aside and let them pass, but not from a sense of white people having more privilege or authority; I was just being polite. However, my friend gently steered me straight so that the white couple were forced to give way to us. I remember so clearly what my Aboagye said: "You never move aside for them. They move aside for you."

This comment struck me at the time and has stayed with me since. Aboagye was a gentle, warm, and cooperative person. It was unusual to hear him speak so forcefully. But, when I consider his West African context, his behavior makes sense. Coming from Ghana, Aboagye was steeped in a colonial/postcolonial culture and worldview. Under European colonial ideology, Black Africans were made subordinate to white Europeans and their descendants, and social norms dictated that Black Africans had to move out of the way of white people. Coming of age during the years of postcolonial revolutions and independence movements across the African continent, Aboagye understood that a refusal to give way was an act of postcolonial resistance. Although we were far from Africa and in a different social-political context, this incident had triggered my friend's colonial trauma and legacy. The more things change, the more they stay the same.

Interestingly, I feel that I am currently experiencing a moment in which I find myself in more and more situations where I feel white people are exercising their privilege by over-occupying public space. For instance, when I am standing at a cash register or receiving help at a store, frequently white people will try to cut in front of me or interrupt my conversations with their own questions. In these instances, I politely ask them to stop, and they do!

So how do we cope with powerlessness and the isms that threaten to dim our divine light? Do we give up and give in? My ancestors would offer a resounding "no!" They'd remind me how they suffered long and hard for me and many others to enjoy the opportunity of the American Dream. Perhaps your ancestors or community have similar empowering reminders for you. I offer the questions below to help you uncover and confront instances in which your divine light may have been dimmed.

Straight Talk: "ISMs That Dim Your Light"

- Describe the "isms" that have dimmed your light either directly or indirectly. What was that impact?

- How do you define personal instances of powerlessness?

- How have experiences of powerlessness affected you and/or your family? How did you manage those situations? How have you managed and coped with those feelings?

- Have there been circumstances where you have shut down the power of others? How did you manage that situation?

- Do you believe you have privileges?

- If yes, please describe them.

- In what areas of your life do you feel powerful?

- Are there ways in which you would like to increase feelings of powerfulness?

Seizing the Path: Healing from Trauma

We must dispel the notion of suffering in silence as a measure of stoicism and strength. For example, it is not necessarily helpful to listen to advice from well-meaning people who say, "just man up," or "stay strong." When we can speak about our pain, we banish the "demons" (the pain, suffering, and shame) associated with trauma. So many closet their suffering for years, the silence and secrecy only intensifying the horror. Some people believe they deserved their suffering because they were repeatedly told they were worthless. In these situations, we find patterns of incest, domestic violence, addiction, and other traumas that have been passed down from generation to generation across both victims and victimizers.

The remnants of trauma are powerful. However, I believe that healing the wounds of our personal traumas, no matter how horrific, are possible via a number of different paths. To begin, I offer the following opportunities for self-reflection.

Straight Talk: Trauma

- *How do you define trauma?*
- *Have you experienced trauma in your life? What are the specifics?*
- *How has that experience(s) impacted you?*
- *Describe the impact and ways it has shaped you and your identity.*
- *If trauma remains a part of your life, describe how it impacts your present?*
- *What ways have you focused on to manage and cope with trauma?*

Quite often, secrecy, shame and fear propel the harmful power among those who abuse. This is why it is so important to validate and own your traumatic experiences. Owning and validating does not mean accepting the role of powerlessness; it does not mean perpetuating your emotional turmoil. My message and feelings are clear: it is important to share, when appropriate, with people who can offer their support and stand with you in the face of your hurt and pain. A full understanding of the nexus of our pain and the multidimensional aspects of trauma may be helpful to our healing processes. You might find it helpful to ask:

- *Do I lack a sense of safety and security?*
- *Do I feel powerless? Fearful?*
- *Low self-esteem and/or self-concept?*
- *Do I feel damaged?*
- *Do I harbor unresolved anger towards the victimizer and others?*
- *Am I perpetuating negative self-scripts about myself?*
- *Have I been making choices in relationships over and over where my needs are not being met?*

The courageous woman impacted by the likes of Crosby, Weinstein, Epstein, and other men who utilized their power and authority to commit abuses, have done much to address the closeting and secrecy surrounding sexual abuse, incest, and rape. The "Me Too" movement has helped to inspire and promote speaking out, while also removing the stigma associated with being a victim of abuse. These women enable other women who may not enjoy the social status or opportunity to be heard. For every woman who has spoken out, there are others who remained silent, feeling retribution and loss of career status. For this reason, it is essential for this important movement to continue around the world.

When we can speak up and admit that we are suffering, part of our healing also involves reconciling ourselves with who and what has hurt us (in some cases, this may include ourselves), as well as our own role in others' hurt. Reconciling is not the same as aligning yourself with the pathology and criminality of your assaulter, and it's not about blaming yourself or others. I'd like to return to the Spiritualist Principle #5: "Personal Responsibility" from Chapter 6. If you recall, as a religious and ethical tenet, "Personal Responsibility" asks individuals to accept ownership of things they have done, thought, or acted upon. We can apply Personal Responsibility to both victims and victimizers. For victims, Personal Responsibility guides us to take ownership over what happened to us and to decide the extent to which we can move forward. Personal Responsibility does NOT absolve victimizers of their crimes, but it can help them to better understand their actions and the consequences of their actions. It can aid us on our journey to forgive ourselves for the harm we may have caused to ourselves and others. The takeaway is that we need to understand the power and presence of our feelings and process them through the psychological, emotional, and cognitive machinery of forgiveness. It is through this process that we can find resolution and peace from the suffering and turmoil we have experienced. What was done to you will never be "okay." But you, dear Reader, are much, much more than "okay." You have always been, you are now, and you will continue to be a beautiful incarnation of divine Spirit—don't you forget it!

But there is a more fundamental message here—that it's quite possible to survive and thrive in the midst of traumatic experiences. The weight of drama and pain, understandable as it is, doesn't have to define us. We don't have to forget about it or quit thinking about it, but it cannot remain the ongoing theme of our lives. I have found it essential to ask—is this serving me well? I ask this question not from a position of unhealthy narcissism, but rather from self-care, self-efficacy and empowerment. And as children of God—a God who loves, cares and protects their children—this is indeed a part of our divine inheritance.

Straight Talk: What To Do If You Are #MeToo

- If you suspect you are a victim of sexual harassment or sexism, know that what happened to you is not your fault. What happened to you was an immoral and illegal act.

- Ensure that you are safe, and speak with someone in your Human Resources Department or legal authorities, depending on the situation.

- Seek whatever level of help you require: medical, emotional, etc.

- Most employers have specific policies and procedures for handling sexual harassment. Familiarize yourselves with these procedures if you haven't already done so.

- Obtain support from trusted friends, loved ones, and/or counselors.

Straight Talk: Healing from Sexual Abuse and Trauma

We often continue to need help throughout our lifetime in order to process the effects of sexual trauma. For some, the experience of sexual violence is like peeling an onion, there are layers upon layers to process due to the profound impact sexual violence exerts upon our body, mind, spirit, relationships, life choices and so much more. Here are some important resources to consider as you continue your healing journey:

- There are times when even a good friend or loved one isn't capable of providing the continual care that you may need. Do you have access to a trusted therapist or counselor?

- Be responsive to your need for healing whenever and wherever you are in your life and development. Our human needs are the same whether we are young adults or facing older age.

- Self-help groups can be enormously helpful and there are many for people experiencing sexual violence. Googling for resources near you can be helpful.

Straight Talk: Creating Your Self-Care Toolbox

Let us take healing and compassionate strategies a step further by encouraging you, the reader, to develop your individualized tools that provide the caring, compassion, and healing you require. I encourage you to craft and design your own healing plan. You will know, instinctively, what will be most helpful and possibly transformative for you. We are all equipped with the inner knowingness and discernment necessary to understand *for ourselves* what will make a difference for our own body, mind, and spirit.

If you had to name healthy and therapeutic strategies, what would you include?

Consider the following examples:

5. *the names of friends or loved ones whom you might contact*
6. *soothing sounds (I love ocean waves!)*
7. *the essence of oils, like lavender*
8. *a warm bath with candlelight*
9. *reading favorite poems or inspirational works*
10. *listening to your favorite music: gospel, classical, R and B, jazz, opera…do you have a favorite?*
11. *taking time to connect with your Higher Power*
12. *designating a special space in your home/personal space devoted to your healing strategies*

It's traditional practice in mental health to advise individual and group therapy for our patients, but such therapies are often not the best first step for some. I have seen many who first needed massage treatments or grief work before embarking on a course of more traditional therapy. Indeed, I have learned that many so-called non-traditional interventions may be helpful. Such alternatives might include, massage, chiropractic, acupuncture, movement therapies, energy work, meditation, grief work, reiki, mediumship and intuitive work. Any one of these might work in conjunction with another traditional or non-traditional practice.

You must ultimately decide what is best for you. You can do as many of these things as you'd like, because this is **your special, individualized toolbox** created to meet your needs. However, I urge you to create this toolbox when you are not in a state of immediate crisis. A crisis is the time for seeking immediate assistance. In the calmer moments, you may find it helpful to assemble this personalized toolbox, so that should another crisis situation arise, you will feel organized, with multiple tools available for you to utilize.

I have personally observed and provided mediumship, trance healing, and intuitive readings that lifted guilt and pain. Yes, indeed, we do have teams of spiritual helpers who love us and are trying hard to help us develop the skills to manage the experiences that impact our souls' evolvement. We are more powerful than we think.

Divine Healing

Our personal and multidimensional relationship with whatever or whomever we consider our Higher Power is the alpha and omega of working towards healing. Call it God, Allah, Jesus, the Buddha. Identify it by the things we see and experience in nature. Call it divinity, spirit force, spirit power. Whatever we name it, surely it is there. The light of divinity resides in me as well as those around me. Many of us are thankful and feel blessed during times of glee and happiness. However, during the tough times, we may feel (and act) estranged from our Higher Power. Yet it is only by understanding there is something bigger, better and more infinite than ourselves that we come to understand that we can be supported, loved and healed by that spirit power. That spirit power that resides in all of us grows as we walk the journey of spiritual evolution and transformation. And as we work to healing ourselves in thought, word, and deed, that same power can help us to harness and utilize the spiritual force that lies within us to love and be loved.

I have found answers to psychological, intellectual and emotional challenges in my relationship with my Higher Power. In part, my spiritual beliefs and connection to a Higher Power come from being raised in a family of faith and belief. I was socialized in a culture of people who have long put their faith in higher powers—this culture includes my enslaved ancestors, as well as our forefathers and mothers in Africa. You may recall the 1977 movie Roots, which follows the saga of Kunta Kinte, an African man captured by slavers and taken to the United States where he is sold as a slave. I often think of the important and touching scene when Kunta Kinte, now making his life in the United States, baptizes his son in accordance with the traditions and values of his West African tribe. He raises his infant son to the sky, asking for blessings and protection, knowing that there was, and will be, something greater. It is a beautiful and meaningful tradition that survived despite the horrors of the Middle Passage. Similarly, as I discussed in Chapters 3 and 4, my own family's mix of Western and non-Western spiritual practices reflects the persistence of African cultural values, even when they are re-mixed into syncretic faith practices.

I truly believe that my Higher Power has come to my aid in times when I felt powerless. When I was active in ministry at a nearby Episcopalian Church, I had a particularly powerful experience. During the singing of the hymn, "I am the bread of life," celebrating the installation of our priest, the congregation raised their hands in praise. As I raised my hands, closing my eyes, I feel a tremendous surge of energy and power enter my body through my hands. At that very moment, I felt intensely blessed and knew all of my troubles would be resolved. That moment remains life-changing.

"This little light of mine, I'm going to 'let it shine!" These lyrics to a well-known gospel song capture the importance of holding onto the healing light of our Higher Power, even when life threatens to snuff it out. There are multiple ways to keep our Divine light ablaze, and I believe we must develop our own set of tools that define and enhance our unique healing path, focused on our individual mind, body, and spirit. For every healing strategy we may come across, both traditional and non-traditional, I believe wholeheartedly in developing a yardstick to measure what is and is not helpful for us. There is empowerment and fortitude in defining what heals us.

Straight Talk: Strategies for Shining On

We've discussed a variety of different tools and techniques, philosophies and traditions, ideas and approaches that may help you find peace and shine on. As you embark on your healing journey, you may be feeling overwhelmed. You may find yourself "stuck" when it comes to your toolbox, unsure of what to try, or when or how. You may be asking yourself, "How will I know if this works?" You can identify what's helpful or not helpful by asking yourself some questions:

- Have I researched these options? What are the benefits and risks?
- What does that inner voice inside me say?
- What are the costs involved? Are they reasonable? Does the healer have a sliding scale?
- Do the interventions seem dangerous or mind-altering?
- Does the intervention seem to be in synch with my core values, my moral and ethical system?
- Do I know others who have tried it? What has been their experience?

Overcoming Common Obstacles to Healing

I would be remiss if I did not mention the barriers to both traditional and non-traditional interventions. These include glaring health disparities, lack of information, lack of insurance, culturally and linguistically unavailable professional staff, mistrust... the list of things which might inhibit access to potentially helpful interventions is long. And therein lies the enormous conundrum: there are so many ways to derail healing before it even begins. Some revolve around being able to truthfully ask and answer the question, "Do I need help?" Others struggle with access—"I need help, but how do I access it? Is it available?" Other people do not receive culturally sensitive treatment from professionals who lack cultural competencies, while some with multiple or very severe traumas get turned away or receive inadequate care from overwhelmed helping professionals. In some communities, especially amongst African Americans, stigma—the prevailing negative opinions around mental health challenges and treatments—prevents people from seeking help. Indeed, in 1999, Surgeon General Dr. David Satcher issued a monumental report on the state of public mental health care in the United States. His report showed how stigma negatively impacts access to care for all Americans. By exploring the historical roots of stigma and linking history to present day realities, we can create a framework for raising awareness and removing the harmful stigmas that stand in the way of equal access to healing and care.

Stigma: The Often Silent Obstacle To Mental Health and Substance Abuse Care Among African Americans

The term stigma derives from Greek, according to the Merriam-Webster dictionary. Defined as a mark of shame or discredit, "stigma most often refers to a set of negative and often unfair beliefs that a society or group of people have about something." The renowned sociologist Erving Goffman has a slightly more specific take on the origins of stigma. In his landmark work, *Stigma: Notes on the Management of Spoiled Identity*, Goffman writes:

> *The Greeks, who were apparently strong on visual aids, originated the term stigma to refer to bodily signs designed to expose something unusual and bad about the moral status*

of the signifier. The signs were cut or burnt into the body and advertised that the bearer was a slave, a criminal, or a traitor— a blemished person, ritually polluted, to be avoided, especially in public places.

Yet often, stigmas are invisible. For example, it is not always immediately obvious if someone has served time in prison or has a disability. Stigmas are associated with things kept hidden and secret because of shame. But the notion of stigmas is more than an individual response to a circumstance or condition. Stigma is a socio-political and economic construct, based on particular societal and cultural norms. It is rooted in environmental and community culture. Therefore, what is considered to be a stigma in the United States may not be a stigmatizing influence in other nations.

The existence of stigma in African American communities has its roots in ongoing mistrust towards various institutions, especially medical and mental health care. During the 1840 census, for example, researchers noted increased rates of insanity among free blacks in the North. This "research" substantiated the need for African Americans to be enslaved, the reasoning being that freedom caused insanity among free African Americans. Or, review many of the historical events discussed in the previous chapter, including the so-called "Drapetomania" diagnosis, the Tuskegee Syphilis Study, and the unlawful and immoral use of the cells belonging to Henrietta Lacks. Clearly, these examples show the harmful and violent effects that socially constructed stigma can exert on people. From medical malpractice to genocide, is it any wonder African Americans fear and distrust the medical establishment? Stigma persists even today. Many feel their best interests will not be looked after by the U.S.A.'s institutions. The glaring lack of African American physicians and clinicians, combined with the lack of cultural competency, both institutionally and among practitioners, exerts an unwelcoming environment for those in need. The larger environment, both its institutions and clinicians, perpetuate a climate of stigma.

When we fail to decouple stigma from the socio-historic, political and economic conditions out of which they have been constructed, it becomes easy to internalize them and believe they are "real." I am certain that there are those of you who can recall that memorable film *Soul Food*. Do you remember "Big Mama's" brother, who remained alone in his room. No one saw him coming or going, but family members knew he was there. Periodically, family members left food outside of his room. Why was he confined to his room? Was he mentally ill? For some African Americans, to suffer from a mental illness is understood as being "strange," and those "strange" folk need to be "hidden" away from polite society. Further, the care duties for such a person are part of the family's responsibility; the family learns to cope with "strange" behavior.

In my own life, growing up in the South Bronx in the 1960's, we certainly had members of our community who were "strange." They looked and acted differently and, at times, were subject to ridicule, jokes, and other devaluing experiences. In her late teens, my own sister suffered from mental illness, a fact that was kept secret among our immediate family. In retrospect, it is unclear why this happened; it was never explained, and I did not have the courage to ask. Would we have kept the secret if she suffered from heart disease or diabetes? Or, if she became pregnant without being married? Unfortunately, the private mental health system, of which we were a part, did not believe that an African American teenager could suffer from Bipolar Disorder, and she was misdiagnosed while under their care. Perhaps such misdiagnoses are another reason why African Americans are often reluctant to seek mental health care.

The idea of having a mental health diagnosis is seen as terribly stigmatizing. I have heard many of my own patients de-emphasize traumas such as childhood sexual and physical abuse, and experiences of neglect and maltreatment. Those African Americans who may be suffering from a major depression dismiss their clinically diagnosable symptoms simply as the "blues" and suffer in silence with many debilitating symptoms such as despair, sadness, insomnia, hopelessness, helplessness, guilt; and for others, anger, agitation and physical symptoms such as pain, headaches, etc. More than once, I have heard that seeing a therapist is seen as a sign of weakness. For many, including some in my own family, accessing mental health care was seen as something that would look bad on their record and prevent them from getting a job. Others have stated that accessing mental health and substance abuse treatment indicates a poor reflection on the family's ability to handle problems, indicating failure. For many who are religiously or spiritually focused, they believe that fasting and praying will handle all difficulties. Although religious and spiritual practices have been found to be helpful in both mental health and substance abuse treatment, fasting and praying alone may not be the sole interventions to address a pressing need. I remember an African American minister who had not been trained in mental health and had not seen such training as a significant part of his ministry. However, he was forever changed when, one sunny afternoon, one of his male parishioners called him in crisis, stating he had a knife and was going to kill himself. This parishioner was severely depressed and could not see a way out of his debilitating feelings. As a result, the minister felt called to step into his leadership, finding ways to bring mental health services to his parish and to educate other ministers.

Again, in my own family, such problems were kept silent until there were legal ramifications. Our family focused on managing the situation through strong advocacy and calling in favors. We often were not able to afford costly substance abuse treatment for our loved ones. I have seen a pattern where many choose self-medicating with alcohol and other dangerous drugs as an alternative to medical and professional help. The ongoing use of these substances becomes a coping mechanism with serious consequences. Sadly, many black mothers and grandmothers silently support the drug habits of their sons, daughters, grandsons and granddaughters, feeling powerless to manage seemingly impossible situations. Their management may be the best way they know how to keep their loved one out of prison. They are often placed in the situation where they feel compelled to lie, pay off the drug dealers, or seek other resources within their community. I remember a client who suffered from severe rheumatoid arthritis and lived on her benefit check, while supporting her son's drug habit by crocheting blankets for sale. She often had to ask her customers for payment in advance because her son needed a fix, and she was frightened. And we must all remember the terrorizing story in the Spike Lee classic, *Do The Right Thing*, when a father (played by Ossie Davis), angry and fed up with supporting his son's (played by Samuel L. Jackson) drug habit, shoots him while his mother (played by Ruby Dee) hopelessly looks on, crying.

When we split off important parts of ourselves as a result of stigma and stigmatization, it impacts our mind, body and spirit, and often these experiences express themselves in other parts of our lives. Isn't it essential that we pay close attention to aspects of not only our physical health but our mental health too? So, what can we all do to eradicate stigma, regardless of which specific community we come from?

Straight Talk: Saying Goodbye to Stigma

1. Ask yourself: Do you engage in self-stigma? Be honest with yourself and those around you.

2. Ask yourself: Have you prevented yourself or members of your family from obtaining much-needed mental health care?

3. Be aware: are you perpetuating the stigmatizing process? Do you use language that denigrates those with mental health and substance abuse problems? Do you diagnose people with conditions (i.e., schizophrenia, bipolar, etc.) even though you are not trained to do so?

4. Do you diminish the personhood of people who have mental health challenges by referring to them by their diagnosis?

5. Get the facts. The computer affords us access to information about physical and mental healthcare. If you don't have access to a computer, visit your local library.

6. Speak with healthcare professionals you trust and obtain information.

7. Ensure you have confidence and trust in your primary care doctor to ask all and any questions. Your primary healthcare provider can be your first access to care and a possible referral.

8. If you have private insurance, be aware of what is covered. Most insurance plans have adopted parity for physical and mental health care. If you do not have health insurance, many communities have ways to access care through public care.

And if you want to do more to actively fight against stigmatizing, consider the following strategies:

- Begin to raise awareness about these issues. Shame and fear keep people quiet. The more people begin to speak, the closer we are to eradicating stigmas. I applaud the efforts of well-known celebrities who have spoken out about their mental illnesses and substance abuses.

- Let people know when they are stigmatizing.

- If you belong to a church, civic or social organization, consider doing a health fair and inviting mental health and substance abuse clinicians to participate. Engage participants in your community in something that is needed and positive. They, too, will have an opportunity to learn.

- Outreach to your local Mental Health Association. Substance abuse services and other resources are a phone call or email away.

- Consider the opportunity to engage in Mental Health First Aid Training. This is a wonderful training opportunity for citizens to obtain knowledge and skills that demystify mental health and substance abuse problems. The training is not designed to have you treat conditions. It is focused on helping individuals to obtain the help they need from a professional. You should contact your County or State Mental Health Department for information.

- Utilize your faith and/or spiritual community to help identify resources. A church in my community developed a resource guide with the names and address for mental health and substance abuse clinicians, many of whom were African Americans.

These are just a few steps towards eradicating stigma in our communities. I assure you it all starts with the power and perspective of one person to eradicate this self-defeating and disempowering phenomenon.

As we have journeyed together through this chapter, discussing healing from so many vantage points, my dear readers may ask whether or not I myself have utilized any of the many interventions and understandings that are chronicled. In order to answer this important question, let me return to the symbol of my worn and weary bucket, the symbol I have returned to throughout this book. Did I turn to any of my own ideas and suggestions when that bucket eventually tipped over, overflowing with grief and trauma in response to the murder of George Floyd and many other black people who made their transition too soon, due to police violence? Have I sought out any of these healing modalities when faced with the reality that a pattern of profiling, racial hatred, and a seemingly irreparable schism between black people and the police continues to exist? How have I managed my own distress when the isms that plague our country continue to exist?

The answer is *yes*. Yes, indeed, I have found many of these ideas extremely helpful. And because my own healing is akin to the peeling of a very large onion, I continue the quest. I continue to seek out healing interventions. I continue to add tools to my toolbox, or different combinations of existing tools. The writing of this very book has been one of those tools! In the face of continued traumatic assaults on my mind, body, and spirit, I find it necessary to increase my inner and outer spiritual bandwidth. Trauma affects us all, regardless of who we are, where we come from, how trained or untrained we are in the management of pain.

We will all be impacted by circumstances that affect us and those we love. There may be times when we feel as if we can't escape these tragedies. We all experience challenges that threaten to dim our beautiful, divine light. In times of chaos, grief, terror and despair, our light may diminish—for some it may feel that the light has gone out completely. However, that is precisely the time to cry out for help, to ask for the sustenance and grace of spirit power to bring you through even the toughest of tough times. Now is the time to erect a powerful bridge for you to cross towards the possibility of healing.

I want to remind my gentle readers that part of healing also includes designing a life that includes experiencing joy and happiness. The journey of managing challenges and assembling your toolbox of healing interventions doesn't have to be arduous! There are opportunities to fill our lives with joy and passion—isn't that also part of our birthright from a loving, caring Mother-Father God? In the following chapter, I will share some life-giving opportunities and strategies for initiating and implementing more joyousness in your life.

Chapter 10

Where Do We Go From Here?

    This chapter was difficult to write. I had the words, and I knew what needed to be said, but I still resisted facing the end of this sojourn. There was a moment where I thought I should just abandon this project, leaving my neonate in utero, un-birthed. As some of my readers might know, a baby in utero has a special and profound experience with its mother. As an infant grows, a mother knows her body and spirit are nourishing her baby into life. It is a sacred and special process. In my own life, I remember the first feeling of life as my little one moved about in my womb and the sense of wonderment I experienced. And so, I hesitated to end the closeness and intimacy writing this book has brought into my life. However, my family, spirit friends, and helpers reminded me: the story that ends here is also a beginning. What do I mean? This chapter is all about celebrating our mind, body, and soul by honoring and infusing the people, places, and things we love most. I explore how we can integrate healing *and* joy in order to craft a life worth living. A life that shakes down to something like one-quarter healing and three-quarters living our lives. In this chapter, the Wise Woman's counsel is all about that three quarters. It's about celebrating new beginnings. So we are exactly where we should be.

A Reminder—Where Have We Been?

Before we move on, it's important for us to take a moment to reflect on where we have been. In the previous chapters, I have endeavored to share information and expand learning around what it means to be African in America. I have pointed out how the distortion of our history and the negation of our humanity, from a system of plantation slavery to police brutality and structural disparities, form the basis of contemporary experiences of trauma. Who among you can forget the horrific trauma of the many deaths of Black Americans at the hands of police and other white supremacist vigilantes mentioned in Chapter 1? Whether it was Derek Chauvin's empty eyes, the senseless murder of Breonna, or the inexplicable so-called "suicide" of Sandra Bland, these horrific instances were proof of how it often feels as if some American police are no different from vigilante slavecatchers, the KKK, White Citizens' Counsel, Proud Boys and QAnon fanatics.

I've explored how injustice and dehumanization show up in our society in the form of racial caricatures—the Pickaninny, Sambo, Uncle Tom, Mammy, etc.—to justify the continued enslavement of black people and validate white supremacy. I've discussed how white supremacy works to undermine the truth of black experiences with lies and evasions that perpetuate the "isms" that attempt to relegate Black Americans to perpetual socio-economic and political slavery.

I am certain there are very few among us who have not experienced traumatic situations, perhaps even intra- and intergenerationally. We, especially people of the African Diaspora, do not often speak of our traumas. If we do, we speak quietly, in hushed tones, or cryptically, refusing to confront the pain that haunts us, our families, and our communities. To give shape and form, faces and names, to histories and demographics that can feel abstract or distant, to speak the stories so often veiled in secrecy, I invited you to share in the vivid and tangible real-life experiences of my ordinary-extraordinary family. Remember Preston, banished from the role of Civil Engineer to cab driver, building superintendent or whatever job he could obtain to provide support for his ever-growing family? And do you recall how, after my family lawfully purchased their home, they were summoned to court for being "undesirable" and had to obtain legal assistance to validate their suitability? And perhaps you will also recollect my struggles to obtain a college education, first being told by white guidance counselors I did not fit college criteria; later, being told by a professor in graduate school: "You people can't write, and you will never become a social worker." (Remember, these incidents happened in the North, not in the deep South where racism ran rampant and the KKK were more powerful than the police). I pray you were impacted by my own experience of being wore down by multiple "isms," culminating in when Derek Chauvin murdered George Floyd in broad daylight for all the world to see.

I also shared many personal and profound examples of "isms" and trauma from my professional career. I have recalled with love, admiration, and honor, the people who crossed my path while facing multiple and simultaneous challenges—incest, rape, racism, sexism, poverty and more. The lives depicted in many of the chapters focused on the harshness, trauma, and unhappiness many of us face, regardless of our race, ethnicity, class, etc.

Lastly, I have attempted to craft and design several healing paths for you. My intention has been to help you gather your own set of tools for surviving and thriving. By now, you know there are endless possibilities along a continuum of interventions. I have lovingly encouraged you to seek, explore and implement your very own trauma-specific healing plan.

Marching Forward with Resilience

We are not meant to live our lives simply trying to get by. As important as seeking our healing path is, it is not everything. When I think about fully living and inhabiting our best lives, I ask: Are there important seeds of wisdom that we can learn from our ancestors? What can we learn from how they sought and found respite?

As part of the Works Progress Administration (WPA) during the Great Depression, the Federal Writers' Project set about collecting the narratives of our ancestors who experienced the dehumanizing of the substantive and, at times, the seemingly hopeless array of soul-killing isms in the United States. Although this project was criticized for employing few Black interviewers, the Project collected more than 2,300 first-person accounts and hundreds of black and white photographs of former slaves.

As one might imagine, these narratives were horrific. They told of families torn apart, rapes, beatings, and crushed bones, amongst other countless horrors. But they also told stories of joy. They told of Saturday evening dancing, falling in love, and stealing moments of precious intimacy. They told of children playing hide-and-seek, skipping stones in creeks, fashioning toys and games where they could, and "finding moments when the movement of their bodies was not governed by anything other than their own sense of wonder." What emerges from these narratives, again and again, is evidence of our divine human drive to find joy and happiness, even in small amounts, no matter what else is happening around us.

I urge you to think about the challenges your ancestors have overcome, be it surviving slavery, the Holocaust, the perils of immigration to America, poverty, prejudices—whatever particular skeletons are rattling around your family's closet. Your ancestors found ways to experience their lives in spite of their challenges. How might you draw inspiration and hope from their lives?

It is essential that we do not allow ourselves to fall victim to the endless barrage of pain the world seems ready to dispense at any moment. The path towards healing should not be our only way of living but rather a part (albeit a significant part) of our lives.

Are there ways in which we can invigorate and inspire ourselves emotionally, physically, spiritually, and culturally? What specific steps can we take to begin this urgent repair? Can we seek people, places and things that help to sustain and flourish our lives? How can we boost our spiritual immune system? For indeed, experiences of peace, joy, and happiness are not just meant for a few of us, but for all of us. How can you sustain the healing plan you have developed in ways that also give you permission to thrive? I'll give you a hint: it starts with self-care.

Self-Care Means Living Your Life Like It's Golden

Despite its current popularity, "self-care" is not a term I use lightly. There are so many things we hold sacred, yet rarely ourselves. Many of us are knee-deep in doing for others, spending little or no time for ourselves beyond our basic needs. It's time to reevaluate this urgent and important aspect of how we live our lives. While not an easy task, it is essential to our well-being and a fundamental part of the divine plan Great Spirit has for us. As Jill Scott's beautiful song, *Living Your Life Like It's Golden*, reminds us, we must live our life like its golden.

To me, "self-care" means, first and foremost, acknowledging and honoring that we are deserving of healing and of happiness. So many of us, particularly women, have been socialized to believe that we are meant to sacrifice our own happiness and well-being for that of others. Indeed, some cultures see the suffering of women as a sign of virtue. And while I am not here to judge other cultures for their ways of being, I do know that ongoing suffering exerts a profound negative effect on our entire being. Self-care is not selfish; it is as vital to our spiritual immune system as vitamin C is to our body's immune system. Know that you, dear Reader, are worthy.

Together, we will find a way to integrate healing into living your desired life and bolstering your emotional-spiritual immune system, so you are well-equipped to handle life's challenges. While I do not pretend to know exactly what will work for you, I do intend to share some of what's worked for me.

Life Celebrations: Big or Small, They Start with You

Life Celebrations

I have often wondered
With a sense of awe and glee
About the number of memorable opportunities
To celebrate just you and me

I look upon those events
Of celebration, jubilation and sensation
Wondering why so often
There are not enough
Momentous occasions

As a tender tot of four or five
I was brought along
To those festive jaunts
Enjoying my elders dancing to the sounds
Ellington, Sach Mo, The Count and their jive
Those Cats and Dolls could really swing
And I loved to watch my people

Twirl and jump
After a taste of
Dewar's, Johnnie Walker, Miller's and other things

Man, they all had on their Sunday best
Hair straight, oiled, curled, cut and waved
Clothes pressed and straight
We were all ready for a Harlem's fest

I would party and dance with them
On these special occasions
Hoping and praying
I would not succumb
To sleepy sensations

And now that I'm all grown up
And can conduct my own participation
It is time for me to plan
These nights of intense celebration

And so I feel a sense of jubilation
That you and yours
Have shared your participation
In this illustrious celebration
Before I say adieu
To this treatise which attempts
To capture my appreciation
For your dedication
To this evening's event

Let's not wait too long before
We decide to meet again
Because tomorrow's not promised
For either of us evermore

I am left without joy and a sense of dislocation
At the possibility
That we may meet in the next year or two
At yet another sad or lamenting occasion

Why don't we think about
More Life Celebrations?
Not needing a reason for elation and jubilation

Perhaps it's more important
For you and I
To come together
And celebrate the joys of life
Living, Loving, and feeling Blessed

So let's not take a vacation
Longer than a week or two
To ponder and develop a plan with sensation
Of another Life Celebration

I wrote the poem above in anticipation of celebrating my 60th birthday. I shared it during this life celebration, feeling blessed and grateful for my loved ones who came together to share in the joy.

While designing this special day, I thought about the particular things that inspire and energize me. I was absolutely not going to hold this celebration in a space where I would have to do most of the work (such as my house)! I wanted my guests to feel special, cherished, and uplifted, but I wanted to enjoy all the joyousness and positive energy, too, without worrying about cleaning or washing dishes. I also encouraged my invitees to dress in their favorite Caribbean colors to complement the theme of the event: Caribbean Dreams. So, I searched for a restaurant that could host about 50ish loving family and friends, where we could eat, drink, and dance. I found a local Indian restaurant to accommodate us.

As guests entered, they were treated to drinks and an assortment of samosas, wings, crudités, and other appetizers. As I welcomed each guest, I introduced them to one another and reminded them that I expected them to be on the dance floor (more than once!). From that entry, we transitioned into a larger space where tables with white tablecloths, linen napkins, and roses in the vibrant colors of orange, turquoise, green, and yellow, awaited us. I had personally selected these colors in advance, with a clear vision in mind for my Caribbean Dreams soiree. The lights were dim, an array of candles on each table providing atmosphere and mood lighting. My special table, with my husband, mother, and children, was placed in such a way so that I could easily interact with all the guests.

The DJ I selected was chosen for his expert musical taste. He and I discussed the musical selections at great length. I selected R&B, hip hop, calypso, and salsa. During the dancing, my son dedicated a special song to me—"Champagne Life" by Ne-Yo. This song has become the soundtrack to my life.

During the main meal, we all enjoyed tandoori chicken, spiced lamb, flavorful rice, rich saag paneer, chana masala, and delicious, warm naan bread to dip into various chutneys and sauces. At the end of the meal, we indulged in rice pudding, fresh fruit, and, of course, a large birthday cake! The staff rolled my cake in, bedecked with sparklers, while everyone sang "Happy Birthday" to me! Before we cut the cake, my husband grabbed the mic and surprised me with a special message. He shared with the audience that his original marriage proposal to me had not been exactly what I wanted. So today, on my birthday, he wanted to set the record straight. With microphone in hand, he got down on his knee, pledging his love and devotion and asking that I marry him all over again!

My mother also gave a passionate speech despite being in the midst of her struggles with dementia. And I made sure to dance individually with each of my special guests over the course of the evening. Towards the end of the night, I read the poem above and individually thanked each guest for coming, for uplifting me and sharing in my special day.

This was a momentous celebration. However, not all our life celebrations need to be on a grand scale. We need to seek life celebrations of all sizes, including those we celebrate alone and those we celebrate with others. Here are some concrete suggestions for making the most of your life celebrations, be they in ballrooms, bedrooms, beaches, or benches.

Celebrations: A How-To Guide

What are the important ingredients in creating a life celebration? It begins with you, dear Reader—your thoughts, your energy, your intention. Did you realize you have immense potential? In fact, you do.

Start with a plan. What do you wish to celebrate, who should be there and what resources are needed? People are often inspired with an invitation—it makes us feel valued and important.

Your celebration does not have to be an extraordinary event. Take the example of mother and sister, both consummate life-celebration organizers, individually and in groups. At one point, my mother had a weekly celebration at our home. We cleaned most of Saturday morning and afternoon. She would then cook an inexpensive meal which was ready once the guests arrived. Guests were asked to bring their favorite drink; she had musical selections in mind, and often seized the opportunity to teach the latest dances to guests. Her life celebrations were always well attended and successful. In the spirit of my family's long traditions of celebrations, both humble and huge, and drawing inspiration from my own 60th birthday bash, here are some suggestions for designing your own special celebration.

The Playlist

Are you a fan of music? Are there songs whose melodies or lyrics have special meaning to you? Do you sing in the shower or while alone in your home or apartment? Are there songs that can literally pull you out of deep feelings of despair and rock you into ecstasy? What are your special songs?

I have found certain music can fill me with a sense of power and inspiration when I've faced major difficulties, even if the song simply reminds me to take a moment and listen. In many situations, this may be the best course of action. Particular songs and lyrics have helped me cry over a lost love, yet gently reminded me that there are many more fish in the sea. Have you allowed yourself to let music and lyrics touch your heart? To gently flow to all the various parts of your mind, body, and spirit, erasing memories and sensations so that it's just you and the music? Have you utilized music to heal and, more importantly, help you thrive? Do you feel the inspiration of Spirit when you hear the mighty roars of Gospel? Can you imagine what it might feel like to effortlessly jump from a plane as you listen to trumpeter Freddie Hubbard's rendition of "Sky Dive"? Are you transported to the European capitals when you hear an intense piano concerto? Yo-Yo Ma's "Bach's Cello Suite No. 1" moves me into a sea of happy tears. Are you propelled to sway your hips and shoulders as you hear the funky beats of R&B? Perhaps you are transported to the islands of Barbados, the Bahamas, or Jamaica when you hear the great Bob Marley croon "One Love." What are some of the musical choices that you feel are, or can be, an important part of your social life celebrations? I encourage you to grab a notebook and jot down the songs that speak especially to you. Make yourself a celebratory playlist.

Food, Glorious Food!

Healthy and balanced eating can be an important part of an enjoyable life and creating a memorable life celebration. For my birthday party, food played an important part, even though food is often treated with ambivalence in our society. We love it, but we hate what it may do to our bodies. Should it be light or on the heavy side? Though I was raised to enjoy the wonderful tastes and flavors of both Caribbean and Southern cooking, as I have grown older, I've learned that many delicious food choices may not be the healthiest. Instead of restrictions, I prefer mindfulness and moderation. Eating with intention and as part of a well-balanced and healthy lifestyle infuses joy into our daily lives and helps to create a memorable life celebration.

Have you taken the time to enjoy your food, savoring the tastes and the smells and not rushing to get on to the next thing? What about the freshness of a good salad with more than enough of your favorite fruits, vegetables, and perhaps nuts? Can you remember and visualize moments when you've taken the time to mindfully eat, enjoying the taste of a sweet, fresh peach on a beautiful torte pastry or the dance of flavors in creole shrimp on top of a mound of flavored yellow rice with a generous portion of black beans on the side?

I can recall the fresh-picked cherries at Pike Place Market in Seattle, Washington, each one sweet and delicious as the next. I remember the beautiful simplicity of the sights and smells of the outdoor market stalls in Nice, France: the humble beauty of peaches and nectarines, the cobblestones streets, and the view of the sea beyond, adding to the beauty and simplicity of the moment, all inviting me to return and return again.

What are your favorite things to eat and drink, dear Reader? When and where do you enjoy these things? Are there opportunities to treat yourself to a special meal that is enjoyable and tasty, perhaps sharing it with a loved one or friend? Do you take time to enjoy these sensory experiences, or do you find yourself rushing to take care of the next thing?

Creating Sacred Spaces, Inside and Out

Designing an atmosphere that is pleasing and uplifting to our eyes is an important part of any celebration. Growing up within an Afro-Caribbean and African American family structure, life celebrations played an important part of my upbringing. It's important to frame what celebrations meant to us in the context of the injustices my family members endured daily. In addition, they worked hard—so hard. Indeed, I would often hear stories of the verbal abuse they suffered, as well as the gross disparities in how they were treated versus their white counterparts. Perhaps to cope with the work week's indignities, weekends were a time to feel special. It was a time to celebrate the joys of life, rather than the traumas and indignations one had experienced during the week. We could also take time to honor one another and provide support, even in just "makin' it" through another week despite "the man." Remember, it takes courage for Black Americans and people of color to keep steady work and provide support for other families; and too often, we don't stop to celebrate and appreciate our everyday bravery and risk-taking.

On the weekends, we bathed, put on our "partyin' clothes," and attended life celebrations for family and community members. Often, these celebrations were spontaneous. Like the children of my enslaved ancestors, I, too, participated in the personal preparations: having my hair done, wearing my favorite, and perhaps only, party dress, and relishing the rare opportunity to stay up beyond my 9:00 pm bedtime curfew. At these celebrations, there was plenty of drinking, eating, and dancing. While my foremothers and forefathers played their hand-crafted musical instruments, we spun records and LPs, dancing to the energy of Count Basie, Ellington, and Satchmo. With our clothes, our food and drink, and our music and dancing, we could feel good about ourselves, despite the negative ways we were depicted in greater society. Our beauty, charm, and value were on display and validated.

So, when the time came to plan my own big bash, I was well-trained! I knew that creating a special and sacred space with the environment I had chosen would play a crucial part in establishing the atmosphere I desired for myself and my guests. During my planning, I carefully considered which colors and things were particularly pleasing to me and that I felt would be important, in fact essential to my life celebration. For my large life celebration, I wanted multicolored roses everywhere, especially the colors of the Caribbean. I asked all who attended to dress in Caribbean colors.

Can a life celebration be part of your healing and thriving plan? When was the last time you organized a life celebration? Have you experienced an inner glow or positive energy when you initiated changes in yourself and your environment, or when you have hosted or attended an event? Or are you perhaps fearful that things will not go well, so you hesitate to sponsor a life celebration?

We all have the power to create and sustain positive energy. I encourage you to take stock of your environment—wherever it is that you will take a moment to celebrate. Can you seek ways to enhance, even in small ways, your space? I'm not talking about extravagance—champagne and chandeliers are optional! A plant, a pillow, a candle, your favorite essential oil, or fresh paint can make a big difference. It does not have to be fancy. One of my esteemed patients had a gathering at her home with black bean dip and punch because that was all that she could afford. However, she wanted to gather people in her home and celebrate. And people came, enjoyed themselves, and this collective enjoyment was contagious and transformed her humble space into a memorable and sacred occasion. Indeed, our enslaved ancestors utilized what they could fashion from what they had or harvested beauty from the natural world to personalize and make sacred their spaces. Flowers, plants, and bushes were all utilized in creative ways. As I mentioned earlier, I continue to be awed and inspired by the ancestors' resilience and determination to seek spaces to be joyous, dance, perhaps laugh and find jubilation, if only in the moment, despite unspeakable traumas and humiliations.

Take a look at YouTube or decorating shows on television for inspiration. Again, this does not have to be an expensive undertaking—start small. Think about how your appearance and clothing choices might play a role in your celebration. Is it time for a new LBD (Little Black Dress) or dapper tie? Even if you cannot afford a new wardrobe, perhaps you can modify what you have with accessories or by pairing items you never thought could possibly go together. Many stores will offer stylists for free. It's important to remember that you are outfitting yourself for you—it does not matter if anyone else will see you and it does not matter what others may think of your choices. It's all about what sacred adornments bring you joy and pleasure.

If these ideas resonate with you, cast off the fear, anxiety, or tension that acts as a barrier to opportunities to celebrate the many joys and energies of living, loving and feeling blessed. May you be reminded that you have access to unyielding love by the God of your understanding.

Ordinary People Extraordinary Deeds
(Poem for Ms. Maya from an ardent admirer; in recognition of a long, one-sided loving relationship)

Let me say at the onset
That my skills and talents as a poet
Are not dependent on
Instruction, Teaching or erudite
Professor's Mind Set

I have never had or want
An academic course
On creative writing, poetry
Or other schools of thought

My rational fear dictates
That the adage "if it ain't broke don't fix it"
Represents my heart and mindset mandate

I speak to you Dear Heart
And all others
In the course of this written expression
From the depths of my mind,
Heart and soul's progression

I hope to articulate my feelings
About you
With understanding and passion
Filled with cascading hues of blue

Poems for me are like giving birth
And Lord knows I've had my share
Cause with the three I had
I surely felt no mirth

Dear Ms. Maya, who would have known
That among the billions of people on earth
There would be one among them
Besides your immediate kin
(Bailey, Grandma, uncle, Mrs. Baxter, your son, etc.)
Who has been imbued with all the knowledge.
Concepts and emotions you have communicated within

You have said on countless times
That your Mom, Brother and others
Have been your greatest fans
But did you know
I count myself among them
That you are totally and unconditionally mine?

You may not know that I have rocked and rolled
With the lyrics and rhythms of the Phenomenal Woman
Found hope and inspiration in "Still I Rise"
And moreover have helped many others
Your long and illustrious life guise

You cannot possibly know how special it was
As I sat alone on a warm summer's night
In New Ark's fair city as you recited
Langston, your life's struggle, and with all
Your might.

Your tears and mine found a way to intermingle
Cause I just knew you were talking
To Me
And I knew then as I know now
That the work of Providence
Would cause my eyes to twinkle

I loved the stories of your special bus
Laughed heartily at the story
Of a lady who almost fainted
And thought longingly of a day
Where I might make your acquaintance

May I join the countless others
You have identified as your daughters?
Although I truly believe that Our Savior
Has already bequeathed you as my long
Distant and long-awaited Mother

I thank God for your life
The sense of empowerment, hope and balm
That you have given so much to others
Without ever knowing the psalms you have spoken
Have soothed so many who were broken

I can go on forever
As this poem has gestated and developed
It did not take nine months like my children who grew

Dear Ms. Maya, please accept my passionate
Heartfelt plea to keep on keeping on
For the sons and daughters throughout the world
Who you do not know but do know
And have blossomed as rich and beautiful flowers
Cause you have loved us so!

I am hesitant to say adieu
There will be many who shout
Please Stop
Because you think you're a poet
But I would really like to go on and on
About how much
I love you

This chapter endeavors to motivate you to confront, reassess and rethink what "ordinary" means. I begin with a spoken-word poem titled, "Poem for Ms. Maya (from an ardent admirer; in recognition of a long one-sided loving relationship)" which speaks to the high regard, respect and praise I have for Maya Angelou. However, I challenge you to ask yourself: prior to her emergence as a spiritual icon, author, civil rights activist, dancer, actress, professor, and so much more, would you have noticed this wonderful woman if she walked past you, perhaps in Stamps, Arkansas or California? Would passengers on the streetcar notice there was genius behind her uniform? Would you have noticed the bright light of creative genius that resided within her body, mind and spirit?

Average or everyday folk who are intrinsically and intimately involved in our day-to-day lives and existence are poorly recognized. We may pass over them, thinking they are just "ordinary." Yet consider what might happen if many of these important people stopped doing their ordinary jobs. I remind the readers of a great play by Douglas Turner Ward called *Day of Absence*. In the play, all of the characters (black people played in white face) are lamenting because none of the black people in the town showed up for work. A hilarious comedy, it also questions what happens when the ordinary people are no longer in our lives. The movie (Director Tate Taylor, 2011) and book *The Help* (Kathryn Stockett, 2009) dramatize a similar theme. We see a town where the black maids are not allowed to use the toilets in the homes of their employers, despite being the very ones who cared for their children, did their shopping, cooked their meals, washed their clothes, and more. Perhaps the most poignant part of the story is the genius of the main character, Aibileen Clark, who knew so much and had so much insight and love. I am also reminded of another ordinary woman, Henrietta Lacks, who has continued to impact the world with the use of her cells for important cancer research.

I would also like to share the tale of two extremely hard-working individuals who were impacted by a story they heard about an orphanage for disabled children in Ghana, West Africa. On their own, they decided to help these children who had been branded with the stigma of being bad omens in their community. This stigma took many forms: a birthmark, an illness, some physical or mental disability, or perhaps the fact that their mother had died in childbirth. With their own resources, my friends traveled to the orphanage, offered their help, shot some video footage, and returned to the U.S. inspired to share their story.

I was so inspired by their experience and their video that I began fundraising myself. I have since provided resources to the children in Ghana, and I continue to do so. This is a prime example of very ordinary people who decided to do something extraordinary.

Yet so often we fail to see the creative light in the ordinary. Take, for example, how students earning average grades are devalued by their teachers and parents. Parents may be upset when their child brings home a report card with all B's, asking "where are the A's??" Sure, some students may not be working as hard as they could, yet there are many for whom B's are perfectly acceptable grades as they work towards seeking and finding the areas of creative genius within them.

Our culture's emphasis on looks and fashion can be particularly damaging for children and teens with only "ordinary" resources. In my own middle school and high school years, I never measured up when it came to clothes and shoes. At that time, you scored points with buying clothes in the "Village" in New York City, and shoes from a shoe line called "Fred Braun" were popular. On one occasion, I was invited to a party and felt oh-so ordinary in my ordinary dress and the ordinary shoes that didn't quite match and weren't quite fashionable. I had sought advice from various family members, trying to figure out a way to make what I had work. I knew asking for a new pair of shoes was out of the question. While I longed for fashionable types of clothing and shoes, my parents shopping arenas were "Alexander's, May's, and Miles (for shoes)." They saw trendy, expensive clothing as second to a good home, great food, and fresh vegetables.

Why did my dress and shoes mark me as "ordinary?" Certainly, no adolescent girl wants to think of herself as "ordinary." Now, as an adult, and with decades of wisdom and professional training behind me, I am encouraging us to re-frame our thoughts about being ordinary.

As we journey towards living our best lives and valuing our time on the earth, let us take stock. Are there ways in which we consciously or unconsciously devalue others and ourselves by only seeing ordinariness? Have we sabotaged our own beauty, gifts, and capacity for specialness? Have we developed unhelpful standards for specialness while trying to attain the unattainable? Have we missed critical opportunities to create and sustain meaningful relationships with those we perceived as lacking that extraordinary glitz and glam?

Ordinary Genius, Ms. Ina.

Is there someone in your life who may seem ordinary but who is actually quite special and impactful? How has that ordinary person affected your perception of yourself and others? Have you shared your admiration for this ordinary-special person? If not, I encourage you to take a moment to review the following words. My poem below, "Ms. Ina," describes the small yet enormous impact of a rather ordinary woman I knew. When she passed to spirit, I wrote this poem in honor of her beauty, grace, loving countenance and impact on my needy heart. May they encourage and motivate you to be a cheerleader for the ordinary-special people in your life.

To Ina, Christ Church Mother, Friend, Nurse, Teacher and Extraordinary Woman

I struggled long and hard
With these thoughts, sentiments, and feelings,
That I failed to utter
In the course of the blessed interactions
Between myself and Our Church Mother

I do not hesitate
To proclaim her as such
Mindful that our small
But mighty congregation
Boasts of many who dutifully care
for us needy neonates

On more than one occasion
Often unexpected

But welcome with glee
She would approach me
With that beautiful smile
Bearing gifts often for my own mother, daughters, and me.

It was always a personalized token
A plant, cosmetics, and hair care products
Which she explained as specialist or clinician
Sustaining our relationship
Which was never ever broken

Even in the midst of her own unrelenting pain and suffering
She committed her body, soul, and spirit
To Our Savior and Lord's mission
With an unending and watchful eye on his vision

Always a nurturer, Our Church Mother
Whose spirit still remains,
Well-spoken, intelligent, possessing a
beautiful countenance and voice
How will we all ever be the same?

I continue to struggle with her loss
I am certain I am not alone
She has left so many who will surely mourn
I pray their pain will not be too much
But surely there will be tears, hurt, sadness and such.

I can still see the seriousness and dedication
exuded when she danced
Surely Judith, Josephine, and Balanchine
Would look with awe and a sense of romance

As Ina weaved with creative glee
The rhythmic pleasure of R and B.
I know the heart of calypso
Was born in her native land
But honey she sure could shake it
Whether DJ or band.

There are many of those among you
That know I speak from the heart.
And so I will end by
Making this on the mark

Our Church Mother is not gone
Or forever lost
She has gone ahead
To prepare a place for you or me
With loving care and dedication
Her essence will always be!

Ms. Ina was a giving human who spread her love without hesitation. She always took the time to inquire how I was doing, and readily shared small gifts, perhaps saying, "your hair looks a little dry; try this conditioner." And, boy, could she dance! I admired her confident connection to, and expression of, rhythm, as if the music was always only playing for her.

I am grateful for the many other people who were a "Ms. Ina" in my life. In past chapters, I spoke of my deep and profound relationship with Mrs. G., who served as my surrogate mom through college, providing me with the support and love I needed to get through four difficult years. I would be remiss if I did not include my English professor, affectionately known as "Ms. Steiner." She was originally from Ohio and had to decide whether to pursue social work or become a college teacher. Ironically, perhaps, being in her course on African American Literature inspired something within me to pursue social work. The various literary avenues we pursued in her class supported my ability to reach deep into the various characters, understanding their thoughts, choices, and decisions. This furthered my ability to go deep within the recesses of the mind, body and spirits of those whom I would later care for and treat. She, too, was, in some respect, an ordinary college professor in a small liberal arts college…and like my other Ms. Inas, quite extraordinary.

So, dear Reader, what are the lessons learned from these examples? If you would, take a moment and recall the beautiful scene from the movie, *Beloved*, which depicts the aftermath of slavery in a particular American town. In the scene I am imagining, an elderly woman, a very wise woman, asks the townspeople to gather in the square. She goes on to deliver a wonderful soliloquy, saying to the townspeople, "Love yourself; hug yourself." I understand this scene as an affirmation of collective worthiness and the creative light of God that lies within us. As we move towards valuing and uplifting the unique and special creations we are, even though we may work in rather ordinary capacities, the creative light, the genius within, will begin to evolve, grow, and make its presence known. I encourage you to look within at your extraordinary ordinariness and to also recognize, utilize, and cleave to those around us who may be considered ordinary but impact our lives in very extraordinary ways.

Breaking Away from the Struggles of Life

I want to tell you the story of how I ended up on a huge cruise ship called *The Breakaway*. Let's go back in time to January 2, 2014…

Like so many, I seemed to suddenly find myself engulfed, and I felt as if there was no way out. I heard myself repeating the words, "I'm feeling very tired," over and over again as well-meaning friends and colleagues asked me how I was doing. I listened as they nodded robotically and blamed holiday preparations or dismal weather and gloomy, sunless skies. But I knew my exhaustion was more than holiday burnout or winter blues.

I am not certain when the rigors of stress and strain began to take their toll on my mind, body, and spirit. Certainly, the pressures of work and home were building up before Jan 2, 2014. In 2013, I began to feel lost in my professional career. I was no longer inspired nor sustained by my work; I knew something was missing. I woke up tired every morning. I had difficulty falling, and staying, asleep. I could not always remember my dreams. Caffeine gave me a quick jolt of energy, but soon faded. No amount of coffee was going to get me through this. I was forgetful, quick to anger, and restless. I found myself overly sensitive to minor slights that I could normally brush aside. I was functioning in a perfunctory way, going through the motions just to get by. I knew there was something keeping me from peace—I just couldn't quite put my finger on it!

It was highly unusual for me not to be able to identify the source of my symptoms and devise healing strategies. Despite my illustrious (if I may say so!) career in mental health and gifts in mediumship and intuitiveness, as previous chapters have shown, I am not immune to stress. I, too, can feel pulled in too many directions, unable to realize when it's time to slow down, or stop, take stock, and intervene.

I tried various interventions, suggestions, and I even considered going back into therapy. I worked hard to find people, places, and things that would offset the void that I was experiencing. Yet, the more I tried to cope, the more my tattered bucket relentlessly overflowed. As 2013 came to a difficult close after many difficult months, I decided that I would like to begin the new year in a different way. I told myself I had to find a way to empty out my bucket of stress, strain, and trauma. I knew I had to break away from it all.

My inner knowingness told me I had to get out of town. So, I perused various getaways that would allow me and my loved ones to be cared for by others. I also looked for something accessible to my home state that did not necessitate air travel; it was the holidays, after all, and I wanted to avoid the challenges and stresses of holiday air travel. Where I live, January is also the coldest and darkest times of the year, so I sought warmth and sunshine. A cruise vacation seemed like the perfect balm for my wounded self. And so, when I heard about a special New Year's cruise leaving from New York City, I knew this was my golden chance to search and seek self-care.

So, I threw myself a lifeline. I boarded "The Breakaway," whose name in bright, primary colors hailed me. There was just so much that I needed to break away from! As I boarded this magnificent ship, I exhaled and burst into tears, sobbing without control. I was letting go, knowing I had arrived to a place where I could find respite. The ship's name was surely no accident. I am reminded of the great saying that accidents are just ways that God shows her/his Divine presence.

How many of you, dear Readers, have found yourself in a similar situation? Have you experienced a time when you felt as if you lacked the resources to keep going? Have you felt as if you are just "getting by," simply surviving life instead of thriving? Have you experienced burnout, overwhelming stress, anxiety, and exhaustion?

There are times when we all must disentangle and unravel the web of stresses and strains life spins around us, in order to find our unique healing strategies. I believe the wisdom of countless physicians, healers, and spiritual teachers who've told me that our bodies are so intricately and divinely designed that we have all we need to heal ourselves.

What's your healing strategy for those times you find yourself sinking into the quicksand of obligations, schedules, and the "all too muchness" of life?

Not all of you may be able to whisk yourself off on a vacation, as I did. However, I encourage you to seek respite. If/when you find yourself constantly saying, "I'm tired" or "I just don't feel like myself," what can you do to soothe and heal yourself? Consider taking an hour or more out of a busy day for self-care ("me time"). Seek out and test a variety of solutions. A lunchtime walk through a park? Perhaps some meditation or aromatherapy oils? Many find solace and nourishment near water, in gardens or libraries or parks. There are many places of respite that cost nothing but will help you reap tremendous rewards.

Once you ease the acute phase of stress, I encourage you to develop an ongoing prevention plan to mitigate future burnouts. Reassess and redesign your day-to-day schedule so that you can devote time for your continued wellness. Life is more than surviving our pain. Wellness means enhancing and sustaining your overall physical, emotional, and spiritual health. And sometimes you just need to break away.

Is this the time for your breakaway? Surely, this is part of God's divine plan for us all.

Seeking Your Happy Place Within

St. Lucia Calls

This poem despite its name
Does not purport to extol or support
The customary verbiage espoused by the tourist industry
Regarding an individual Caribbean Island's fame

I had the good fortune
To be taught to hear my inner voice
Which in retrospect emanates
From Our Lords' wisdom and plan
In spite of our choice

St. Lucia called me
I am not completely sure why
But when I suggested this venue
To my beloved spouse
He did not utter a cry

When we arrived after a lengthy ride
It was not love at first sight

*As the island's general demeanor
Was not in line with
My mind's culinary delights*

*A gentle rain slowly fell
There were clouds
No hint of sun
And at that point
I was not sure we would have fun
As we journeyed from south to north
Moving carefully through the maze of roads,
Breathtaking foliage, and views
Guided by our esteemed driver and navigator
We placed our faith and trust as he drove among the mews*

*We looked in wonderment
At the mountains, oceans, and spectacular sights
That we tried to hold onto
With all of our might*

*Once arriving at our seven-day home
We scanned the beauty of this venue
The resort's staff focused on the dinner menu
We were offered delicious rum punch
But not one thing to munch*

*I continued to focus on the positives
Secretly praying that I was not wrong
Again trusting this inner voice
Which articulated a melodious song
Dear, hear as you read this written expression
Please keep this though in mind*

That often than not
Don't be mindful of your first impression

The island's spectacular beauty and charm
Impacted us more than you can imagine
It helped to initiate a personal metamorphosis
That continues to this day
To insulate me from the negative effects of harm

I am certain there was some secret nectar
Administered to known visitors, which permeated
Mind, body and spirit
Which was specially brewed with a charm that said
Protect her!

I can't begin to even describe
The sights smells sounds
That reeked of the multicultural and diverse hands
Of Africa, France, England and other lands

I want you to ride with me as I recalled a simple voyage
With the bright and beautiful sun in the blue sky
Destined to the ports of Castries, Marigot, Soufriere,
and the mineral baths
Riding along with a gentle breeze that caressed my shoulders
Ever so slowly as if making love in between the boulders

I would be remiss if I did not recall
The sensual taste of mackerel, cod fish, pork and fruits

So delicious and tasty
I am currently seeking a way to pursue

The highlights of this wonderful journey
Are too numerous to recall
The warm and friendly black and brown faces
Said it all
If the opportunity exists
For you and yours to seek a piece of heaven
Amidst the stress and strains of the things we must to
Only seek a way to persist

Please listen to your inner voice
God speaks to us all
You will have to be quiet
Cause I am certain of this
St. Lucia should be in your midst

Dearest Reader, shall we continue our important discussion of creating and sustaining a life that is golden? In a previous chapter, we danced with the idea of devoting one-quarter of our lives to healing and the remaining three-quarters to our actual existence, including seeking, learning, and implementing the important ingredients that represent a joyful existence.

As we have seen, there are so many ways we dismiss our yearnings; we often forget or deny ourselves the opportunity to dream and manifest those dreams, even when just a few small steps could make a huge impact on how we experience joy. In this section, I want to share with you the importance of nurturing some of those inner yearnings—specifically your soul's need for places where you feel alive, safe, challenged, and comforted. I call these places your "happy place within." Your happy place might be a real location. But it might also be more of a state of mind that you can retreat to and immerse yourself in, wherever you are physically in the world. For me, my happy places are both inner and outer. Since childhood, I've sought happiness and joy through reading as well as in imagining (and then undertaking) travel.

As a youngster, I devoured books, often completing an entire book in a single day. I found joy in the lives and experiences of fictional characters. By immersing myself in the lives of each character, I grew in my own identity and expanded my perceptions and experiences. I learned what the characters learned; I was exposed to their trials, triumphs, successes, and failures, while imaginatively traveling to and experiencing a variety of times and places and socio-political-economic circumstances. I was especially drawn to Black authors, whose books I could find at our local library. The library was a place of wonder and adventure, where I could fulfill my ever-present need to read, understand, and explore.

My love of travel has a similar origin story. My mother served as the Office Manager at the U.S. Passport Office in Rockefeller Plaza, New York City, where thousands entered her office daily seeking the necessary travel documentation (at that time, in the 1960s, an individual had to come in person to obtain and/or renew their passport!). My visits to her office provided glimpses of the possibility of travel. I snuck peeks at the glitz and glamour of celebrities who frequented the office with urgent travel requests. I prayed I might cross paths with the likes of Jackie Kennedy, Douglas Fairbanks Jr., and, of course, Duke Ellington—and I did! These experiences fueled my imagination in the way that immersing myself in fictional worlds and lives did. For a brief moment, I yearned for a career in the Foreign Service. Mimi, a close friend of my mother's, lived and worked in Japan. She would often send me beautiful kimonos. These exotic artifacts from far-away lands only increased my curiosity about the world and deepened my yearning to travel.

I was fortunate to have opportunities to travel with my family as a youngster. I remember shorter trips and excursions to parts of Long Island, Martha's Vineyard, Washington DC, South Carolina. No matter how small the trip, seeing and experiencing something new always felt like an adventure to me. We also traveled to Barbados when I was fourteen, a trip that was significant in my personal growth and development. It was not only my very first experience being on an airplane; it was my first experience visiting someplace foreign yet familiar.

I relished in the preparation—the planning and packing, even the smallpox inoculations that were recommended at that time. On the day of our travel, we dressed up in our Easter finery, including a flowered hat. I enjoyed each moment of the flight on British Airways—even the food tasted good to me! But, what can you expect from a kid who enjoyed TV dinners and Sara Lee chocolate cake!? Alongside a large number of British people, we stayed at a guesthouse that offered breakfast, tea, and dinner. The food was delicious and plentiful, expertly prepared by Bajan cooks. In particular, I ate pumpkin fritters at breakfast (they're somewhat like pancakes but even tastier) until I thought my stomach would surely burst. Afternoons were spent on the beautiful beach, visiting family, friends and tourist attractions. At that time, Barbados was still under English rule. Later on, I remember a discussion regarding the impending move towards independence, which eventually happened in 1966. It was during this trip that I met a young woman and her brother who were vacationing from Guadalupe. The brother, who was quite handsome, shared his political views on Cuba, which were quite the contrast to what I had learned at home in the U.S. about the terrors of communism. I remember him saying that Castro's regime helped people to learn to read, which challenged and expanded the stories I had heard. It was through experiences such as these that travel and my encounters with different people, places, ideas, and things helped widen my worldview and develop my perceptions about myself and my place in this wide, wonderful, weird world.

My hunger to seek unknown and foreign places has remained an important and essential part of who I am and who I wish to be. As I watch airplanes soar across the skies, I feel inspired and excited to plan a new trip.

You may not be able to afford to jump on a plane whenever your heart desires, but there are other ways to satisfy this urgency. I remember one year in particular when I was short of funds but had an upcoming vacation from work. Instead of traveling, I went to a different park each day with a sandwich and cool drink. These small adventures helped to satisfy my need to go out and experience something new. The point is this: a lack of financial resources doesn't mean putting off your need to seek those happy places that make your heart sing.

There are additional and important things that can help you develop joy within. Let us explore the impact of service to others as a way to seek—and find—a happy place.

Infusing Service and Gratitude

I would like to begin the end of this chapter—and this book—with three important quotations:

> "If I can help somebody, then living my life will not be in vain." –*If I Can Help Somebody* by Alma Androzzo (1945), one of Dr. Martin Luther King Jr's favorite hymns.

> "The best way to find yourself is to lose yourself in the service of others." –M.K. Gandhi

> "There is no joy and no service that can match helping others." –*The Philosophy of Silver Birch* spoken through Maurice Barbanell

Why these three quotes, dear Reader? Each of these statements comments on the importance of infusing our lives with service to others. For those among you who have joined me in this reading adventure, I extend the concept of service to you as a way of moving beyond life's challenges. I offer you the opportunity to consider how being of service to others as part of your life's journey may be a part of your own healing and, ultimately, your own joyous contentment.

My convictions around the importance of service are drawn from my own life experiences. As I have shared with you in previous chapters, I seemed destined to be of service. There has never been a time in my life when I stumbled onto a problem that I did not try to solve. Rarely have I seen suffering and not felt compelled to help in some way. Could this be an essential part of my DNA? Was I born with this keen and urgent desire to help individuals manage their hurts, seen or unseen? My experience suggests that I am instinctively an active listener—an ear for those in need.

Yet, my commitment to helping others has also been inspired by others and the decisions they've made. I urge those among you who are experiencing the pangs of grief to read the brief story by the prolific Chilean writer Isabel Allende, "In Giving I Connect With Others." Allende, who I read as a somewhat metaphysical writer who often focuses on the spiritual practices of people living in various parts of South America, is a remarkable storyteller. This story, the tremendous loss she suffered and the ways in which she coped, etched themselves into my body, mind and spirit. The story is about her daughter, Paula, who had been a volunteer for women and children, working six days a week, eight hours a day, devoting her life to others. Upon her untimely death, dying in the arms of her mother, Isabel was overcome with an intense and severe grief for a year. Yet, in the course of a thoughtful and reflective process, Isabel discovered that despite her loss, she remained the same person with the same values and instincts and the same sense of integrity. And, in the course of this process, she discovered a way out of her grieving process from the way her dear Paula lived her life. Isabel found, "you only have what you give. It's by spending yourself that you become rich."

In my own life, I have found Isabel's observation to be stunningly accurate. Around 2012-2013, two talented and gifted individuals of my acquaintance decided to create a film about a special orphanage in Ghana. With little knowledge of the film itself or the orphanage, I instinctively knew this work needed to be shared. I encouraged the filmmakers to submit their film to a local film festival. It was accepted! I joined the screening and, as I watched this film, I felt as if children in the film were speaking directly to me. Now for those of you who believe we can receive messages from those in spirit, I will share a memory from a mediumship training in 2011. I received a messaged that Our Beloved Mother wanted me to be an instrument of her work in helping children. Further, I was told that an opportunity would come for me to help children who needed my specific help. As I watched this film, I knew that Our Beloved Mother was directing me to the needs of these children.

The *Nazareth Home For God's Children* (also known as *Sister Stan's Children)* is a refuge for unwanted children, many of whom also suffer from a disability or medical problem. Some of the mothers of these children died in childbirth, a stigma borne by the surviving children in Ghanaian culture. The orphanage's founder, Sister Stan, had been an administrative assistant, with little knowledge of children. However, she was approached by an imam who was concerned about the welfare of children in her community, especially those who seemed to have been abandoned to die. With little to no resources, the Sister worked to create a space for them. Over time, she accepted infants, kids, and teenagers into a place where they would be welcomed and cared for.

These children inspired the following poem:

Our Spirit Children

I have often talked about the struggle in life
In poems, prose, and narration,
The things that haunt
Challenge and plague us
Without hesitation

This may cause us to feel
We have been struck with a knife
There are so many who challenge our minds and thoughts, saying

Hey—there is always opportunity with crisis
But some of these struggles we need the likes
Of the Egyptian Princess Isis!

This particular poem
Was one of these struggles
I readily admit it put me
In a somewhat muddle

Not sure of going right or left
Up or down, in or out
East or West
My goodness what a struggle!

But somehow-someway
I visualized the gentle swirls
Twirls of sacred incense
We often see

As it danced
Sacred dance like
Vapor from steaming tea
Seeking its divine destination
Settling somehow in me

I must share a secret of small aspect
Divinity was foretold
Many years before
By one of the sisters of the light
Who gently whispered

Our Blessed Mother has so much in store
You will be called Mother
By many children who you did not bore

These children are in need
Of your love, support, and so
Much more!

Most assuredly, their tremendous need
Will touch your soul's core

And so when two gentle and creative hearts
Approached me with their dream
I felt I had no choice
But to join
In their extraordinary party
Of delicious ice cream

And so when I saw the multicolored rainbow
Of laughing spirit children
With hearts and minds of gold

I recoiled in horror as I heard their stories
Of neglect, abuse, and many needs
All alone in the cold without a friend indeed

And I thought of Our Blessed Mother's voice
And was sure I must do what I am told

So my plan is to shower
Their beautiful spirits with love, food, clothing,
Shelter and education
As these things will surely help them
All towards their particular vocation

And as they grow, mature and succeed
I will certainly watch with glee
And respectfully beg you
To join with me.

After seeing the film and hearing their remarkable story, I went about fundraising in order to visit the orphanage and bring badly needed resources. I was fortunate to receive monetary gifts from many at the Journey Within Church, friends, family members and others who just wanted to be a part of this endeavor. Unexpectedly, it was around this time that I saw a brief advertisement for a trip to Ghana for alumni of my undergraduate college. I contacted the organizer and was welcome to join the group. The organizer promised me a visit to the orphanage.

As I prepared for my trip, I packed suitcases with things the children might need: school supplies, clothing, first aid items, soap, toothpaste, shampoo, and healthy candies. But nothing could have prepared me for the on-the-ground experience of being in Ghana and meeting these children.

Ghana, once called "The Gold Coast," is a beautiful country with a host of different geographies, including mountain ranges, ocean and beautiful coastlines, markets teeming with people, products, and energy, and enormous and meaningful historical sites attesting not only to the talents, abilities and resources of their population but also to a history of colonialism, enslavements and resource depletion. The visit to the country itself was overwhelming and emotional.

Yet, my actual visit to the orphanage will be forever etched in my mind's eye. Upon entering the facility, the children were waiting for me. They welcomed me, carried my suitcases and give me a seat in their shadowed courtyard. I received a tour of the building, which was in quite a state of disrepair. Despite the grim surroundings, the children were thrilled to see me. During my initial visit, they couldn't stop talking and singing hymns. I could feel their evident love for me and for each other. Eventually, Sister Stan drove up in an old pick-up truck with provisions, and the children excused themselves to help unload the truck and carry items into the kitchen. I saw children as young as toddlers helping without needing any prompting!

I had brought a substantial amount of money and suitcases filled with lots of items they needed, but it was I who received so much. I was showered with love, respect and compassion from *Sister Stan's Children*. I was encircled in their ocean of community, and I marveled at what this one woman had created with such meager resources. I vowed to continue to help, joining so many who find they receive more than they give when they are in service to others.

To this day, I have continued my yearly gifts to the children and staff. The amount of the gift is not important—it is the energy that is resplendent with caring and compassion. This remains an important and essential personal undertaking. *Sister Stan's Children* and I urge you to seek your personal and meaningful way to enlarge, revitalize, and magnify your lives by the enormous opportunity to serve and be of service. You will surely receive so much more than you give, and you will remain changed forever.

Being Your Own Philanthropist

It is through giving without expecting anything in return that we give ourselves the enormous opportunity to expand our spiritual bandwidth. This is an opportunity, if we so choose, to connect with our higher selves and the sense of the God force that resides within ourselves—whomever or whatever we feel is the God of our understanding. When we offer something, whether big or small, to someone in need, without fanfare or recognition, the change in energy is palpable. Take time to watch the bright faces of those who receive our gifts and open yourself to sensing the difference it makes, even if it's fleeting. I promise you will connect with optimism and hope.

Sharing something of ourselves (time, money, a smile, a small gift) supports and encourages us to be mindful of the gifts we have. It allows us to see and appreciate daily resources that we might take for granted—access to fresh water and food, medical care, clothing and more. Yet, many of these daily necessities are inaccessible to others, even people in our own communities. There are so many around us who are in need.

Recently, I have been encouraged to be more keenly aware of women in supermarkets who have to make difficult decisions to feed their families. I have noticed that when their children ask for small treats, some women are unable to purchase them. Once, I realized, after the fact, that I may have witnessed a woman shoplifting in order to provide her children with the tokens they were asking her for. If I could go back in time, I would have offered her a few bucks. However, after that experience, I became more mindful and have started to share small amounts of money to supplant a needy woman's resources. As of this writing, I met a woman in a Dollar Store whose children were asking for a small toy. I gave her what I thought the toy would cost and she answered me in Spanish with such an outpouring of emotions, you would have thought I had given her much, much more. These tiny gestures are usually not much of a sacrifice and yet have a profound and lasting impact on our emotional and spiritual well-being.

Straight Talk—Being Your Own Philanthropist

A sense of wanting to share or give to others begins with the individual.

- Pay attention to your feelings. Encourage and allow your feelings to dictate the extent to which something is important to you.

- Focus especially on your heart space where, emotionally and energetically, the love for yourselves and others resides. This space also contains your capacity for empathy, compassion and forgiveness.

- If you find there are blockages within you or you don't feel yourself comfortable in a space of giving and/or gratitude, allow yourself the time for exploration and healing.

Once you have found yourself in a space of readiness, start on the small side. Ask yourself: where is my path and sense of love for others, my compassion and forgiveness? Is it with the elderly, children, disabled individuals, those suffering from traumas? Is it with environmental causes? Social justice issues? For some, service may involve joining a group; for others it can be individual or solitary work. It is completely up to you to decide what feels best.

Review and be mindful of your resources. For example, are you able to provide financial resources? Or would you rather volunteer your time? There are as many different paths of giving and service as there are causes in need. Find a way that is sustainable and manageable for you and what you are realistically able to do.

The most important thing is to develop a plan, whether it be on-the-spot-paying for a person's lunch while you are having your lunch, paying the tolls for the person behind you, or offering to do a favor for a friend are all examples of your brand of philanthropy, keeping in mind that there are so much more!

As you find yourself encouraged and motivated to love yourself and love others through giving your resources, you will absolutely find that you receive so much more than you give. I can recall, without hesitation, how the children in the orphanage greeted me with love and affection, well before I offered the many gifts I had planned to share. I can recall the love and appreciation one of my best friends expressed as I worked along with others cleaning her house as she prepared to move. She was much too sick to do it, and I relished in the opportunity to help her. I found another opportunity to help a man who was obviously homeless, whose affect and demeanor changed when I offered him ten dollars and suggested he get a coffee or something to eat. And I don't want to forget the many individuals in local shelters when it was my family's turn to cook dinner. We offered with pride our tasty, home-cooked meals and put the same quality into the cooking that we would have if we were cooking for ourselves!

Perhaps it was my maternal grandmother's insistence that we abide by the Golden Rule—do unto others, as you would have them do unto you—that propelled me into the space of giving. She fully inhabited that space of generosity, often sharing the words, "feed the hungry, shelter the homeless and clothe the naked." She felt it was her responsibility to enact and implement help for others. Perhaps I have inherited her sense of giving. Whatever your reasons may be, I encourage you, dear reader, to explore this opportunity to design how your healing space takes place. I promise you, whatever you give you will receive (and more!). And, most importantly, you will remain absolutely changed forever.

acknowledgements

Many of the lessons I have learned came to me through the words of loved ones, even if I did not apprehend their significance at the time. My gratitude to the beings who have shepherded me on my journey. Much love and thankfulness to my family members who have transitioned, as well as the many angels, helpers, orishas, healers and guides who have and continue to help me. I am continually blessed by their loving encouragement, support, and expert teaching abilities and, yes, their criticism. I thank the many teachers and mentors who have guided my spiritual evolvement over the last fifteen years, including those people and situations that have caused me pain and discomfort. Jerome Carter, a good-hearted soul who has also made his transition, introduced me to numerology. He held weekly conference calls, teaching a group of us numerology while also helping to create a strong sense of community between us. I remain in contact with many of the participants. Again, I remain in contact with another teacher and group participants led by medium, healer, and shaman, Kerrie O'Connor. I refer to these participants as "Sisters in Spirit" or, at times, "Divine Divas." Following my workshop, I continued studying with James Van Praagh, and he has helped me to awaken abilities within me such as transfiguration. He is the type of teacher who will walk you successfully through any new venture. Over the years, he has become a member of my family and I with his. Through James, I have been introduced to additional world-renowned mediums, intuitive healers and spiritual teachers. I have learned and experienced so much from them and my relationships have expanded internationally throughout the world. If you ever have the opportunity to visit The Journey Within Spiritualist Church in New Jersey you will meet Rev Janet Nohavec, one of the most compassionate people I know, who taught me the importance of power and strength in my mediumship. Under her mentorship, I also expanded my abilities as a healer and deepened my understanding of the role of healing in mediumship. I have also initiated and will continue studies with the Spiritualists' National Union International. This wonderful community introduced me to Spiritualism and have helped enormously to develop my skills. There are far too many tutors to mention; however, Jan, Margaret, Paul, Cathy, Chris, Suzanne, and Alan, you all have made a difference. Juliet Joan, an inspiring and motivating teacher, helped me to seek and find my abilities in inspirational speaking and mediumship.

I have shared a meal, the platform and numerous workshops with Mavis Pittilla and Jean. Mavis inspired my love of mediumship, urging me to walk fearlessly into mediumship and to see every reading, whether on platform or one-to-one as an adventure. She has taught me not only techniques but also the professionalism of mediumship.

My dear brother and friend Colin Bates imbued me with confidence when doubt creeped into my consciousness and nagged at me, suggesting I might not have the "right stuff." Both Brian Robertson and Simon James have a special place in my heart, as they were the first mediums to bring forth anyone from my family at a service. During that experience, they brought forth Grandma Edith and spoke extensively and evidentially about her cooking. I felt that if she decided to come through with them, they must be good folks, as she was an excellent judge of character. Brian and Simon ushered me into the importance of ethics, fundamentals, and provided me with an understanding of the historical nature of mediumship and how widespread the use of mediums was in England, the United States, and throughout the world. I have had classes and observed the work of the gifted Stella Upton, who helped me locate a lost person. I would be particularly remiss if I did not praise my brother, friend, and teacher Tony Stockwell, who has become part of our family. Tony has done so much to push me out of my comfort zone in mediumship and trance and has also helped me to develop my skills in teaching, inspirational speaking, and platform work.

I did not have courage to pursue the arduous credentialing process that the Spiritualists' National Union requires. To that end, I must share that Ann Marie Bond pushed me to understand the extent to which I had the absolute right stuff to obtain those credentials. She is an outstanding teacher and mentor and certainly led the way for others and myself.

I have had the wonderful opportunity to initiate and deepen my practice of mediumship, and especially trance. To that end, my eternal thanks to my brother, Chris DeSerio, and John Goodey, Debbie Nicholson, Simone Key, and Arthur Plumpton. My gratefulness to John for connecting me with my dear Great Grandfather Cesar bringing forth the message that I must complete this book. Simone also publically indicated my ability in trance and this too has propelled me onwards. My year-long mentorship in trance and teaching with the renowned Helen DaVita skyrocketed me into understanding and experiencing the connection between myself and spirit practitioners. She told me I was born to do this work and I am grateful for her skill and encouragement.

Tutors and teachers are important, however, peers are also essential, and I have benefitted from my relationships with other students, teachers, and leaders like dear Patty and Reverend Joe at The Journey Within, SNUI, where I gained support, understanding, and knowledge; to my many friends who joined me on this path of learning and provided immense love and support, especially my loving Sister Friend Latifu; Sister Friends Sandra, Carmen, and Ivory, my adopted Godchild and right hand.

I am grateful to my Wednesday Development Group—Gretchen, Ann, Judy, Barbara, and Maria, who comforted and helped me through grief and despair, Other important and meaningful friends including Elizabeth, Lilah, and Brother Louis, whose healing and inspiration continue to uplift me, dear Chrissie, a marvelous teacher and friend, Brother Jeffrey, who travels with me in the path of diversity and culture in spiritual practice, Catherine, my adopted daughter, Candice, Jenny, Carolyn, also my Sis Friend and explorer in mediumship, music and the divinity of Orishas, Gloria, Fredrick, who has guided and helped me more he knows, Helen, Monique, who inspired me to have fun, my Sister Friends Betty, Ivory, and Michaelle who contributed immensely to The Mediums of African Ancestry, our wonderful and meaningful diverse learning community on Facebook, and dear Tonya, who forecasted the writing of this book. To many others, your supportive energies have sustained me and helped me to soar. I am eternally grateful to prayer warriors and healers Ivory, Latifu, Juliet Joan, Michaelle, Annekee, Patti, and many others who interceded for me in times of illness, including four bouts of COVID-19.

To my loving parents, husband, who has supported my dreams and goals beyond belief, our children, have and continue to provide me with unending upliftment, and many family members, I am deeply grateful and blessed by your love and support. To my editors, designers, typists, especially Pamela, and others who provided their talent, expertise, and care—thank you for your intense support, flexibility, and strong belief in this sojourn. I offer my unending gratitude and love to Dr. Jennifer Reimer, who was initially brought into my path surely by Spirit and Spirit-helpers who knew I would benefit from her support and guidance. Her editorial leadership without making me feel that my voice was unheard essentially propelled me to do what needed to be done. When you read this, dear Jennifer, know that our hearts, our minds, body and spirit are inextricably linked forever. I am eternally in a space of gratitude for all that I have been given from others. And certainly most essentially I offer my sincere appreciation to my publisher and her staff Dr. Heather Sanders at A Sanders Publishing Company. I so appreciate Dr. Sanders for not only taking a chance with a relatively new author but, more importantly providing me with intense support, attention and guidance. I am truly grateful. I am grateful for the immense support, direction and technical skill from Kai Henderson and her team in the marketing of my book. Kai is a Digital creator, and founder and CEO of Public Relations Rock Stars. When she initially offered her help I didn't truly believe her, however she has offered creative and unyielding support in all aspects. I am also grateful to the members of our group who also have been extremely supportive, and generous sharing of ideas and perspectives.

There's wisdom in recognizing our limits, discerning the things we can control and the things over which we have no control. My connection to a higher power has, time and again, brought me through tragedy and dehumanization. This connection holds me and sustains me when I feel like drowning in the floods of hopelessness. I believe in my heart in a loving and caring Mother-Father God who wants us all to seek happiness and contentment—an essential part of the divinity that lies within and outside of us.

And, finally, I must thank Mother-Father God for continual blessings of wisdom and love.

References

Langston Hughes, "I, Too," in The Collected Poems of Langston Hughes, Arnold Rampersad and David Roessel, eds., (New York: Penguin, 1995), 46. Originally published in Hughes' first volume of poetry, The Weary Blues, 1926.

"Life of Medgar Evers," Medgar Evers College, The City University of New York, accessed June 22, 2023, https://www.mec.cuny.edu/history/life-of-medgar-evers/.

"What to Know About Daniel Prude's Death," The New York Times, September 4, 2020, updated October 9, 2020, https://www.nytimes.com/2020/09/04/nyregion/rochester-daniel-prude.html.

"What to Know About the Death of Daunte Wright," The New York Times, February 21, 2022, https://www.nytimes.com/article/daunte-wright-death-minnesota.html.

Heather McGhee, The Sum of Us: What Racism Costs Everyone and How We Can Prosper Together (London: Oneworld, 2021).

George Lipsitz, The Possessive Investment in Whiteness: How White People Profit from Identity Politics (Philadelphia: Temple University Press, 2006).

Matthew Frye Jacobson, Whiteness of a Different Color: European Immigrants and the Alchemy of Race (Cambridge: Harvard University Press, 1999).

Kimberle Crenshaw, "Demarginalizing the Intersection of Race and Sex: A Black Feminist Critique of Antidiscrimination Doctrine, Feminist Theory and Antiracist Politics," University of Chicago Legal Forum, 1, no. 8. (1989), http://chicagounbound.uchicago.edu/uclf/vol1989/iss1/8.

Andrew Hacker, Two Nations: Black and White, Separate, Hostile, Unequal (New York: Scribner, 2003).

Jane Dailey, Glenda Elizabeth Gilmore and Bryant Simon, eds, Jumpin' Jim Crow: Southern Politics from Civil War to Civil Rights (Princeton: Princeton University Press, 2000).

David M. Oshinsky, Worse than Slavery: Parchman Farm and the Ordeal of Jim Crow Justice (New York: Free Press, 1996).

Donald Bogle, Toms, Coons, Mulattoes, Mammies, and Bucks: An Interpretive History of Blacks in American Films (New York: Bloomsbury, 2016).

James W. Loewen, Sundown Towns: A Hidden Dimension of American Racism (New York: New Press, 2005).

For further information, see the Pinetree Institute online: https://pinetreeinstitute.org/aces/

Dr. Kristina Muenzenmaier, "Childhood Abuse and Neglect Among Women Outpatients With Chronic Mental Illness," Psychiatry Online, 1 April 2006. https://doi.org/10.1176/ps.44.7.666

Bessel van der Kolk, MD. https://www.besselvanderkolk.com

Allan Weiland, "Opinion: I Saw the Horrors of the Pre-Roe Era. Let's Never Go Back," Buzzfeed, June 7, 2019, https://www.buzzfeednews.com/article/allanweiland/i-saw-the-horrors-of-the-pre-roe-era

Rebecca A. Clay, "Are you experiencing Compassion Fatigue?," American Psychological Association, June 11 2020. Updated July 11, 2022. https://www.apa.org/topics/covid-19/compassion-fatigue#:~:text=Compassion%20fatigue%20occurs%20when%20psychologists,Traumatology%20Institute%20at%20Tulane%20University.

Maya Angelou, And Still I Rise (New York: Random House, 1978).

"White Eagle First Steps on a Spiritual Path," in White Eagle's Introduction to Inner Wisdom. (The White Eagle Publishing Trust, 2009), 47,48.

"The Power of Sankova," Berea College – Carter G. Woodson Center, accessed April 8, 2023, berea.edu/cgwc/the-power-of-Sankofa.

"Critical Race Theory," NAACP Legal Defense Fund, https://www.naacpldf.org/critical-race-theory-faq/. Critical Race Theory, or CRT, is an academic and legal framework that denotes that systemic racism is part of American society — from education and housing to employment and healthcare. Critical Race Theory recognizes that racism is more than the result of individual bias and prejudice. It is embedded in laws, policies and institutions that uphold and reproduce racial inequalities.

Rebecca Bayeck, "Unsung History of the Kingdom of Kongo," New York Public Library, November 2, 2021, accessed April 8, 2023, https://www.nypl.org/blog/2021/11/02/unsung-history-kingdom-kongo.

Joshua J. Mark, "Virginia Slave Laws and Development of Colonial American Slavery," World History Encyclopedia, April 27, 2021, https://www.worldhistory.org/article/1740/virginia-slave-laws-and-development-of-colonial-am/.

Henry Louis Gates Jr., "How Many Slaves Landed in the U.S.?" PBS, accessed March 23, 2023, https://www.pbs.org/wnet/african-americans-many-rivers-to-cross/history/how-many-slaves-landed-in-the-us/.

Samuel A. Cartwright, "Report on the Diseases and Physical Peculiarities of the Negro Race," The New Orleans Medical and Surgical Journal (New Orleans, Weld & Co, 1850), Internet Archive, 691-715. https://archive.org/details/neworleansmedica7185unse. Ibid, 708.

Nancy Krieger, "Shades of Difference: Theoretical Underpinnings of the Medical Controversy on Black/White Differences in the United States, 1830–1870," International Journal of Health Services, 17, no. 2, 197-342, (April 1987), accessed April 8, 2023, https://journals.sagepub.com/doi/10.2190/DBY6-VDQ8-HME8-ME3R3.

Brynn Holland, "The 'Father of Modern Gynecology' Performed Shocking Experiments on Enslaved Women," History, updated December 4, 2018. https://www.history.com/news/the-father-of-modern-gynecology-performed-shocking-experiments-on-slaves.

Eric Lott, Love & Theft: Blackface Minstrelsy and the American Working Class (New York: Oxford University Press, 2013).

Although there are sports team owners who identify as minorities, at the time of this writing, none are African American. Mind-boggling race-based disparities exi Avery J. Chapnick, "How the NFL disadvantages Black coaches," 1A WAMU, NPR, November 1, 2022, https://the1a.org/segments/how-the-nfl-disadvantages-black-coaches/.

"Profile: Black/African Americans," U.S. Department of Health and Human Services, Office of Minority Health, accessed February 19, 2023, https://minorityhealth.hhs.gov/omh/browse.aspx?lvl=3&lvlID=61.

"K-12 Disparity Facts and Statistics," United Negro College Fund, accessed February 17, 2003, https://uncf.org/pages/k-12-disparity-facts-and-stats.

"Civil Rights Data Collection, Data Snapshot: College and Career Readiness," U.S. Department of Education Office for Civil Rights, Issue Brief No. 3 (March 2014), https://www2.ed.gov/about/offices/list/ocr/docs/crdc-college-and-career-readiness-snapshot.pdf.

King Davis, "Special Report: America's First Asylum for African Americans Marks 150th Anniversary," Psychiatry Online, July 29, 2020, accessed April 8, 2023, https://doi.org/10.1176/appi.pn.2020.8a23.

King Davis, "Dr. King talks about his digital archiving project," YouTube video (2020), https://www.youtube.com/watch?v=-IUdlmK32kg.

Vanessa Jackson, "In Our Own Voice: African American Stories of Oppression: Survival and Recovery in the Mental Health System," University of Dayton, accessed March 23, 2023, http://academic.Udayton.edu/health/01status/mental01.htm.

"A Treasure Trove of Historical Data on the History of Mental Illness Among African Americans," February 6, 2014, The Journal of Blacks in Higher Education, https://www.jbhe.com/2014/02/treasure-trove-of-historical-data-on-the-history-of-mental-illness-among-african-americans/.

Britt Peterson, "A Virginia mental institution for Black patients, opened after the Civil War, yields a trove of disturbing records," March 29, 2021, The Washington Post, https://www.washingtonpost.com/lifestyle/magazine/black-asylum-files-reveal-racism/2021/03/26/ebfb2eda-6d78-11eb-9ead-673168d5b874_story.html.

Lorna Hines-Cunningham, "Critical Themes in Mental Health Treatment of African Americans: Past, Present, and Recommendations for the Future," Behavioral Health News, January 2, 2023, https://behavioralhealthnews.org/critical-themes-in-mental-health-treatment-of-african-americans-past-present-and-recommendations-for-the-future/.

"What does a human rights failure look like?" North Carolina Human Rights History - 1990s, accessed March 23, 2023, https://storymaps.arcgis.com/stories/ffcf92cd511c46fcbf19fff09c1d5883.

Elizabeth Nix, "Tuskegee Experiment: The Infamous Syphilis Study," History.com, May 16, 2017, updated December 15, 2020, https://www.history.com/news/the-infamous-40-year-tuskegee-study.

"The Legacy of Henrietta Lacks," Johns Hopkins Medicine, https://www.hopkinsmedicine.org/henriettalacks/.

"Social Determinants of Health," U.S Department of Health and Human Services, https://health.gov/healthypeople/priority-areas/social-determinants-health.

NBC New York Broadcast, "Why Local Leaders Want Funds From Infrastructure Bill to Fix Cross Bronx Expressway," November 9, 2021, https://www.nbcnewyork.com/news/local/why-local-leaders-want-funds-from-infrastructure-bill-to-fix-cross-bronx-expressway/3389019/.

"Asthma and African Americans," (2019), Department of Health and Human Services, Office of Minority Healthy, https://minorityhealth.hhs.gov/omh/browse.aspx?lvl=4&lvlid=15.

Linda Villarosa, "Why America's Black Mothers and Babies Are in a Life-or-Death Crisis," New York Times Magazine, April 11, 2018, https://www.nytimes.com/2018/04/11/magazine/black-mothers-babies-death-maternal-mortality.html.

"Infant Mortality and African Americans," (2020), Department of Health and Human Services, Department of Health and Human Services, Office of Minority Health, https://www.minorityhealth.hhs.gov/omh/browse.aspx?lvl=4&lvlid=23.

Monica K. Goyal, Nathan Kuppermann and Sean D. Cleary, "Racial Disparities in Pain Management of Children with Appendicitis in Emergency Departments," November 2015, JAMA Network Pediatrics, https://jamanetwork.com/journals/jamapediatrics/fullarticle/2441797?resultClick=1.

"Mental Health Status," Department of Health and Human Services, Office of Minority Health, Source CDC 2021. https://www.minorityhealth.hhs.gov/omh/browse.aspx?lvl=4&lvlid=24.

"Income and Poverty in the United States: 2019," United States Census Bureau, Table A-1, B-1, accessed February 22, 2023, https://www.census.gov/library/publications/2020/demo/p60-270.html. Wealth is different than money. Wealth refers to the combined level of all assets and is indicative of financial strength.

"Labor force characteristics by race and ethnicity, 2019." U.S. Bureau of Labor Statistics, BLS Reports. December 2020, accessed February 22, 2023, https://www.bls.gov/opub/reports/race-and-ethnicity/2019/home.htm.

C. Percheski and C. Gibson-Davis, "A Penny on the Dollar: Racial Inequalities in Wealth among Households with Children," Socius, 6, June 1, 2020, accessed April 8, 2023, https://doi.org/10.1177/2378023120916616.

Dorothy A. Brown, "College isn't the solution for the racial wealth gap. It's part of the problem," The Washington Post, April 9, 2021, https://www.washingtonpost.com/outlook/2021/04/09/student-loans-black-wealth-gap/.

Paul Kiel, "Debt and the Racial Wealth Gap," The New York Times, December 31, 2015, https://www.nytimes.com/2016/01/03/opinion/debt-and-the-racial-wealth-gap.html.

"Homeownership rates show that Black Americans are currently the least likely group to own homes," USAFACTS, July 28, 2020, updated March 21, 2023, accessed April 15, 2023, https://usafacts.org/articles/homeownership-rates-by-race/.

"Reducing the Racial Homeownership Gap," 2017, Urban Institute, accessed April 15, 2023, https://www.urban.org/policy-centers/housing-finance-policy-center/projects/reducing-racial-homeownership-gap.

Kriston McIntosh, Emily Moss, Ryan Nunn and Jay Shambaugh, "Examining the Black-white wealth gap," Brookings, February 27, 2020, accessed March 2, 2022, https://www.brookings.edu/blog/up-front/2020/02/27/examining-the-black-white-wealth-gap/.

David C. John, "Disparities For Women and Minorities in Retirement Saving," Brookings, September 1, 2010, accessed April 8, 2023, https://www.brookings.edu/testimonies/disparities-for-women-and-minorities-in-retirement-saving/.

"On the Persistence of the Black-White Unemployment Gap," CAP Center for American Progress, February 24, 2020, https://www.americanprogress.org/article/persistence-black-white-unemployment-gap/.

Karen Yuan, "Working While Black: Stories from black corporate America," Fortune, June 16, 2020, accessed March 2, 2022, https://fortune.com/longform/working-while-black-in-corporate-america-racism-microaggressions-stories/.

Jason Del Ray, "Bias, disrespect, and demotions: Black employees say Amazon has a race problem," Vox, February 26, 2021, accessed March 2, 2022, https://www.vox.com/recode/2021/2/26/22297554/amazon-race-black-diversity-inclusion.

Marianne Bertrand and Sendhil Mullainathan, "Are Emily and Greg More Employable Than Lakisha and Jamal? A Field Experiment on Labor Market Discrimination," (2004) The American Economic Review, 94(4):991-1013.

"4 Hiring Bias Study Statistics That May Shock You," IQ Partners Inc., December 10, 2020, https://www.iqpartners.com/blog/4-hiring-bias-study-statistics-that-may-shock-you/.

Christian E. Weller, "African Americans Face Systematic Obstacles to Getting Good Jobs," CAP, December 5, 2019. https://www.americanprogress.org/article/african-americans-face-systematic-obstacles-getting-good-jobs/.

Jason Del Ray, "Bias, disrespect, and demotions," Vox, February 26, 2021, accessed March 2, 2022, https://www.vox.com/recode/2021/2/26/22297554/amazon-race-black-diversity-inclusion.

Debjani Mukherjee, ed., "Microaggressions in Clinical Training and Practice," Wiley Online Library, PM&R, (August 1, 2019) vol 11, 9, 1004-1012, https://onlinelibrary.wiley.com/doi/10.1002/pmrj.12229.

Del Ray, "Bias, disrespect, and demotions."

Niki Monazzam and Kristen Budd, "Incarcerated Women and Girls," The Sentencing Project, April 3, 2033, accessed April 18, 2023, https://www.sentencingproject.org/fact-sheet/incarcerated-women-and-girls/.

Yuan, "Working While Black."

Amir Vera, "White woman who called police on a black man birdwatching in Central Park has been fired," CNN, May 26, 2020, accessed March 2, 2022, https://www.cnn.com/2020/05/26/us/central-park-video-dog-video-african-american-trnd/index.html. The interviewee references an incident in Central Park (New York City), between a white woman (Amy Cooper) walking her dog without a leash and a black man (Christian Cooper, no relation) birdwatching in May 2020. The two exchanged dialogue about Ms. Cooper's unleashed dog, which was in violation of Park rules. She said she felt threatened and called 911. Video footage records her as saying, "I'm going to tell them there's an African American man threatening my life."

The Sentencing Project, About Us, accessed March 2, 2022, https://www.sentencingproject.org/about-us/.

Ashley Nellis, "In the Extreme: Women Serving Life Without Parole and Death Sentences," The Sentencing Project, September 22, 2021, accessed March 2, 2022, https://www.sentencingproject.org/publications/in-the-extreme-women-serving-life-without-parole-and-death-sentences-in-the-united-states/.

Ashley, Nellis, "The Color of Justice: Racial and Ethnic Disparity in State Prison," The Sentencing Project, October 13, 2021, accessed, March 2, 2022, https://www.sentencingproject.org/publications/color-of-justice-racial-and-ethnic-disparity-in-state-prisons/.

Niki Monazzam and Kristen Budd, "Incarcerated Women and Girls," The Sentencing Project, April 3, 2033, accessed April 18, 2023, https://www.sentencingproject.org/fact-sheet/incarcerated-women-and-girls/.

Michelle Alexander, The New Jim Crow: Mass Incarceration in the Age of Colorblindness, (New York: The New Press, 2012), 73, 224.

Joshua Rovner, "Racial Disparities in Youth Incarceration Persist," The Sentencing Project, February 3, 2021, accessed February 23, 2023, https://www.sentencingproject.org/publications/racial-disparities-in-youth-incarceration-persist/.

Dorothy Otnow Lewis, "Race Bias in the Diagnosis and Disposition of Violent Adolescents," American Journal of Psychiatry (published online April 2006), vol 137,10, https://ajp.psychiatryonline.org/doi/abs/10.1176/ajp.137.10.1211.

Innocence Staff, "The Lasting Legacy of Parchman Farm, the Prison Modeled After a Slave Plantation," Innocence Project, May 29, 2020, accessed February 23, 2023, https://innocenceproject.org/news/the-lasting-legacy-of-parchman-farm-the-prison-modeled-after-a-slave-plantation/.

"It's Time to End the Racist and Unjustified Sentencing Disparity Between Crack and Powder Cocaine," The Leadership Conference on Civil and Human Rights, November 30, 2021, accessed February 17, 2023, https://civilrights.org/blog/its-time-to-end-the-racist-and-unjustified-sentencing-disparity-between-crack-and-powder-cocaine/.

"Findings: The results of our nationwide analysis of traffic stops and searches," Stanford University, accessed July 5, 2023, https://openpolicing.stanford.edu/findings/.

Magnus Lofstrom, Joseph Hayes, Brandon Martin and Deepak Premkumar, "Racial Disparities in Law Enforcement Stops," Public Policy Institute of California, October 2021, https://www.ppic.org/publication/racial-disparities-in-law-enforcement-stops/.

Nazgol Ghandnoosh, "Black Lives Matter: Eliminating Racial Inequity in The Criminal Justice System," (2015) The Sentencing Project, https://www.sentencingproject.org/app/uploads/2022/08/Black-Lives-Matter.pdf.

Andrew Johnson, "December 3, 1867: Third Annual Message to Congress," UVA Miller Center, https://millercenter.org/the-presidency/presidential-speeches/december-3-1867-third-annual-message-congress

Bobby Harrison, "5th Circuit upholds Jim Crow-era law written to keep Black Mississippians from voting," Mississippi Today, August 24, 2022, https://mississippitoday.org/2022/08/24/felony-conviction-voting-ban-mississippi/.

Aaron Randle, "America's Only Successful Coup d'État Overthrew a Biracial Government in 1898," History.com, October 7, 2020, updated May 10, 2023, https://www.history.com/news/wilmington-massacre-1898-coup.

A National Historic Landmarks Theme Study, "Civil Rights in America: Racial Voting Rights," (2007, revised 2009), NPS, https://www.nps.gov/subjects/tellingallamericansstories/upload/CivilRights_VotingRights.pdf.

Debra Michals, ed, "Fannie Lou Hamer," National Women's History Museum, 2017, https://www.womenshistory.org/education-resources/biographies/fannie-lou-hamer.

David Dennis Jr., "The Day the Civil Rights Movement Changed," The Atlantic, June 2022, https://www.theatlantic.com/magazine/archive/2022/06/medgar-evers-death-civil-rights/629639/.

National Archives, "Confrontations for Justice," Eyewitness: American Originals, accessed April 8, 2023, https://www.archives.gov/exhibits/eyewitness/html.php?section=2.

Nancy Abudu, "Seven Years After Shelby County vs. Holder, Voter Suppression Permeates the South," SPL Center, June 25, 2020, accessed April 8, 2023, https://www.splcenter.org/news/2020/06/25/seven-years-after-shelby-county-vs-holder-voter-suppression-permeates-south.

Lawrence Goldstone, "America's Relentless Suppression of Black Voters," The New Republic, October 24, 2018, https://newrepublic.com/article/151858/americas-relentless-suppression-black-voters. Jelani Cobb, "Voter Suppression Tactics in the Age of Trump," The New Yorker, October 29, 2018, https://www.newyorker.com/magazine/2018/10/29/voter-suppression-tactics-in-the-age-of-trump.

"North Carolina Fact Sheet: A Pattern of Blocking Access to the Polls," Lawyers Committee for Civil Rights, accessed April 18, 2023, https://www.lawyerscommittee.org/north-carolina-profile/.

Alisa Chang, "In Rural N.C., New Voter ID Law Awakens Some Old Fears," NPR, August 16, 2013, https://www.npr.org/2013/08/16/212664895/in-rural-n-c-new-voter-id-law-awakens-some-old-fears.

Richard Fausset, Nick Croissant and Mark Leibovich, "Why The Georgia G.O.P.'s Voting Rollback Will Hit Black People Hard," The New York Times, March 25, 2021, accessed March 7, 2022, https://www.nytimes.com/2021/03/25/us/politics/georgia-black-voters.html.

Robert P. Jones, et al, "American Democracy in Crisis: The Challenges of Voter Knowledge, Participation, and Polarization," PRRI: Research, July 17, 2018, https://www.prri.org/research/American-democracy-in-crisis-voters-midterms-trump-election-2018/.

Vann R. Newkirk II, "Voter Suppression is Warping Democracy," The Atlantic, July 17, 2018, accessed March 7, 2022, https://www.theatlantic.com/politics/archive/2018/07/poll-prri-voter-suppression/565355/.

Jamelle Buie, "This is Jim Crow in New Clothes," The New York Times, March 19, 2021, accessed March 2, 2023, https://www.nytimes.com/2021/03/19/opinion/raphael-warnock-voting-rights-resonstruction.html.

David Satcher, "Mental Health: Culture, Race, and Ethnicity—A Supplement to Mental Health: A Report of the Surgeon General," (2001) U.S. Department of Health and Human Services, Washington, D.C., https://drum.lib.umd.edu/bitstream/handle/1903/22834/sma-01-3613.pdf?sequence=1&isAllowed=y.

Merriam-Webster Dictionary, s.v. "stigma," accessed February 27, 2023, https://www.merriam-webster.com/dictionary/stigma..

Erving Goffman, Stigma: Notes on the Management of Spoiled Identity, (New York: Touchstone, 1986 reissue), 1.

Vanessa Jackson, "An Early History - African American Mental Health," University of Dayton, updated March 10, 2010, https://academic.udayton.edu/health/01status/mental01.htm.

Clint Smith, "Stories of Slavery, From Those Who Survived It," The Atlantic, March 2021, https://www.theatlantic.com/magazine/archive/2021/03/federal-writers-project/617790/.

Jay Allison and Dan Gediman, eds., This I Believe: The Personal Philosophies of Remarkable Men and Women (New York: Holt Paperbacks, 2006), 13-15.

about the author

Lorna J. Hines is a Licensed Clinical Social Worker, Spiritual Practitioner, Certified Medium, Intuitive Counselor, and acclaimed speaker with over four decades of experience at the intersection of mental health, trauma recovery, spirituality, and social justice. With a master's degree in social work and an academic background that includes more than twelve years as an Associate Adjunct Professor at New York University's Silver School of Social Work, Lorna has shaped the next generation of clinicians while pioneering integrative approaches to healing.

Her academic work has focused on cultural and linguistic competence, trauma-informed care, and holistic recovery. As a thought leader, she has presented nationally and internationally on topics including systemic trauma, ancestral healing, grief, and wellness. Lorna's career includes senior leadership roles in the New Jersey Department of Human Services and the New York State Office of Mental Health, where she was instrumental in developing large-scale trauma recovery initiatives and post-9/11 support systems.

In addition to her extensive behavioral health credentials, Lorna is credentialed by the Spiritualists' National Union International in mediumship and spiritual demonstrating. She has shared her intuitive gifts at the Omega Institute under the tutelage of notable mentors and is featured on platforms such as FindACertifiedMedium.com and Helping Parents Heal.

Her debut book, *Straight Talk from a Wise Woman: Trauma, Tears, and a Healing Path,* offers a deeply personal and professionally grounded roadmap for healing from unseen wounds. With compassion and clarity, Lorna guides readers on a path beyond pain and powerlessness—toward peace, purpose, and personal restoration.

A lifelong advocate for vulnerable populations, Lorna dedicates a portion of her proceeds to the Nazareth Home for Children in Ghana, West Africa. Whether in clinical settings, academic classrooms, or spiritual circles, her mission is the same: to empower individuals to heal, grow, and rediscover their divine path.

Learn more at *www.lornajhines.com*

A SANDERS COMPANY

Made in the USA
Middletown, DE
23 June 2025